# The Kaizen Event Planner

## Achieving Rapid Improvement in Office, Service, and Technical Environments

Karen Martin and Mike Osterling

*Claribel*
*Best wishes for rapid*
*continuous improvement.*
*Regards,*
*Mike Osterling*
*January, 2008*

**Productivity** Press

New York

Most Productivity Press books are available at quantity discounts when purchased in bulk. For more information, contact our Customer Service Department (888-319-5852). Address all other inquiries to:

Productivity Press
444 Park Avenue South, 7th Floor
New York, NY 10016
United States of America
Telephone: 212-686-5900
Fax: 212-686-5411
E-mail: info@productivitypress.com
ProductivityPress.com

*Library of Congress Cataloging-in-Publication Data*

Martin, Karen.
    The Kaizen event planner : achieving rapid improvement in office, service, and technical environments / by Karen Martin and Mike Osterling.
        p. cm.
    Includes index.
    ISBN 978-1-56327-351-3 (alk. paper)
    1. Organizational effectiveness.   2. Industrial efficiency.   3. Waste minimization.
4. Production management.   5. Manufacturing processes.   I. Osterling, Mike.   II. Title.
    HD58.9.M378   2007
    658.5′15—dc22

                                                                    2007032450

11   10   09   08   07   5   4   3   2   1

# CONTENTS

# ACKNOWLEDGMENTS

If there was ever a cross-functional process, writing a book is it. First and foremost, we thank our employers and clients who have provided the "learning laboratories" in which we could experiment with applying lean principles and tools in nonmanufacturing environments, and test our theories about process design, team dynamics, measurement, and sustainability. A special thank you goes to the clients who pushed us to create the standard work materials on the CD that accompanies this book and one client whose processes provided the analytical need that led to our development of metrics-based process mapping, introduced in Chapter 12. This tool has proven highly effective in identifying and eliminating waste in office, service, and technical environments.

We remain indebted to colleagues with whom we have collaborated, and those who continue to challenge our thinking and deepen our understanding of what the Toyota Production System is *really* about.

A very special thank you goes to Nima Nekoui who transformed our content for the standard work tools into an intuitive and visually pleasing product that far exceeded our expectations.

The team at Productivity Press has been stellar in helping us package our experience into a book. Thanks to Maura May, Michael Sinocchi, Bob Cooper, Ed Hanus, Karen Gaines, and Lara Zoble. Thanks also to Gary Peurasaari and Sandra Kear who provided editorial direction and helped our words flow, and to all the other people who work tirelessly behind the scenes.

But the largest thank you, by far, goes to our families and friends who provided much appreciated support throughout the project, and demonstrated exceptional patience as we holed ourselves up in our offices for more than a year.

# PREFACE

In writing this book, we had to make a number of difficult decisions. Just like a Kaizen Event, our first decision concerned scope. We were tempted to include information about how to apply the specific improvement tools, such as pull systems, work balancing, and standard work, to name a few. But we decided to narrow our scope and focus specifically on what we considered the continuous-improvement community's greatest need: how to plan and execute Kaizen Events and conduct post-event follow-up. Productivity Press and other publishers offer a number of excellent resources, and professional associations and seasoned consultants can help you design and implement the actual improvements. That said, we did include sample value stream maps for a purchasing process in Chapter 1, and a section on map interpretation because we feel strongly that the bulk of your Kaizen Events should be closely tied to a future state value stream map and implementation plan.

Our second major decision concerned how much information to include about the Toyota Production System (TPS), lean enterprise principles, the plan-do-check-act (PDCA) cycle, and other philosophies and approaches that have played a strong role in the development of Kaizen Events as an improvement implementation strategy. While a fair number of readers may be new to lean terminology and concepts, many of our manufacturing-based readers likely have extensive TPS knowledge and experience applying lean enterprise principles and tools. For those in the former group (and those in the latter group who need a refresher), you may wish to read seminal works, such as James Womack and Daniel Jones' *Lean Thinking*, Jeffrey Liker's *The Toyota Way*, or Masaaki Imai's *Gemba Kaizen* or *Kaizen: The Key to Japan's Competitive Success* to gain a greater appreciation for kaizen's roots. It would be a mistake to move forward with Kaizen Events without a firm grasp of TPS and lean principles. We sincerely hope that Chapter 1 delivers enough introductory information to set the stage for holding successful Kaizen Events and whets your appetite for continuous learning to deepen your understanding of TPS and lean.

The final decision, closely tied to the previous one, concerned how much Japanese terminology to include. This was not an easy decision for us to make because we feel passionate about lean's roots and the metaphorical nature of the Japanese language. But we wanted the book to be accessible to individuals and, in some cases, entire organizations that are firmly rooted in Western culture and don't share our appreciation for Eastern ways. Further, we continue to meet resistance from well-meaning professionals in nonmanufacturing industries who believe that TPS and lean can't possibly apply to them because they're not manufacturers. Therefore, we find it more effective to initially limit what many perceive as manufacturing-specific terminology, then integrate the Japanese terms and Lean vernacular as the practitioner begins to recognize that it is not a question of whether they manufacture goods; it's about *process*—and offices, service organizations, and technical staffs all have their own versions of a production line. So, with some reluctance, we have limited the use of Japanese terminology in the book itself, but those such as *muda, gemba, poka-yoke, kaikaku*, etc., are included in the glossary, which can be found both in Appendix A and on the accompanying CD as a printable PDF file.

A final note for those of you in manufacturing: While this book focuses on office-related improvement efforts, many of the concepts and tools apply to production-specific Kaizen Events as well.

Enjoy the journey to becoming a kaizen-thinking and kaizen-behaving organization. We invite you to share your experience with us at *http://www.kaizeneventplanner.com/*.

# INTRODUCTION

In the world of continuous improvement (CI), kaizen may perhaps be the most misunderstood concept. We've heard executives refer to their organizations as "kaizen organizations" when there is little evidence of ongoing improvement being designed and implemented by the workforce. We've seen organizations refer to their value stream mapping activities as Kaizen Events. We've also attended conferences where seasoned continuous-improvement professionals refer to kaizen as a specific tool for reducing lead time or creating process capacity rather than what it is: a continuous-improvement philosophy and business management approach for making small, incremental progress on a daily basis. Kaizen sets the stage for the workforce to effectively apply specific improvement tools. When practiced on a daily basis, this process can transform an organization's culture.

But even those who truly understand the essence of kaizen often struggle when it comes to execution. Applying the kaizen philosophy at a tactical level on a daily basis isn't as easy as it seems it should be—especially here in the West. At its core, kaizen is about people and respect for human dignity. Today's organizations are complicated ecosystems comprised of independent-minded people with varying needs, experience, goals, understanding, priorities, and responsibilities. When we add the challenges associated with daily firefighting, excessive multitasking, functional organizational structures, unclear roles and responsibilities, and changing organizational priorities to this system, it's no wonder that many organizations struggle with how to use kaizen to improve bottom-line performance, the work environment, and ultimately, their position in the marketplace.

Kaizen Events—the subject of this book—offer an effective way to train organizations to break unproductive habits and adopt the kaizen philosophy while, at the same time, achieve breakthrough performance and unprecedented results. Through Kaizen Events, cross-functional teams learn how to make improvements in a methodological way. They learn how to apply specific improvement tools, establish relevant metrics programs, and sustain their gains. Most importantly, they learn how to work with one another to solve problems rapidly and in a highly effective way. After a Kaizen Event ends, these team members become ambassadors for change, spreading their learned behaviors across the organization.

With each Kaizen Event, the pool of ambassadors grows, fueling a cultural shift that begins to place *improvement* as the organization's top priority and increasingly authorizes the workers themselves to design and implement tactical level improvements. After a series of many Kaizen Events that reach into various operating units, organizations are often better positioned to begin practicing daily kaizen. But while Kaizen Events provide the focus, structure, and skilled facilitation that enable daily kaizen to become standard practice within an organization, the need for Kaizen Events never goes away. Even the most seasoned organizations benefit from using Kaizen Events for making larger scale, rapid improvements, which are best achieved in a structured setting with a sequestered, cross-functional team.

Although many U.S. manufacturers have been holding Kaizen Events since the early nineties, the approach is fairly new to office, service, and technical environments. And while these settings present unique challenges, we have seen their Kaizen Events produce even more dramatic results than those from manufacturing-based events. In two to five days, Kaizen Event teams in office, service, and technical environments regularly reduce throughput time by 60 percent, improve quality by 80 percent, and increase capacity by 20 percent.

But these impressive outcomes don't magically appear. Kaizen Events in these settings require more planning, skillful execution, and follow-up than their manufacturing counterparts. The teams are often larger, and they are often less familiar with cross-functional problem solving, less comfortable with the concept of standard work, and more isolated from the customer who ultimately determines value. In addition, relevant current state performance data is often difficult to obtain.

As we began facilitating Kaizen Events in office areas within manufacturers and in nonmanufacturing environments (e.g., healthcare, information technology, financial services, distribution, insurance, engineering services, oil and gas production, government, military, and construction), we discovered the need for detailed standard work for planning and executing Kaizen Events in environments that weren't accustomed to the structure that Kaizen Events require. When we looked around for existing materials, we discovered a market void and created our own set of tools. As we began sharing these tools with clients and conference attendees, they asked us to make them publicly available.

At the same time, we grew increasingly concerned with two observations. First, many organizations were (and still are) relying too heavily on external consultants to drive their continuous-improvement efforts and seemed reluctant to develop a pool of internal resources to facilitate Kaizen Events and other improvement activities such as value stream mapping. But an organization will never become self-sustaining if it doesn't develop its own cadre of continuous-improvement experts. Further, it's difficult to achieve momentum and sustain gains if activities only occur when an outside consultant is on site.

Our second concern stemmed from the growing number of organizations that tell us they are holding Kaizen Events, but the only outcome is a *plan* for implementation, not actual implementation—a defining element for a Kaizen Event. While we value what we refer to as "rapid planning events," they are not Kaizen Events and should not be referred to as such. So, with tools in hand and concern for retaining the original theme and objectives for Kaizen Events, a book was born.

## HOW TO USE THIS BOOK

This book is organized into four parts. Part I provides background information about the Toyota Production System (TPS), the lean philosophy, and the difference between the practice of ongoing, daily kaizen and Kaizen Events. For those of you who are new to TPS and lean, Chapter 1 includes a sample value stream map, so you can see how Kaizen Events fit into a larger strategic improvement plan.

Parts II, III and IV center around the planning, execution and post-event follow-up phases of the Kaizen Event, which form a macro plan-do-check-act (PDCA) cycle. Within the execution phase, lies a micro PDCA cycle as teams design, test, modify, implement, and monitor their improvements.

In looking at Part II, you may wonder why it would take seven chapters to discuss planning an event, but the *success of a Kaizen Event is directly related to the quality of the upfront planning*. Do not succumb to the temptation to skip this vital section to get to the "meat" of the matter. Part II may require even more of your focused attention than the rest of the book. Through your thorough understanding about who should lead events, how to scope them properly and select an effective team, and how to properly communicate event details, you will be positioned for success.

Part III addresses event execution and introduces a new process mapping technique we refer to as *Metrics-Based Process Mapping* (MBPM), which combines the metrics components from value stream mapping with the swim-lane structure of functional process maps. This mapping approach, described in Chapter 12, has proven a powerful addition to our improvement tool belt. It enables teams to perform a deep dive and "get into the weeds" with a process, which results in powerful current state analyses, which lead to effective solutions. We use this mapping technique in about 50 percent of the Kaizen Events we lead.

Part IV addresses essential post-event follow-up activities and techniques to assure sustainability. Most events generate a short list of activities that need to be completed immediately following the event, such as conducting makeup training on the improvement for the workforce that may have been out of the office during the Kaizen Event. The sustainability section provides direction concerning process audits—including how often audits should be conducted and by whom—and the role of metrics in driving ongoing improvement.

You may wish to read the final chapter in the book, Creating a Kaizen Culture, before you begin the book. While Kaizen Events are an effective implementation strategy for *any* type of organization, the outcomes are often directly related to the organization's readiness for the commitment and discipline required by the approach. Kaizen Events significantly test an organization's ability to handle rapid change. They reflect current culture and reveal organizational weaknesses like no other improvement tool. Through having the courage to look into the mirror that Kaizen Events provide, organizations can make quantum leaps in their desire to become lean enterprises. But looking into the mirror isn't always easy, and requires a committed leadership team. Chapter 19 includes a change management matrix that addresses the key elements for effective change—essential understanding for those of us who seek to shift culture—and the desired leadership behaviors that will set you on a path to success.

## THE CD

The book is structured around a set of Excel-based tools and templates that can be found on the CD included at the back of the book. These tools are designed to serve as standard work for planning and executing Kaizen Events, and conducting post-event follow-up. The CD instructions for use, which follow this introduction, describe how to use these interactive tools most effectively. You may not need every tool for every event. We encourage you to take a careful look at what's available, each tool's intended use, and then make an informed decision based on your specific needs. We hope you find the tools as helpful to the rapid change process as we have. While we've tested them extensively and have used them in many Kaizen Events, we practice continuous improvement on a daily basis. So if you discover the need for additional tools or discover an opportunity for improving the ones provided, please contact us at *http://www.kaizeneventplanner.com*. The CD also includes additional documents and templates you may wish to print and refer to as you read the book, or to include in your internal training efforts.

## OTHER LEARNING MATERIAL

The book also contains a number of other learning tools to support your development as continuous improvement leaders and Kaizen Event facilitators. Appendix A includes a glossary of commonly used lean enterprise terms and acronyms. An electronic version of the glossary is included on the CD, so you can print it for distribution or as a learning aid during training sessions. Appendix B lists a wide variety of resources available to you to practice continual learning. To continue your professional development, read, attend workshops and conferences, form communities of practice, and join user groups. The Internet, your local library, and booksellers offer a wealth of information. Through continuous learning, we strengthen our skills as CI leaders and model the behavior we encourage others to adopt.

This book has been a labor of love. While the seed was planted from our personal needs as consultants, it has evolved into what we hope will provide substantial support to others who seek to make rapid improvements and shift organizational culture through Kaizen Events. We're relatively certain that we haven't hit on every aspect of holding Kaizen Events, but we hope we have captured the largest issues and have addressed them in an accessible way. Enjoy, freely share your knowledge, get results, reflect, and continue learning. Ultimately, that's what improvement is all about.

# CD INSTRUCTIONS FOR USE

The CD included at the back of the book contains a file—Kaizen Event Tools—that contains practical tools and standard work templates to help you plan and execute successful Kaizen Events and perform necessary follow-up activities. In addition, the CD includes a folder containing several full-size versions of the graphics that appear in the book. This material is included in case you want to print them to take notes as you read the book and/or use them for training purposes.

The CD files are:

- **Kaizen Event Tools** (Excel file)
- **Additional Materials Folder**, which includes:
    - **Current and Future State Value Stream Maps**—This file contains the sample value stream maps described in Chapter 1. You may want to print these to refer to as you read Chapter 1.
    - **Kaizen Commandments**—These "rules," which are discussed in Chapter 11, help ensure a successful event. You may want to distribute these rules to the kaizen team and/or post them in kaizen central.
    - **Key Mapping Metrics**—This table, introduced in Chapter 12, lists the most common mapping metrics used to measure the current state and projected future-state performance for either macro-level value stream maps or micro-level process maps.
    - **Certificate of Achievement**—This certificate, referred to in Chapter 17, can be modified for your organization and either printed as is or the borders can be removed and you can print on certificate paper available through any office supply store or specialty company such as Baudville, www.baudville.com, 800-728-0888.
    - **Lean Terminology**—This reference guide, which appears as Appendix A in the book, includes the most commonly used lean terms and acronyms.

## KAIZEN EVENT TOOLS—GENERAL INFORMATION

These interactive Excel-based tools, which provide standard work for planning and executing Kaizen Events, form the backbone of this book. Detailed instructions and best practices for using the tools are described throughout the book. The matrix on the following page lists the tools, their tab numbers on the Excel file, the Kaizen Event phase in which they will likely be used, and the chapter in the book in which the tool's use is first introduced.

### File Type and File Naming Conventions

The Kaizen Event Tools file—named "Kaizen Event Tools.xlt"—is an integral part of this book and serves as the standard work for planning and executing successful Kaizen Events,

| Kaizen Event Phase | Tab | Tool | Chapter |
|---|---|---|---|
| Pre-Event Planning | 1 | Kaizen Event Charter | Chapter 3 |
| | 2 | Planning Checklist | Chapter 3 |
| | 3 | Team Formation Matrix | Chapter 6 |
| | 4 | Supplies Checklist | Chapter 7 |
| | 5 | Communication Worksheet | Chapter 8 |
| Event Execution | 6 | Execution Checklist | Chapter 10 |
| | 7 | Improvement Ideas | Chapter 10 |
| | 8 | Sustainability Plan | Chapter 17 |
| | 9 | 30-Day List | Chapter 17 |
| | 10 | Parking Lot List | Chapter 17 |
| | 11 | Kaizen Event Report | Chapter 17 |
| | 12 | Final Presentation Agenda | Chapter 17 |
| Post-Event Follow-up | 13 | Post-Event Activities | Chapter 18 |
| | 14 | 30-Day Audit Report | Chapter 18 |
| | 15 | 60-Day Audit Report | Chapter 18 |

as well as laying the groundwork for improvement sustainability. This file has an .xlt suffix, indicating an Excel template file type. Templates offer the user a degree of protection against inadvertently overwriting the master file. In addition, a template creates a convenient way for creating multiple derivations for each of your Kaizen Events. We recommend that you modify the template to create an organization-specific template. For example, you could preload the Team Formation and Communication worksheets (Tabs 3 and 5) with the functional departments within your organization. Store the new template in a safe and accessible place, such as a shared drive. You may want to create a master folder to house all information related to Kaizen Events, with subfolders for each event. When saving the company-specific master file, rename the file with language that clearly indicates it's a master. In the "save as type" window (directly below the file name window), select "template" from the drop-down choices. The file will retain the ".xlt" extension.

For each Kaizen Event, you can perform the "save as" function and give the tools a unique file name for that event. When you do this, the file name will then carry the regular Excel file extension—".xls." We recommend you include the event name and start date (e.g., Accounts Receivable 2007-08-15) in the file name.

## Macros

The tools contain several macros. Therefore, when you open the file, you will receive a message warning you that macros are embedded in the file. Select "Enable Macros" to ensure the best functionality. If your computer's macro security settings are set to "high" or "very high," you will need to change the security settings to medium before you'll be able to enable the macros so the tool will operate properly.

Because of the macros, when you exit the tool you will be asked whether you want to save changes, *even if you haven't made any changes*. If you have made changes and want to save them, select "yes." If you have not made any changes to the file, or have made changes that you do not wish to save, select "no."

## Tools Organization

The file, which Excel refers to as a workbook, contains 15 different standard work tools/templates, which Excel refers to as "sheets." You can access each sheet by clicking the appropriate tab along the bottom of the Excel workspace. The tabs are color-coded according to the Kaizen Event phase in which the tools are typically used:

| Tab Color | Phase |
| --- | --- |
| Blue | Pre-event planning |
| Yellow | Event execution |
| Lavender | Post-event follow-up |

# KAIZEN EVENT TOOLS: NAVIGATION TIPS

While detailed information about each specific tool's use can be found within the book's chapters, the following navigation instructions provide general information about the tool structure and function. The instructions for use are not intended as Excel training. Rather, the instructions assume users possess a basic understanding of Excel.

## Cell Color Coding

All cells are color coded to indicate the cell's format, functionality, and what action, if any, the user should take:

| Cell Color | Action |
| --- | --- |
| Yellow | These are the *only* cells that will accept direct data input from the user. On those tools containing pre-populated lists, we have included blank yellow cells so you can add activities or items that are unique to your organization (e.g., cells C14 –C17 in the "Planning Checklist" sheet). |
| White | White cells contain descriptions of activities or items in a list and are "locked" to prevent inadvertent deletions, formula revisions, or cell reformatting. |
| Black or gray | These cells contain section, column, or row labels and are also locked, preventing alteration. |
| Salmon/tan | For user ease, salmon-colored cells are auto-populated from other cells within the workbook. For example, once the top three sections of the Kaizen Event Charter are completed, all corresponding cells, on the subsequent tools, auto-populate with the information entered into the charter cells. If you need to update the information in any of the tools' fields that drive from the charter, you'll need to modify the information in the charter first as it's the driving document. Metrics-related salmon-colored cells auto-populate based on programmed formulas that auto-calculate once data is entered into the driving yellow cells. The salmon cells are also locked. If the source cell information is altered, the |

salmon cells will update automatically. More detailed information about this feature is included in the auto-populate section.

## Cell Content

When more content is entered than the cell's size allows, one of two things happen, depending on the format of the particular tool: 1) the font size automatically shrinks to accommodate additional text, or 2) the text wraps within the cell. Cells are limited in size to encourage concise communication. When possible, we opted for the "text wrap" feature. If text wrapping would alter form layout, we used the "shrink to fit" feature. In this case, the font will be reduced to the size necessary to fit all text into the space available. Again, we encourage brevity but not at the expense of clarity.

If you want to create a list within a single cell, such as the Boundaries and Limitations cell (C11) on the Kaizen Event Charter (Tab 1), press alt + enter after each item to move to a new "line" within the cell.

## Insert Comment

Any time you need to explain a *yellow* cell's contents further, you may insert a comment by right clicking on the cell. A small red triangle appears in the upper right corner of the cell to indicate a comment exists. To view the comment, simply left click on the cell (making it "active") and the comment will appear. To delete the comment, right click in the cell and select "delete comment." You may also insert and delete comments from the menu bar by selecting "insert," then select "comment."

## Check Boxes and Progress Boxes

Place the cursor over the check box and left click once to check the boxes that appear on several of the tools containing lists. To remove the checkmark, simply left click again.

On the 30-Day List's progress section, if you delete the number on the progress box quadrant that indicates the appropriate degree of completion for the particular task, the quadrant color will change from yellow to green. You may delete the cell contents by left clicking the cell to make it active and pressing the "delete" key or right clicking in a cell and selecting "clear contents." To change the color back to yellow, enter the corresponding value (1, 2, 3, or 4).

## Footers

Each tool includes a footer that contains up to three pieces of information. The file name and the tool's tab number appear in the left position of the footer. For tools with multiple hard copy pages, the page numbers appear in the center position. If you print the Planning Checklist, page numbers will appear as "Page 1 of 4," "Page 2 of 4," etc. If you print a one-page tool, the printed copy will not include a page number.

If you select "entire workbook" before printing, the hard copy will be paginated sequentially: "Page X of 26." The entire workbook is 26 pages. Footers are protected and may not be altered. Please note that the Excel print option defaults to "active sheet," so if you want to print the entire workbook (entire set of tools), you need to highlight all of the tabs or select "entire workbook" before printing.

The right position of the footer includes a copyright: © 2007 Karen Martin and Mike Osterling.

## Protection

All sheets are protected. In addition, all cells with the exception of yellow cells have been locked to prevent alteration. Yellow cells—intended to be filled in by the user—are "unlocked" and color coded yellow. This formatting restriction is intentional, designed to prevent you from inadvertently deleting key information, creating inoperable formulas or reformatting the cells.

## Auto-Populate Feature

Certain cells on the various tools serve as source cells that, when data is entered, automatically populate corresponding cells on the same or subsequent tools. Cells that receive this automatic population are color coded salmon (Excel refers to this color as tan). For example, once the executive sponsor's name is entered into cell H3 on the Kaizen Event Charter, it will automatically populate the Executive Sponsor cell on the Planning Checklist, 30-Day List, and all other sheets that include the executive sponsor's name. Another example is when the Event Start Date is entered into cell F4 on the Planning Checklist, the "Due Dates" in column D auto-populate, based on a calculation that includes the Event Start Date and the suggested timing for that activity (four weeks prior to the Kaizen Event, three weeks prior, etc.).

Metrics-based examples appear on the Event Report, and the 30- and 60-Day Audit Reports, in which formulas automatically calculate the projected change and percentage of action items completed. In addition, metrics information entered in the Event Report auto-populate the corresponding cells on the audit reports.

## Insert Pictures

When completing the Event Report sheet, you will notice two sections where you may insert graphs, charts, or pictures. Since this sheet is protected (as are all of the sheets), pictures cannot be inserted using typical Excel commands. To insert pictures, an "insert picture" feature has been added. To use this feature, click the "insert picture" button. After selecting the desired picture file, a pop-up message will appear prompting you to select the cell into which you'll insert the picture—simply type in the cell address (e.g., L7) or click on the desired cell. The picture will auto-size to fit within the selected cell. To enlarge or shrink the image, you may use the standard picture editing commands (e.g., crop and rotate).

## Kaizen Event Tools Licensing Information

The Kaizen Event Tools file is licensed for a single user. Separate copies of "The Kaizen Event Planner" must be purchased for anyone who enters data into or edits the file. No purchase is required for users who only view the file contents.

When the Kaizen Event Tools file is opened for the first time, a pop-up box will appear containing an End User License Agreement (EULA), which specifies the terms and conditions of this license. If you prefer not to see the pop-up box each time the file is opened, you may check the box "Do not show license message at start-up" and "Agree." You may view the EULA at any time by clicking the "License Agreement" button in the top right corner of the Kaizen Event Charter (Tab 1).

If you are distributing the file for viewing purposes, the pop-up box containing the EULA should be activated so the recipents understand the terms and conditions of the license. To reactivate the EULA pop-up, click on the "License Agreement" button in the top right corner of the Kaizen Event Charter (Tab 1) and uncheck the "Do not show license at start up" box.

# PART I

# Lean and Kaizen: An Overview

# CHAPTER 1

# LEAN ENTERPRISE PRINCIPLES

To thrive during strong economic times and survive the inevitable downturns, organizations must continuously improve their ability to deliver high-quality goods and services as quickly as possible—and at the lowest cost. At the same time, they must develop new capabilities, attract and retain a talented workforce, and provide a safe working environment. As market demands, technological advancements, and new business requirements challenge companies to adapt quickly, they need to apply new continuous-improvement tools to create the agility and flexibility necessary to become increasingly responsive to their customers and stakeholders.

But most organizations are plagued with one of two problems at the core of their culture. First, most organizations do not respond quickly. They take so much time analyzing and planning for change that, by the time they are ready to execute it, the parameters under which they were operating have changed, requiring further analysis and planning. The arduous cycle begins again, resulting in little or no meaningful change. Potentially worse, some organizations ignore the altered conditions and move forward, implementing suboptimal improvements.

The second problem arises when organizations behave in the opposite manner—they implement knee-jerk improvements that are not well planned, do not involve all the key stakeholders, and do not connect to the organization's overall strategy. Interestingly, many of these organizations view themselves as responsive and boast at the speed at which they implement change, but then find themselves coping with poor morale, disconnected processes, shrinking margins, and dissatisfied customers.

The Kaizen Event is an effective tool for moving past "analysis paralysis," tying improvements to a larger strategy, and involving all the necessary perspectives to create relevant, measurable, and sustainable improvements. The Kaizen Event is a *two- to five-day focused improvement activity during which a sequestered, cross-functional team designs and fully implements improvements to a defined process or work area.*

While many manufacturers have achieved tremendous improvements using Kaizen Events, the approach often generates even more dramatic results when applied in office, service, and technical environments. In environments where the "product" is difficult to see, the workforce is often disconnected from both internal and external customers, measurement has not been the norm, and significant waste exists. Because these areas directly impact the quality and speed at which organizations are able to deliver goods and services—and, ultimately, their profitability—they are ripe for properly run Kaizen Events. But before exploring the nuts and bolts of this approach, it is necessary to see how Kaizen Events fit into the essential business management philosophy that businesses and organizations must adopt to succeed in today's marketplace: *lean thinking.*

## LEAN THINKING

The story of lean thinking began in the early 1900s in Japan with the Toyoda family business, the Toyoda Automatic Loom Works, which developed a key business principle known as *jidoka*. Jidoka loosely translates as automation with a human touch and involves building in quality as you produce goods and deliver service. Jidoka focuses on enhancing human beings' ability to perform value-adding work, which creates a more humane and positive workplace. Working by trial and error and getting your hands dirty was another important Toyoda family principle. Before you can truly understand a situation or problem, you must go to the area in which the work is being done (*gemba*) and see it for yourself.

In 1930, the Toyoda family established the Toyota Motor Company, which integrated a second key business concept: *just-in-time* (JIT), producing goods and providing services only when needed and only in the quantity needed. Toyota adapted the *continuous flow* manufacturing methodology developed at Ford Motor Company and the *pull* concept (producing to replenish only what has been consumed) used by U.S. supermarkets to maintain low inventories while consistently meeting customer demand. The two principles of *flow* and *pull* were essential to the early success of Toyota, steering them past the wasteful pitfalls of a mass production *push* system that results in overproduction and high inventories. The concepts of jidoka and just-in-time form the two pillars of the Toyota Production System (TPS).

After WWII, W. Edwards Deming, the American statistician who developed the concept of Total Quality Management (TQM), began teaching his philosophy in Japan and Joseph Juran began working directly with Toyota. Influenced by Deming and Juran, Taiichi Ohno led Toyota's philosophical development. Toyota also adopted the scientific approach for problem solving that Deming adapted from Walter Shewhart's work, commonly referred to as the Deming Cycle or Plan-Do-Check-Act (PDCA), and the WWII training program from the United States, Training Within Industry (TWI). These elements formed the basis for the kaizen revolution of democracizing Japanese management and empowering the workforce to continuously identify, design, and implement improvements, no matter how small or large.

By consistently producing high-quality and reasonably priced products, Toyota accelerated its market share gains through the 1980s to their preeminent position today. The book *The Machine that Changed the World* (Womack, Jones, Roos, 1990) revealed Toyota's successes and introduced the Toyota Production System (TPS) to the manufacturing world. The authors contrasted the two production paradigms—batch (mass) production versus continuous flow—and identified TPS as a state-of-the-art business management approach for manufacturing and service delivery.

James Womack and Daniel Jones further developed the lean paradigm in their book *Lean Thinking* (1996), which identified five major lean principles: *value, value stream, pull, flow,* and *perfection*. Table 1-1 describes each principle and the role Kaizen Events play in realizing each principle.

**Table 1-1.** The Five Lean Principles and Their Relationship to Kaizen Events

| Lean Principle | Definition | Relationship to Kaizen Events |
|---|---|---|
| *Specify Value* | Value is defined from the external customer's (end user's) perspective. Knowing what the customer values and is willing to pay for helps differentiate which activities are truly required. | In a Kaizen Event, the team looks at the process targeted for improvement and identifies activities as value-adding, non-value-adding, or necessary non-value-adding. The order of priority for improvement is: 1) *eliminate* unnecessary non-value-adding activities; 2) *reduce* necessary non-value-adding activities; and 3) *optimize* value-adding activities. |
| *Identify the Value Stream* | A value stream represents all value-adding and non-value-adding activities that are required to deliver a product (good or service) from request to delivery (and ultimately, to receipt of payment from the customer). Value stream maps are commonly used to help organizations identify opportunities to improve performance through waste elimination. | The future state value stream map and resulting implementation plan provides direction in identifying where Kaizen Events should be used to implement improvements. |
| *Create Flow* | Flow occurs when a product (good or service) moves through a series of process steps without stopping. Identifying and eliminating non-value-adding activities is the key to achieving continuous flow: processing one unit of work at a time with no waiting or delays between or within process steps. | A common goal in Kaizen Events is to create flow through waste elimination. An essential activity is having the team view the process as though they were the material, data, or paperwork being passed through the system—or the thing or person receiving service—and identifying all the stops along the way. After determining why the stops occur, the team members are able to use relevant lean tools to improve flow. |
| *Pull from the Customer* | Pull is a scheduling methodology used to reduce process lead times. Pull is a key tenet within most flow systems, and is also a necessary strategy in situations where flow cannot yet be realized. Pull is based on the concept whereby consumption of resources triggers the replenishment of that resource. That is, the upstream supplier doesn't produce anything until the downstream customer signals a need and has available capacity to begin work. | Pull is often achieved most easily during Kaizen Events, since a cross-functional team can ensure that both supplier and customer requirements are taken into account. Pull systems include one-piece flow, FIFO lanes, and kanban. |
| *Seek Perfection* | In the pursuit of perfection, the company must continuously strive to eliminate all waste along all value streams to achieve continuous flow. The more a lean-seeking company works on the other four principles, the greater ease it has in identifying additional opportunities for improvement. | Learning is most effective if accompanied by "doing." Kaizen Events are an effective means for the workforce to learn new tools, practice real-world application in a facilitated environment, and become better prepared to implement other improvements in the future. Holding multiple Kaizen Events for the same process gives the team the opportunity to learn about and apply more advanced tools. |

In the 1990s, fueled by Womack's findings and Toyota's continued success at capturing a progressively greater market share, U.S. automotive companies began adopting selected aspects of lean thinking and TPS with varying degrees of success. Many other types of manufacturers followed suit, first in high-volume/low-variation environments, then later in custom job shop settings. Success in the latter category led practitioners to see the parallels between high-variation manufacturing and non-manufacturing processes. Today, lean thinking has spread to healthcare, government, research organizations, food service, education, construction, information technology, nonprofit organizations, financial services, and law enforcement, to name a few. All of the success stories report the same results: The journey to becoming a lean enterprise generates *rapid* and *sustainable* organizational improvements that far surpass traditional approaches. The reasons are attributable to lean principles, which:

- use customer-defined value to drive the way in which an organization delivers services or manufactures goods;
- use lead time as a primary metric to identify opportunities and drive improvement;
- seek ways to improve the entire value stream, from request to delivery, rather than optimizing individual components of a delivery system;
- engage the entire workforce in shortening lead time and improving quality through the elimination of waste;
- seek out root causes to performance problems and apply innovative solutions that exploit existing resources before considering capital expenditures;
- generate rapid and sustainable results, often through the proper use of Kaizen Events;
- improve organizational performance by building organization-wide accountability, standards, discipline, and trust.

One can visualize this integrated approach to operational excellence using the principle components of a house, including the foundation, pillars, bricks, and roof. Adapted from the original Toyota Production System house that was developed by Taiichi Ohno disciple Fujio Cho, and further refined by Jeffrey Liker in *The Toyota Way*, Figure 1-1 illustrates how lean principles and tools can build upon each other to achieve optimal organizational performance.

Those familiar with the TPS house will note that speed and quality, the pillars around which the house is built, represent the concepts of just-in-time and jidoka on the traditional TPS house. Also, two people-based outcomes specified in the figure—motivated workforce and customer loyalty—sandwich the tactical tools that are used to achieve flow, and flow is achieved when both speed and quality are present. Finally, it's important to note that daily kaizen and Kaizen Events are part of the foundation of building the lean enterprise house, and serve as the tactical means to implement lean principles.

The remainder of this chapter looks more closely at the first two lean principles—value and value stream, the first and second layers in the house's foundation—which are essential in driving the need for improvement and creating a relevant strategy. The other three principles—flow, pull, and perfection—form the core of the kaizen philosophy and are discussed throughout the book.

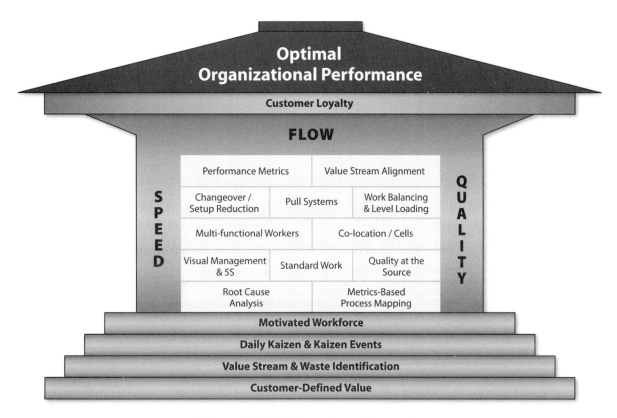

**Figure 1-1.** Building a Lean Enterprise

## DEFINING VALUE—ELIMINATING NON-VALUE-ADDING ACTIVITIES

Lean thinking defines value from the external customer's perspective. In processes that have intermediary internal customers and/or multiple external customers, view your processes first from the end user's perspective. "What does this customer (end user) value and is, therefore, willing to pay for?" That is, if the customer knew the incremental cost for a particular activity, would he or she be willing to pay for it?

A mature lean organization views every activity through the customer lens. It seeks to identify, from the customer's perspective, all activities that are *non-value-adding and that, therefore, merely add operational expense.* Theoretically, from the customer's perspective, every activity that does not add value to the service or good is waste, and the organization should eliminate it.

But classifying waste as non-value-adding (NVA) is not always that straightforward. A lean enterprise understands that some activities are *necessary non-value-adding*—though they are non-value-adding through the eyes of the external customer, they are essential to properly operate the business. Activities that are necessary to meet regulatory requirements and accreditation standards fall into this category, as do many activities within support departments that do not provide direct value to the customer, such as human resources, information technology, finance, legal, etc. In these areas, the goal becomes to *reduce* the effort required to assure 100 percent compliance and proper operation of the business.

Table 1-2 shows how lean thinking reverses the way improvement efforts have been traditionally prioritized. With this new perspective, the first priority is to eliminate unnecessary NVA, followed by reducing necessary NVA, and then optimizing value-adding activities. In many cases, the traditional approach—which focused on helping people perform the value-adding work faster—created quality, safety, and morale problems that exacerbated the organizational performance issues that drove the need for improvement in the first place. Toyota has turned this thinking on its ear.

**Table 1-2.** Lean Versus Traditional NVA and VA Activities

| SHIFTING THE FOCUS OF IMPROVEMENT ACTIVITIES | | |
|---|---|---|
| **Type of Activity** | **Lean Approach** | **Traditional Approach** |
| Unnecessary non-value-adding | 1st Priority—Eliminate | Often unrecognized, hidden, or accepted as is |
| Necessary non-value-adding | 2nd Priority—Challenge and reduce | Accepted as required |
| Value-adding | 3rd Priority—Optimize as necessary | Top improvement priority, primary focus |

While optimizing value-adding activities is important, lean thinking shows that faster and more dramatic results occur by first eliminating NVA activities—in part, because the traditional view did not consider this aspect when evaluating how to improve a process. The outcomes from eliminating NVA are measurable and wide ranging, including faster delivery, improved quality, freed capacity, and reduced inventory—all of which lead to greater customer loyalty, market share and reduced expenses. *Collateral benefits* that result from eliminating non-value-adding work include improved interdepartmental and interpersonal relationships, safer working conditions, and reduced workforce frustration—all of which create a work environment that attracts and retains a talented workforce, which, in turn, leads to further business growth.

Toyota's Taiichi Ohno identified seven major types of non-value-adding activities, also known as *muda* or waste: 1) overproduction, 2) waiting, 3) defects (errors), 4) overprocessing, 5) inventory, 6) movement (motion), and 7) transportation. Many lean practitioners have since added an eighth waste, 8) underutilization of people, to underscore the degree to which many workers are not being utilized to their fullest potential. But these eight wastes are not the direct targets for elimination. Root cause analysis reveals that they are merely symptoms of underlying problems. To truly eliminate the waste, you have to identify and eliminate the relevant root causes for the waste that is preventing flow in the value stream. Simply looking for and even addressing the "symptoms" in suboptimal processes will not effectively eliminate waste.

Table 1-3 lists the eight wastes as they frequently appear in office, service sector, and technical environments. One waste often causes another, multiplying the problems exponentially. For example, motion may result in batching, which produces waiting. We often inadvertently

**Table 1-3.** Eight Wastes in Office, Service, and Technical Environments

| Waste | Explanation | Evidence | Risks | Common Root Causes |
|---|---|---|---|---|
| **Overproduction** | Producing too much, too fast or too soon.<br><br>Upstream supplier pushes work to downstream customer regardless of whether he or she has the capacity to work on it. | Build up of work-in-process (WIP) between process steps.<br><br>Build up of queues, people waiting, etc. | Excessive lead times (also referred to as throughput and turnaround time).<br><br>Unnecessary complexity and confusion due to reprioritization of tasks and the development of multiple tracking systems. | Lack of focus on entire value stream.<br><br>Push environment.<br><br>Individual performance is valued more highly than team/value stream performance.<br><br>Ignoring downstream bottlenecks. |
| **Waiting** | People waiting for people.<br><br>Information, product, or equipment waiting for people.<br><br>People waiting for information, product, or equipment. | "The thing" passing through the system stops.<br><br>Idle people.<br><br>Idle bottleneck equipment. | Extended lead times, long work days, and paid overtime.<br><br>Unnecessary capital expenditures for equipment. | Too many handoffs or approvals required.<br><br>Push environment.<br><br>Suboptimal use of equipment.<br><br>Unbalanced workloads.<br><br>Lack of cross-training. |
| **Overprocessing** | Doing more to anything than the customer is willing to pay for. | Inspections, audits, and reviews.<br><br>Redundant tasks, duplicate data entry, rewriting, etc.<br><br>Too many handoffs; multiple approvals. | Excessive lead times.<br><br>Low productivity.<br><br>Frustrated workforce. | Lack of trust between individuals and departments.<br><br>Unclear understanding of customer requirements.<br><br>Too many or too few software applications, which result in workaround development. |
| **Defects** | Internal or external suppliers providing incomplete or incorrect information or material. | Correcting information that has been supplied.<br><br>Adding missing information that should have been supplied.<br><br>Clarifying information that should have been clear when supplied. | Errors become defects that require rework, a 100% NVA activity.<br><br>Produces dissatisfied customers, frustrated workers, lost productivity, and extended lead times. | Nonstandard work.<br><br>Poor training.<br><br>Lack of visual work instructions and job aids.<br><br>Poor communication between internal upstream suppliers and downstream customers about customer requirements and performance. |

*(Continued on next page)*

**Table 1-3.** Eight Wastes in Office, Service, and Technical Environments, *continued*

| Waste | Explanation | Evidence | Risks | Common Root Causes |
|---|---|---|---|---|
| **Inventory** | Excess paperwork, supplies, materials, equipment, etc. | Stockpiles of supplies, forms, materials, etc. Disorganized storage areas. | Reduced cash flow. Lost productivity due to searching. Excess Space. Damage. Obsolescence. | Just-in-case thinking. Unreliable or burdensome purchasing process. Unreliable suppliers. |
| **Motion** | Movement of people. | Hand carrying work product. Functional layout. Traveling to shared equipment. Searching for information; seeking information clarification. | Reduced capacity to perform value-adding work, which produces increased staffing requirements. Injury. | Poor layout. Lack of cross-training. Insufficient equipment. |
| **Transportation** | Movement of "things" — paperwork, electronic information, material, drawings, equipment, and supplies. | Hand carrying. Traveling to shared equipment. Searching for information; seeking information clarification. | Damage or loss during transport. Delay in work being available. | Poor layout. Lack of cross-training. |
| **Underutilization of people** | Not utilizing the full capacity of the individual — knowledge, skills, aptitude, and creativity. | Excessive reviews and approvals. Specialized workers and sole-service providers. Processes designed by managers or select few workers. Excessive hand-offs. | Frustrated and unfulfilled workforce. Absenteeism. Turnover. Excessive handoffs and delays. | Difficulty in "letting go" and allowing workers to design and implement improvements. Lack of trust in ability of workforce to perform. Lack of training. Siloed thinking. |

create the waste of overprocessing, such as approvals, reviews and audits, to cope with the waste of errors. Overproduction creates a buildup of inventory, work-in-process, and queues—which, in turn, produces waiting. And so on.

A surprising finding about waste is how tiny pockets of seemingly insignificant waste add up over time. For example, an organization with *1,500 employees*, each earning an average of *$22 per hour*, estimated that each employee spent at least ten minutes a day looking for information on shared drives, or looking for the equipment and supplies necessary to perform their tasks. When they calculated the impact of this problem, they were shocked. Disorganized shared drives and storage areas were costing this company *41.7 hours* of wasted time per year, per employee. Viewed another way, each employee could take an additional week of vacation with no appreciable loss to the organization. Or the company could absorb growth that would have traditionally required thirty additional full-time employees, without adding a single worker—a potential cost avoidance of *$1.4 million*.

Table 1-4 provides two additional examples of seemingly minor office waste that, when viewed over the course of a month, quarter, or year, result in significant performance losses.

**Table 1-4.** Two Additional Examples of Waste in the Office

| Motion Waste | Overprocessing Waste |
|---|---|
| A department was having difficulty meeting customer demand and the supervisor wanted to hire two additional employees. Her boss resisted. Upon analysis of the processes, she was able to handle the growing workload with no additional employees being hired and, at the same time, improve departmental morale dramatically. Here's how: the staff had to walk **788 feet** to a printer. And they did this **31,200 times** per year, which translates into **4,656 miles per year**.<br><br>Assuming a one mile per hour walk pace (a slow but surprisingly common finding in offices due to interruptions along the way and waiting for shared equipment to become available), the motion translated into **582 days** of non-value-adding time, which equals approximately **2.2 FTEs** (Full-time Equivalents). By reorganizing the departmental layout, they were able to move the printer adjacent to the workstations, which freed them to handle an increased workload without hiring additional staff. And the staff was thrilled to eliminate an activity they had long complained about. | This case illustrates a surprisingly common waste—excessive handoffs and approvals—in which eight approvals were required for a purchase requisition before a purchase order could be generated. Current state analysis revealed that each approval took approximately three minutes to complete. Yet the requisitions waited from **four hours** to **five days**, depending on the reviewer. During a Kaizen Event, each approval was reviewed for its necessity. As a result, six of the eight approvals were eliminated, and overnight the organization reduced its turnaround time from **10 days** to **2.25 days**—a **77.5% improvement**—greatly increasing the speed in which workers were able to receive the supplies and material they needed to perform their work. And there was no quality loss from eliminating the redundant handoffs. |

Many organizations are likely to have similar types of waste riddled throughout their processes, slowing customer responsiveness, increasing operational expense, and producing worker frustration. A few wasted minutes here and there can add up to significant productivity losses and increased costs over the course of time. So how does a lean-seeking company go about uncovering these eight wastes? By following the second lean principle: identifying the value stream.

## MAPPING THE VALUE STREAM

Value stream maps are invaluable tools for visualizing macro-level process steps, identifying the waste in those steps, and creating a desired *future state* (sometimes referred to as the "ideal" or "desired" state). It's beyond the scope of this book to teach you how to map value streams and there are several excellent resources available on that topic. In *Learning to See* (Rother and Shook, 2003), the authors provided a systematic approach for analyzing the current state of a value stream and designing a future state for manufacturing operations. *The Complete Lean Enterprise* (Keyte and Locher, 2004) and *Value Stream Management for the Lean Office* (Tapping and Shuker, 2003) are excellent guides for mapping value streams in nonmanufacturing environments.

The CD that accompanies this book includes printable sample current and future state value stream maps for a purchasing process to show the connection between value stream mapping and Kaizen Events. Readers are encouraged to print a copy of these maps to refer to while reading the rest of this section.

Value stream maps are visual storyboards. Limited to an $11'' \times 17''$ piece of paper, the current state map documents how the process is currently being performed and helps visualize waste, revealing opportunities for improvement. It represents a snapshot in time—the process as it exists on *the day that you map*—and sets the foundation for designing the future (desired) state. The future state value stream map is a management-level strategic plan. It illustrates the value stream, as you envision it three to six months in the future, and the improvements necessary to fully realize the future state. Some practitioners encourage mapping teams to create longer-term future states, but when mapping a value stream for the first time, shorter implementation time frames are advised (especially in office and service environments), as this practice drives a bias toward action. Table 1-5 defines the common value stream mapping icons that provide necessary shorthand for visualizing a process.

Value stream maps illustrate three major types of information: information flow, product flow, and a timeline. The upper portion of the map typically contains information flow—both verbal and electronic—and depicts how information is passed through the system. How is work scheduled? Which IT systems are involved?

The bottom portion of the map depicts the macro-level process steps for product flow. Typically, each block represents a series of micro-level tasks that are performed before there is a break in the timeline due to a buildup of work-in-process (represented on the value stream map by an inventory triangle), queues, or delays of any sort. Often, the delay is due to handoffs to a different work team or functional department.

**Table 1-5.** Common Value Stream Mapping Icons

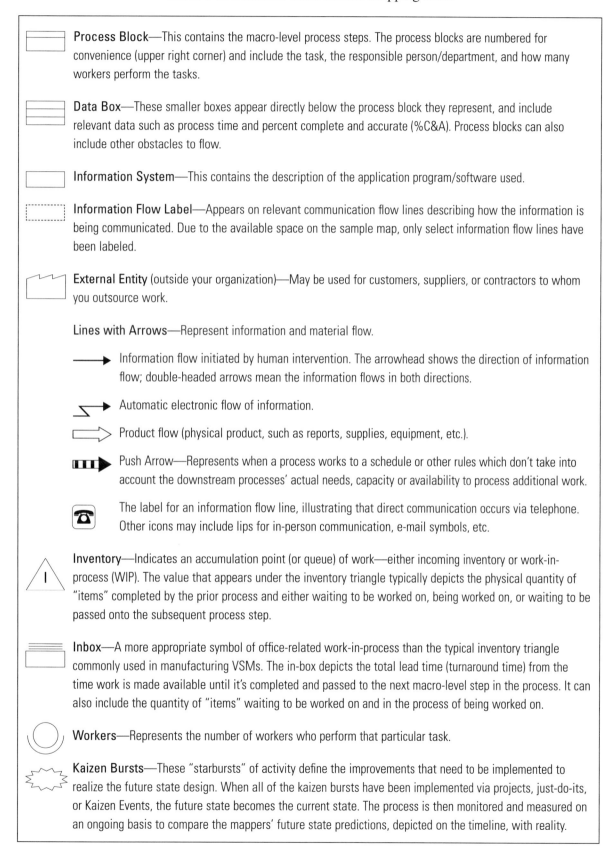

**Process Block**—This contains the macro-level process steps. The process blocks are numbered for convenience (upper right corner) and include the task, the responsible person/department, and how many workers perform the tasks.

**Data Box**—These smaller boxes appear directly below the process block they represent, and include relevant data such as process time and percent complete and accurate (%C&A). Process blocks can also include other obstacles to flow.

**Information System**—This contains the description of the application program/software used.

**Information Flow Label**—Appears on relevant communication flow lines describing how the information is being communicated. Due to the available space on the sample map, only select information flow lines have been labeled.

**External Entity** (outside your organization)—May be used for customers, suppliers, or contractors to whom you outsource work.

**Lines with Arrows**—Represent information and material flow.

Information flow initiated by human intervention. The arrowhead shows the direction of information flow; double-headed arrows mean the information flows in both directions.

Automatic electronic flow of information.

Product flow (physical product, such as reports, supplies, equipment, etc.).

**Push Arrow**—Represents when a process works to a schedule or other rules which don't take into account the downstream processes' actual needs, capacity or availability to process additional work.

The label for an information flow line, illustrating that direct communication occurs via telephone. Other icons may include lips for in-person communication, e-mail symbols, etc.

**Inventory**—Indicates an accumulation point (or queue) of work—either incoming inventory or work-in-process (WIP). The value that appears under the inventory triangle typically depicts the physical quantity of "items" completed by the prior process and either waiting to be worked on, being worked on, or waiting to be passed onto the subsequent process step.

**Inbox**—A more appropriate symbol of office-related work-in-process than the typical inventory triangle commonly used in manufacturing VSMs. The in-box depicts the total lead time (turnaround time) from the time work is made available until it's completed and passed to the next macro-level step in the process. It can also include the quantity of "items" waiting to be worked on and in the process of being worked on.

**Workers**—Represents the number of workers who perform that particular task.

**Kaizen Bursts**—These "starbursts" of activity define the improvements that need to be implemented to realize the future state design. When all of the kaizen bursts have been implemented via projects, just-do-its, or Kaizen Events, the future state becomes the current state. The process is then monitored and measured on an ongoing basis to compare the mappers' future state predictions, depicted on the timeline, with reality.

The timeline, traditionally drawn as a saw tooth visual with peaks and valleys, may also be drawn as a single straight line and includes the two primary time metrics:

1. *Process time*—the time it actually takes to perform the task, and includes both "touch time" and "think time" for processes that are analytical in nature. Process time is also sometimes referred to as cycle time, though cycle time has several meanings and can be confusing when used in non-manufacturing environments.

2. *Lead time*—the elapsed time from when the work is made available until it is completed and passed on to the next step in the process. Lead time is also sometimes referred to as throughput time, turnaround time (TAT), or clock time.

An additional metric that measures quality throughout the process—*% Complete and Accurate (%C&A)*—is also included. Table 1-6 contains definitions for these metrics, as well as a calculated quality metric (rolled first pass yield) that are helpful in analyzing the current state and establishing a baseline from which to measure improvements. These and other key mapping metrics are discussed in greater detail in Chapter 12 during the introduction to *metrics-based process mapping*.

**Table 1-6.** Key Metrics for Value Stream Mapping

| Abbreviation | Metric | Description |
|---|---|---|
| LT | Lead Time | The elapsed time from the time work is made available to a person, work area, or department until it is made available to the next person, work area, or department in the process. LT = PT + Waiting/Delays. Typically expressed in hours, days, weeks, and months. |
| PT | Process Time | The typical touch time it takes to complete an activity if the worker was able to work on one job uninterrupted. Also referred to as touch time or cycle time. In office and service environments, PT is often expressed in minutes or hours. |
| AR | Activity Ratio | PT/LT x 100 = The percentage of time work is actively being worked on (including analysis, discussion, and physical transformation). 100-AR = the percentage of time work is sitting idle. Note: In manufacturing, this metric is often referred to as %VA (percent value-adding). Our concern with this label is that it carries with it an erroneous assumption that all of the process time is value-adding, when this is rarely the case. |
| C&A | Percent Complete & Accurate | The percentage of occurrences in which a person, work area, or department releases work that doesn't require the downstream customer to correct the information supplied, add information that should have been supplied, or clarify information that should have been made clear upfront. |
| RFPY | Rolled First Pass Yield | The product of all of the process block's C&A (in its decimal form) expressed as a percentage. Rolled First Past Yield represents the percentage of time "the thing" (i.e., paper, data, people) passes through the process completely "clean," requiring no rework (which includes correcting, adding, or clarifying information that should have been complete and accurate when it reached the downstream customer). |

Traditional mapping convention places the customer icon in the upper right-hand corner of the map and the supplier icon in the upper left. But in many non-manufacturing processes, the customer and the supplier are one and the same—especially if the customer is internal to the organization. In this case, you may prefer to center the customer block at the top of your map.

Figure 1-2 shows the current state value stream map for a purchasing process. The map depicts the value stream—from order to delivery—for nonrepetitive purchases of less than $5,000. The driver for the mapping activity came from members of the engineering group, who complained that they were not able to meet project deadlines because it took too long to get the supplies they needed. So the customers for this process are the 31 engineers—the "requisition originators"—who collectively initiate approximately 615 requisitions per year for nonrepetitive supplies and material purchases.

At the time the current state map was created, the average lead time for the engineers to receive the materials they had ordered was 28.4 business days (5.7 weeks). During those 28 days, the requisition and the subsequent purchase order that the requisition evolves into were only being worked on ("touched") for a total of 65 minutes (process time). As a result, the process had an overall *activity ratio* (the percentage of time work is being done to or concerning "the thing" passing through the process) of 0.5 percent—which means that the customer request was being worked on less than one percent of the total lead time.

Another finding was that, of the ten macro-level steps the requisition went through, five of them were inspection steps, in the form of review. In these steps, no physical transformation of the requisition was occurring. If you were this organization's external customer, would you consider these reviews value-adding? If you were one of the engineers (internal customer), would you consider it value-adding—or even necessary—to have others review your work?

You'll note that, for many of these reviews, the requisition sat for a full day before undergoing a five-minute review. Further, we see that excessive lead times at blocks four, eight, and nine created bottlenecks where work-in-process had accumulated. It took the systems engineer (who travels 50 percent of the time) an average of one work week to complete a five-minute review, and once the requisitions reached the corporate purchasing area, they sat for another two weeks (three and seven business days at blocks eight and nine, respectively) before the purchase order (P.O.) was generated and submitted to the supplier. It then took the supplier another two weeks before they shipped the order.

Another thing we see is that six separate software programs or systems are utilized in this process, which prompted the mapping team to wonder: Was there a way to streamline the system aspects of the process?

An additional issue was that a severe quality problem existed. The overall quality performance of this process is reflected in a rolled first pass yield of only five percent. That is, only five out of 100 requisitions passed through the process "clean"—with no rework required—on the first attempt. Interestingly, the mapping team discovered that the bulk of the quality issues in the process were generated by the customer. This is a surprisingly common finding in office- and service-related processes where, traditionally, upstream and

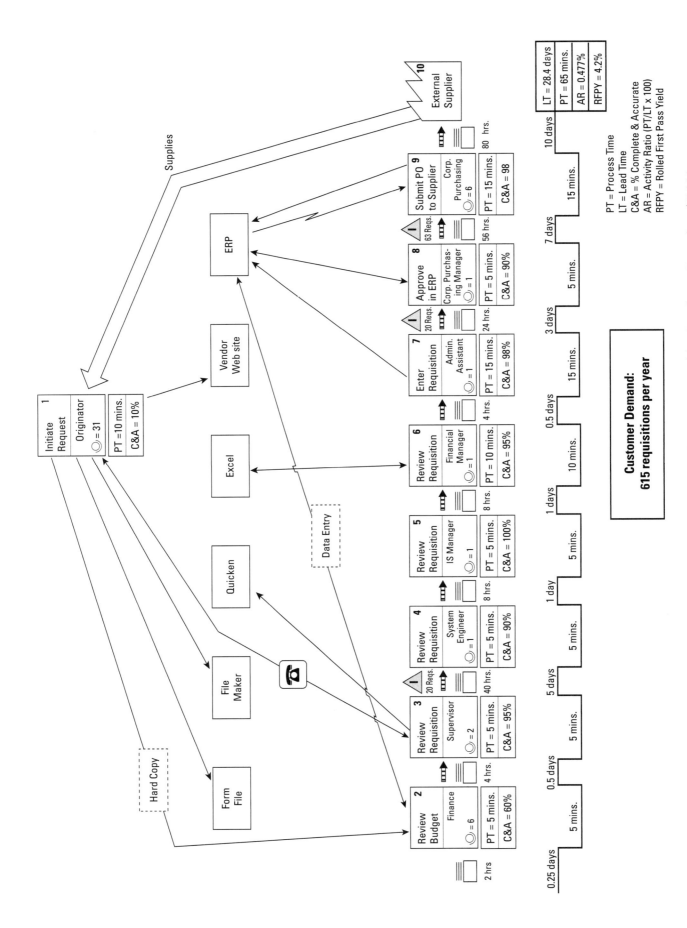

**Figure 1-2.** Current State Value Stream Map: Purchasing—Nonrepetitive Purchases Less than $5,000

PT = Process Time
LT = Lead Time
C&A = % Complete & Accurate
AR = Activity Ratio (PT/LT x 100)
RFPY = Rolled First Pass Yield

| LT = 28.4 days |
|---|
| PT = 65 mins. |
| AR = 0.477% |
| RFPY = 4.2% |

**Customer Demand:
615 requisitions per year**

downstream process workers—the internal suppliers and customers within the process—haven't talked about requirements nor measured quality output along the value stream.

And finally, an issue not reflected on the map itself but revealed through the mapping process was that, at the time of mapping, the overall morale in this organization was quite low, resulting in high turnover in two areas. The originators were consistently frustrated by how long it took to get the material they needed for their projects, and the corporate purchasing department was chronically overwhelmed with a backlog of requisitions waiting to be processed.

So in creating the future state map, the mapping team focused on three desired outcomes: shortening the lead time, improving overall quality, and eliminating the bottlenecks to improve flow and reduce workforce stress and frustration.

Figure 1-3, the future state design, includes several key improvements: reducing the number of reviews, creating a higher quality product entering the process (more complete and accurate requisitions), and eliminating the bottlenecks—all of which greatly reduce lead time and improve quality. Note that the mapping did not create a *"perfect state"* with this future state map. Additional opportunities still existed, such as delivery lead time from the outside supplier, which has since been addressed. Reducing supplier lead time further improved the engineer's experience of the process (improving retention), shortened the response time to the external customer, reduced expenses as the cost of expediting was eliminated, and improved quality as ineffective shortcuts were eliminated.

Table 1-7 contains a summary of the current state metrics and the mapping team's projections for value stream performance when all of the kaizen bursts have been implemented and the future state is fully realized.

**Table 1-7.** Projected Future State Results

| Metric | Current State | Projected Future State | % Improvement |
|---|---|---|---|
| LT | 28.4 days | 12.3 days | 56.7% |
| PT | 65 mins. | 30 mins. | 53.8% |
| AR | 0.48% | 0.51% | 6.3% |
| RFPY | 4.2% | 71.0% | 1,590% |
| # Steps | 10 | 5 | 50% |
| # IT Systems | 6 | 3 | 50% |

The future state map isn't designed to include micro-level details about how specifically to implement the improvement—those decisions fall to the Kaizen Team or others implementing improvements. Rather, the kaizen bursts on the future state map illustrate *what* improvements need to be implemented to realize the future state and form the foundation of the implementation plan (Table 1-8). The implementation plan categorizes improvements based on the best type of implementation approach for that particular improvement. Just-do-its (JDI)

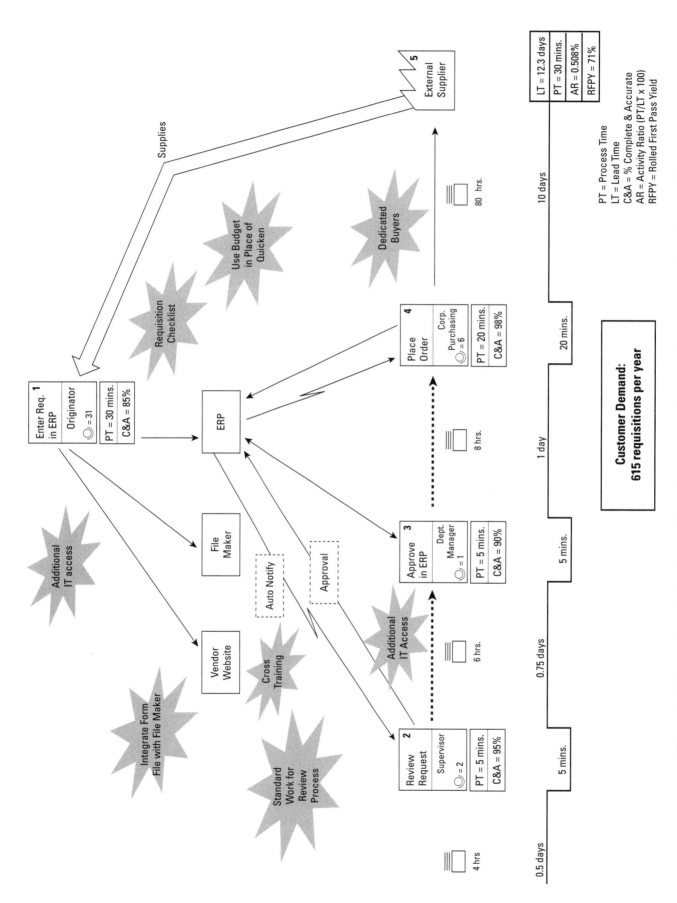

**Figure 1-3.** Future State Value Stream Map: Purchasing—Nonrepetitive Purchases Less than $5,000

Table 1-8. Future State Implementation Plan

## FUTURE STATE IMPLEMENTATION PLAN

| | | Implementation Plan Review Dates | |
|---|---|---|---|
| Executive Sponsor | Allen Ward | 2-Nov | 14-Dec |
| Value Stream Champion | Karen Louise | 16-Nov | 28-Dec |
| Value Stream Mapping Facilitator | Thomas Albin | 30-Nov | 11-Jan |
| Date Created | 10/5/2007 | | |

| Block # | Goal Objective | Improvement Activity | Type* | Owner | Implementation Schedule (weeks) 1–12 | Date Completed |
|---|---|---|---|---|---|---|
| 1, 3, 6, | Reduce number of IT systems by 50%; orginator to corp PT to 40 min. | Integrate FormFile data with MasterFile system | Proj | Dianne M. | ↑ (weeks 8–11) | |
| 2, 4–6 | Reduce number of review/approvals by 66%; orginator to corp LT = 1.25 days | Put in place standard work for requisition review | KE | Ryan A. | ↑ (weeks 3–8) | |
| 7 | Eliminate handoff to admin. assistant; originator to corp LT = 1.25 days | Define standard work and cross-train orginators in use of ERP | KE | Sean M. | ↑ (weeks 5–8) | |
| 1 | Improve %C&A from originator to 85%; RFPY to 71% | Create checklist for initiation of requsition, integrate into form | KE | Ryan A. | ↑ (weeks 5–8) | |
| 3 | Reduce number of IT systems by 50% | Eliminate use of Quicken | JDI | Dianne M. | ↑ (week 2) | |
| 8, 9 | Reduce LT through corporate purchasing group to 1 day | Put dedicated buyers in place (by commodity) | PROJ | Sam P. | ↑ (weeks 5–7) | |
| | | | | | | |
| | | | | | | |
| | | | | | | |

### APPROVALS

| Value Stream Champion | Value Stream Mapping Facilitator |
|---|---|
| Signature: | Signature: |
| Date: | Date: |

| Executive Sponsor |
|---|
| Signature: |
| Date: |

*JDI = Just-do-it; KE = Kaizen Event; PROJ = Project

are simple improvements that take a day or less to complete. Projects (PROJ) include activities that will take weeks or months to complete. Improvements best suited for Kaizen Events (KE) are those that are most effectively implemented in two- to five-day focused activities by sequestered, cross-functional teams. These improvements are often bundled together and implemented during a single Kaizen event.

One final general note about value stream mapping: It is as much an art as it is a science. While mapping conventions exist, and it's important to stick with convention as much as possible so that a wider number of people can interpret your maps, the art of value stream mapping—especially in office, service, and technical environments—is knowing when to break with convention for the sake of creating a clear, concise map that serves its purpose: visualizing the process, illustrating the need for improvement, and defining an action plan for implementing the defined improvements.

Value stream maps have proven to be effective tools to heighten leadership's level of awareness regarding the opportunities for improvement. These maps are also invaluable for defining what tactical-level activities need to take place to accomplish leadership's vision for value stream performance. The kaizen philosophy and Kaizen Events are being used around the world to execute improvement in support of that vision. So what are the characteristics of kaizen and Kaizen Events? Read on.

# CHAPTER 2

# KAIZEN CHARACTERISTICS

Kaizen is a Japanese word that, loosely translated, means to take apart (*kai* = change) and put together in a better way (*zen* = good). The term, commonly used in Japan, moved into mainstream American business language when Masaaki Imai's book *Kaizen: The Key to Japan's Competitive Success* was published in 1986. But only through repeated applications of lean principles and tools has the West begun to understand the true meaning of kaizen, which goes far beyond process improvement.

Kaizen, or continuous incremental improvement, refers to a philosophy—a way of thinking and behaving. It's about empowering and unleashing the creative power of people who actually do the work, in order to design more effective and efficient processes—*and not requiring leadership's hands-on involvement in doing so*. Practicing kaizen on a daily basis infuses lean thinking into the organization's DNA, fueling the shift to a continuous-improvement culture—an essential element in high-performing organizations. Ideally, everyone in an organization—from senior leadership to frontline workers, and from those delivering value to customers directly to those supporting the delivery of value—begins to "think lean" and apply kaizen every minute of the day. The true purpose of kaizen is to humanize the workplace, eliminate hard work (both mental and physical), and teach the workforce how to effectively solve problems *as they arise*, by using a scientific and learn-by-doing approach. At its core, kaizen is far more about people and human dignity than it is about specific process design.

Kaizen *Events*, on the other hand, are formalized activities that organizations use to achieve rapid and dramatic improvements (*kaikaku*) and progressively shift their culture. Kaizen Events create a structured environment in which teams learn how to identify waste and apply specific lean tools to eliminate it. In this "learn-by-doing" environment, teams become more comfortable with their authority to make improvements, and leadership learns to let go of the tactical details for which frontline workers are best suited. Under the guidance of a skilled facilitator, Kaizen Events generate rapid results, relying on the creative power of a cross-functional team to design and implement innovative ways to perform work, often reaching breakthrough performance levels.

Well-executed Kaizen Events deliver results at unprecedented speed and magnitude. Table 2-1 shows the typical outcomes for two- to five-day Events.

Putting these into financial terms, actual kaizen teams have achieved the following results during a single two- to five-day Kaizen Event:

- A healthcare organization created the capacity to earn $1.2 million more in annual revenue without adding additional staff or equipment.

**Table 2-1.** Typical Results Achieved by Kaizen Teams

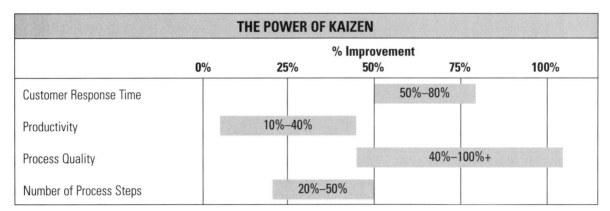

| THE POWER OF KAIZEN | | | | | |
|---|---|---|---|---|---|
| | % Improvement | | | | |
| | 0% | 25% | 50% | 75% | 100% |
| Customer Response Time | | | 50%–80% | | |
| Productivity | 10%–40% | | | | |
| Process Quality | | | 40%–100%+ | | |
| Number of Process Steps | 20%–50% | | | | |

- A publicly traded medical device manufacturer reduced its turnaround time to process complex sales orders from 7.5 days to less than two days, improving the company's cash flow significantly, and delighting its customers and shareholders.

- An administrative department, with an opening for two FTEs, discontinued its search because the Kaizen Team freed enough capacity to do the work with the staff they had—and with less stress than when they were fully staffed.

- An oil industry supplier doubled its output in a given time period, at half the original cost.

- A healthcare organization reduced patient care delays from 35 percent of its cases to 15 percent, improving patient loyalty and, by extension, assuring ongoing revenue.

- An engineering department reduced the engineering change notice process from 36 days to less than five days (85 percent reduction in lead time), and creating the capacity to process 50 percent more change notices with no additional staffing.

- A financial services organization reduced its application review turnaround from 19 days to 11 days (42 percent improvement in customer responsiveness) and reduced the collective process time to verify customer information from 19.3 to 8.5 months per year (56 percent improved capacity).

- A department about to incur significant expense by leasing additional storage space discontinued its plans by freeing half of its existing storage space.

Kaizen Events deliver consistent results: faster turnaround, improved productivity, better quality, and reduced expenses—all of which lead to greater customer loyalty, market share, and profitability. In addition to these directly measurable improvements, a wide variety of collateral benefits exist that, while they may be tougher to measure, are equally important in producing high-performing organizations. Enhanced job satisfaction results when workers engage in more meaningful work with less stress. Kaizen Events also result in better working relationships between individuals and departments and the workforce becomes more valuable to the organization. When staff members understand how work is done and build their expertise beyond their defined work areas, they become better decision-makers and problem-solvers in the process. And an important side benefit of having a well-developed workforce is that word gets out. Before long, the organization becomes an employer of choice and is able to attract and retain a talented workforce.

Arguably, the more important result from using the Kaizen Event approach is the culture shift it initiates over time. Leadership begins to let go of tactical-level involvement so they can finally focus on strategic thinking, creating proactive solutions, and removing obstacles to their staff's success. Trust is built. Transparency becomes a way of life, rather than covering up problems. The blame game ends. Communication improves. Everyone works together to solve problems rather than only caring about his or her piece. And, most importantly, the customer takes his or her rightful place in an organization's psyche.

Another reason Kaizen Events are so powerful is that they teach the organization how to solve problems through the scientific approach of plan-do-check-act (PDCA), one of the cornerstones of the Toyota Production System. In a properly executed PDCA improvement cycle, the focus is on *seeking* perfection rather than *waiting* for perfection, and on being approximately right rather than exactly wrong. You avoid analysis paralysis through strict time management and accelerated movement to the next stage in the cycle.

As illustrated in Table 2-2, the PDCA cycle is present at two levels in Kaizen Events. The three phases of Kaizen Events—planning, execution, and follow-up—complete a macro-level PDCA cycle. Within the Event itself (the execution phase) lies a micro PDCA cycle. Further in this book, Part II of this book focuses on the "P" in the macro cycle, Part III focuses on "D," and Part IV includes both "C" and "A." The micro PDCA cycle begins in Chapter 12 and concludes in Chapter 18.

**Table 2-2.** Plan–Do–Check–Act's Role in Kaizen Event Management and Execution

| PDCA (Deming Cycle) | Macro-level PDCA (Entire Kaizen Event Process) |
|---|---|
| *Plan:* Determine process objectives and methods for achieving them | Plan and prepare for the Kaizen Event; obtain baseline data as needed |
| *Do:* Design and implement improvements; train workers | Observe and analyze the current process; design the improved process; test, standardize and document the new process; train workforce |
| *Check:* Measure the impact of the improvements | Monitor process performance; conduct 30-day audit |
| *Act:* Make further improvements as necessary by repeating the PDCA cycle | Evaluate process performance, compare with Value Stream objectives, make further improvements as needed |

| Micro-Level PDCA (Execution Phase) |
|---|
| *Plan:* Study the micro-level current state; identify, select and prioritize improvements |
| *Do:* Design the improved process |
| *Check:* Test the improved process |
| *Act:* Modify the improved process as required, standardize and document the new process, train the affected workforce |

Building on the cornerstone characteristics of the kaizen philosophy identified by Imai, successful kaizen efforts (whether through daily practice or formal events) have common features that can be divided into two categories as shown in Tables 2-3 and 2-4: 1) the philosophical and people aspects of kaizen, and 2) the methodology used to design and implement improvements.

**Table 2-3.** Philosophical and People-Related Kaizen Characteristics

| |
|---|
| Leaders embrace their primary role as strategists and delegate tactical decision making to the workers, creating a top-driven, bottom-executed improvement model. |
| Communication throughout the organization is timely, thorough and relevant, and clearly defines what action, if any, the recipient is required to take and the time frames for doing so. |
| A passion for improvement permeates the organization. |
| An awareness exists that even well-performing processes and work environments can be improved upon. |
| "Patient persistence" drives the organization's continuous-improvement efforts. |
| The organization thinks long term and globally with a bias toward local, incremental action. |
| The organization promotes a spirit of "calculated experimentation" and creates a structured environment for encouraging workers to "challenge everything," which promotes innovation and reduces the risk of stagnation. |
| The organization promotes discipline, precision, and standardization as core values. |
| The *process* for problem solving is held in higher regard than the solutions themselves. |
| Employees are motivated to reap small rewards associated with incremental change and recognize that small improvements add up over time. |
| Employees receive recognition for small improvements as well as breakthrough efforts. |
| The organization views the delivery of its products and services in value streams, and seeks to connect traditionally siloed (functional) work areas through process design that links upstream and downstream workers. Improvements are designed to optimize the whole rather than one isolated area. Ultimately, compensation and incentives are based on value stream performance, not on the performance of an individual or a particular functional department. |
| Accountability includes rewards for performing to standards—and consequences for performing otherwise. |

**Table 2-4.** Methodology-Related Kaizen Characteristics

| |
|---|
| Performance metrics emphasize leading (vs. solely lagging) indicators and incorporate operational (vs. solely financial) metrics. |
| Relevant, standardized workforce education (to develop *knowledge*—how we *think*) and training (to develop *skills*—what we *do*) is provided on an ongoing basis to both new and existing employees. New hire orientation includes indoctrination into the organization's continuous-improvement philosophy and information about how it expects its employees to perform in that environment. |
| Processes are monitored consistently and adjusted as needed. |
| Decisions are data driven. |
| The Plan-Do-Check-Act approach (Deming cycle) shapes problem-solving and improvement activities. |
| Problem solving occurs through cross-functional teamwork. |
| Short management time frames enable real-time performance assessment and adjustments as needed. |
| All processes are performed according to documented standard work. |
| Visual management and controls are evident throughout the organization. |

Of course, just as you cannot go out and purchase "lean DNA" to shift your culture, you cannot expect your employees to begin to "think lean" and adopt the kaizen philosophy overnight. Transforming your organization will take years of relentless commitment to workforce education and training, and proper facilitation in the use of lean tools to create flow by eliminating waste in every process. But you don't have to wait years to realize tangible benefits. Once you begin using Kaizen Events on your lean journey, the results can be immediately palpable and measurable. The proven tool for learning the kaizen philosophy and reaping immediate results is the *properly facilitated Kaizen Event.*

## A PROPERLY FACILITATED KAIZEN EVENT

A Kaizen Event, also referred to as a Kaizen Workshop, Kaizen Blitz, Breakthrough Kaizen, or Rapid Improvement Event, is a powerful tool for accelerating improvement. It's a structured team activity designed to remove waste and implement improvements in a defined work area or process, all within a few days.

As Geoffrey Mika explains in his manufacturing-focused *Kaizen Event Implementation Manual*, Kaizen Events enable organizations to unlock "the talents and abilities of workers, allowing decisions to be made at the lowest possible level in the organization, in the quickest time, by the people who know the situation best."[1] This differentiates Kaizen Events from value stream mapping, which provides *strategic* direction—*what* needs to happen—and involves leadership. Kaizen Events are *tactical*, focusing on *how* to execute the strategy, utilizing the people closest to the work (see Figure 2-1). This is the cultural shift that can be the most profound and the most challenging to realize: In a lean enterprise, leadership is responsible for creating strategy and the workforce is authorized to design and implement the tactical solutions required to execute leadership's strategic plan. This frees leadership from the day-to-day minutiae so they can focus on performance measurement, strategy, and removing operational obstacles, and at the same time, the workforce knowledge base and level of fulfillment grows exponentially. A key element in high-performing organizations—and required for rapid and sustainable improvement—is alignment between tactics and strategy and the clear division of responsibilities.

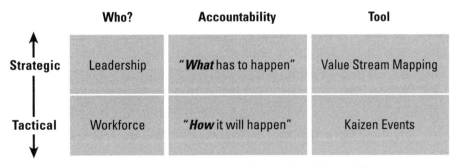

**Figure 2-1.** Improvement Roles for Leadership and Workforce

---

1. Mika, Geoffrey. *Kaizen Event Implementation Manual*, 4th ed. Dearborn, MI: SME, 2005, p. 11.

This tactical focus is why properly executed Kaizen Events solve problems quickly and succeed in consistently delivering sustainable results. The approach relies on cross-functional teamwork, implementing improvements in real time, and learning by doing. A familiar Chinese proverb sums up the kaizen philosophy: *Tell me and I'll forget, show me and I may remember, involve me and I'll understand.* The Kaizen Event is characterized by a number of attributes that, when followed, enable teams to consistently outperform established expectations, and make this improvement approach fundamentally different from traditional models.

## Thirteen Kaizen Event Characteristics

People regularly assert that their company runs Kaizen Events on a regular basis. Yet, with deeper probing into their activities, that is often not the case. Companies often fail to use strict rules and standards to plan and execute Kaizen Events, often generating merely a *plan* for improvement rather than actually implementing changes. Part II of this book covers specific standards and best practices for successful Events. But first, an introduction to the attributes of a properly run Kaizen Event:

1.  *Value stream driven.* Individuals, departments, and entire organizations are typically well-intentioned when they seek to make improvements. However, they often do so without considering the full value stream and, as a result, either sub-optimize the process when viewed as a whole from the customer's perspective—or worse, actually create new problems for workers upstream or downstream from the improved area. Lean thinking challenges people to make improvements that will truly impact the customer's experience—both external customers and those internal customers that receive work output from the area being improved. Linking your Kaizen Events to a future state value stream map and implementation plan enables a holistic view of customer value and minimizes the risk of sub-optimization. (Note: A value stream map is not always a prerequisite to a Kaizen Event, but those cases are relatively rare.)

2.  *Total employee involvement.* Traditionally, organizations have relied too heavily on leadership or outside consultants for executing process-level change. Lean thinking asks, "What value do leaders or consultants really bring?" "Are they better suited than workers for designing improvements?" The answer is usually no. Certainly, leaders and consultants have important roles to play, but the primary members on Kaizen Teams are the people who are working the process daily. In most settings, the people doing the work know what needs to change, but traditional improvement processes have not provided them with the proper platform to participate in actualizing their ideas. Encouraging teams to seek the wisdom of ten rather than the knowledge of one promotes inclusive decision making and, as a result, more innovative and sustainable solutions. An important aspect of the kaizen philosophy is to use measurable objectives and a learn-do model to develop teamwork and build an improvement skillset in your front-line workers, which further increases organizational flexibility and responsiveness to changing demands.

3.  *Cross-functional teamwork.* Kaizen Events leverage the power of involving upstream suppliers, downstream customers, and subject matter experts, as well as objective

"outside eyes" in problem solving. Figure 2-2 shows that, if you were planning a Kaizen Event to improve a process at step 3, the Kaizen Team would likely include representatives from steps 1, 2, 4, and 5. In addition to these internal suppliers and customers, you often benefit by including external suppliers and customers.

Leveraging the perspectives and experience of a cross-functional team has many benefits. First, it dissolves interpersonal and interdepartmental tension that may exist prior to a Kaizen Event, in large part because individuals and departments don't understand one another's needs and don't regularly solve problems together. Working on a defined problem provides everyone with a full understanding of how the process works and what the true needs are. From here, the team generates the best solutions, strengthening working relationships in the process. As a Kaizen Team member from Flagler, Florida, said: *"For once we built bridges instead of walls."*

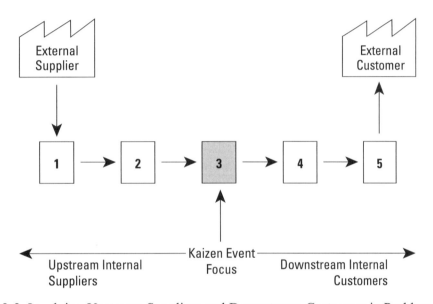

**Figure 2-2.** Involving Upstream Suppliers and Downstream Customers in Problem Solving

Cross-functional teamwork also ensures that improvements will benefit the entire value stream and not just one work group or department. In traditional improvement activities, decisions are often made without considering the impact on upstream suppliers or downstream customers. A cross-functional Kaizen Team minimizes the risk of making changes that do not improve the overall process.

The increased knowledge base the team acquires during the Event is one of the most significant Kaizen Event outcomes. Prior to Kaizen Events, typically no single team member understands the full range of process steps being analyzed and improved. It's difficult to design meaningful improvements when no one person can explain how the work is truly accomplished from point A to point Z. By the conclusion of a Kaizen Event, the organization typically gains six to ten process experts, because all of them have participated in analyzing, designing, and implementing improvements—and they all understand how the concept of customer value affects process design. So, in addition to better solutions, the organization develops a more knowledgeable workforce, which creates job fulfillment and organizational flexibility.

4. *100 percent focus.* The Kaizen Event model requires a sequestered team, so they are able to focus completely on the problem that they are trying to solve. Therefore, leadership must relieve Kaizen Team members of their normal duties for the full duration of the Kaizen Event. Sequestering makes a strong statement that the organization is serious about improvement and is one of the key requirements for achieving the rapid results for which well-executed Kaizen Events are known.

5. *Short duration.* Kaizen Events usually last for two to five days. While this may seem like a long time to sequester people from their normal duties, it's actually a short time period when compared with the length of time the defined process problems have typically existed and will likely continue to exist without the Kaizen Event. Also, the amount of work that's accomplished and the learning that occurs in only two to five days far exceeds that which is experienced in most traditional improvement activities and training programs. Sequestering a team is a small sacrifice, especially given current state process performance issues and the positive financial impact that the problem-solving activity typically resolves (freed capacity that can generate increased revenue, reduced expenses, and reduced workforce turnover, to name a few).

6. *Aggressive objectives.* To assist the team in achieving and maintaining focus, measurable objectives must be set, based on what members believe performance *should* be—based on customer expectations and market requirements—rather than what a team thinks is possible, given their historical experience making improvements through other means. These *stretch objectives* provide clear direction regarding expected outcomes and generate breakthrough performance from teams, which fuels the ongoing use of Kaizen Events across the organization.

7. *Creativity before capital.* Kaizen Events are low cost by design, guiding teams to create effective change while leveraging existing resources (workforce, equipment, software applications, etc.). This Kaizen Event characteristic produces rapid returns with little investment and creates more innovative solutions to most problems. With a resource-intensive improvement approach, the tendency is to fix problems with more people, equipment, or other capital-intensive resources, which often masks the waste that exists and stifles creativity. And, since implementation is an expected Kaizen Event outcome, you want to avoid delays due to acquisition time frames. Further, improvement teams often point to system and software weaknesses as the reason for process issues and focus on data needs instead of looking at the underlying process itself. The best IT solutions are borne from creating waste-free processes, which are then automated to optimize the activity—not the other way around. As Taiichi Ohno said, "We start our kaizen efforts by looking at the way our people do their work because it doesn't cost anything."[2]

---

2. Imai, Masaaki. *Kaizen: The Key to Japan's Competitive Success.* New York: McGraw-Hill, 1986, p. 83.

8. *Waste elimination.* Kaizen Events place greater emphasis on eliminating non-value-adding activities than improving speed in performing value-adding (VA) activities. You want to eliminate the eight wastes embedded in the work sequence that are causing the greatest pain and that will produce the most immediate results. This does not mean that implementing improvements to accelerate VA activities is off limits—it just means that optimizing value-added work is not the primary focus for Kaizen Events.

9. *Rapid decisions and real-time buy-in.* "Think long, think wrong," is an adage that forms the foundation for the decision-making process during a Kaizen Event. A painful pitfall of traditional improvement approaches is the slow pace of decision making and gaining leadership's authorization to proceed. Further, the longer we take to make a decision, the more doubt enters into the equation, clouding our judgment and causing us to second-guess ourselves. For this reason, Kaizen Events are designed to include real-time, rapid decision making by:

   - collecting the necessary data before and during the Event;
   - using the cross-functional team's various perspectives and time limitations to drive quicker decision making;
   - breaking the usual patterns of slowness that often hinders the improvement process (which also begins the process of shifting organizational culture);
   - obtaining real-time leadership buy-in through the use of interim briefings (explained fully in Chapter 10).

   Through these means, analysis paralysis is avoided, and teams can move forward quickly, the cornerstone to generating rapid results.

10. *Full implementation.* Many organizations are proficient at analyzing and planning, but lack the sense of urgency and discipline required for executing plans. This is why a properly executed Kaizen Event requires a skilled facilitator—one who can drive full implementation of the team's breakthrough improvements. In fact, the only failed Kaizen Event is one in which no measurable change occurs during the Event, where the improvement is scheduled to occur "offline" at some point after the conclusion of the Event. In an eight-to-five office environment, if the Event ends at 5 p.m. on a Wednesday afternoon, the process should be performed differently at 8 a.m. Thursday morning. This event characteristic requires that everyone involved receive new process training *during* the Kaizen Event so that they arrive at work the following day (or the next shift) fully prepared to perform their work in the improved way.

11. *New process training.* The training required to achieve full implementation during a Kaizen Event is provided in a just-in-time manner, often in highly innovative ways. If you need to train a staff of 300 how to complete a newly improved time sheet or a nationwide sales department on a new process for producing quotes, chances are you won't be able to pull 300 workers into a conference room for a traditional one-hour training program. Training requires as innovative thinking as process design itself does. Chapter 16 includes how-to information for designing and delivering effective

just-in-time training to large numbers of employees, often in geographically dispersed locations.

12. *Built-in sustainability*. Change is difficult, and to achieve sustainability, we must confront our human tendency of returning to the way we've always done things. Kaizen Events address this issue in several ways: 1) thorough current state analysis and clear improvement objectives; 2) total employee involvement; 3) real-time leadership and peer buy-in regarding changes; and 4) the development and execution of a solid Sustainability Plan, discussed in Chapter 17. Assuring sustainability requires design input from the affected parties upfront, clear ownership for ongoing monitoring and adjustments as necessary, and organizational discipline to follow through on sustainability activities that often take a back seat to daily firefighting. The Sustainability Plan is the tool for gaining commitment for and monitoring these post-event activities.

13. *Workforce development*. A final characteristic of Kaizen Events is that significant workforce development occurs at the same time the team is achieving results. Within the Kaizen Event, the PDCA cycle is repeated several times, and each time it's employed, the team learns by doing. A skilled facilitator will not "tell" the team what to do. Instead, he or she asks questions and provokes discussions that lead the team to solutions *that they themselves identify*. Further, the team learns new problem-solving techniques and how to apply specific improvement tools through a train-apply-train-apply format. Through this approach, the workforce learns how to apply the kaizen philosophy on a daily basis, creating a group of "true lean believers" to carry the message to others in the organization and serve as a potential pool of facilitators for future internal improvement.

As these thirteen characteristics demonstrate, a properly run Kaizen Event is a shaping tool to transform the way an organization thinks, behaves, designs, and views its work. It authorizes and empowers the workforce to make change, freeing leadership to focus on strategy and create proactive solutions, rather than using command and control tactics to micromanage their workforce. It frees leaders to become mentors, which may be uncomfortable for them during the early transition months. But eventually an enlightened leadership team embraces their new role, realizing that it allays common leadership complaints such as, "Why do I have to decide everything?" and "Why doesn't my staff take the ball and run with it?" and "I don't have enough time to get all of my work done."

But executing an effective Kaizen Event requires proper planning, a critical success factor in determining the degree to which teams will achieve productive results. Part II of this book includes the step-by-step process for this critical phase in the Kaizen Event process—the "P" in the macro-level PDCA cycle.

# PART II

# Kaizen Event Planning

# CHAPTER 3

# PLANNING ESSENTIALS

Benjamin Franklin said it best: "By failing to prepare, you are preparing to fail." Franklin's proclamation is especially true when planning a Kaizen Event. The success of an event is often directly related to the quantity and quality of upfront planning. The P in the plan-do-check-act (PDCA) cycle also emphasizes the significance of planning, which includes scoping the Event, identifying the required resources, defining objectives, and scheduling the leadership briefings and workforce training sessions that will occur during the Event. Adequate planning saves you from using valuable time during the Event to define the team's mission, search for data, or find last minute coverage for team members. When the Event begins, you want to hit the ground running and maintain that momentum throughout the Event.

Planning for a Kaizen Event must begin *at least four weeks* prior to the Event. A six-week planning cycle is recommended for organizations that are new to Kaizen Events or those who are just beginning to hold Kaizen Events in their office, service, or technical areas. In only two situations should a Kaizen Event be attempted with less than four to six weeks of planning:

- The organization has experience holding highly cross-functional Kaizen Events.
- The organization is holding short events with narrow scopes and the prospective team members have flexible schedules.

As an organization matures with Kaizen Events, the planning time frame can often shorten, but a four-week planning cycle is still recommended.

## EVENT LEADERSHIP AND PLANNING TOOLS

Most Kaizen Events are planned and executed by up to five individuals who serve as *event leaders* and fill specific roles:

1. executive sponsor
2. value stream champion
3. facilitator
4. team lead
5. event coordinator

Depending on the organization, the Event scope, and whether an internal or external facilitator is used, five separate individuals may not be necessary to fill these roles for all events. These roles, which we'll collectively refer to as *event leaders* throughout this book, are discussed in detail in Chapter 4.

The event leaders—or at least a subset of them—should meet on a regular basis during the four- to six-week event-planning period to assess progress and assure all necessary activities have been completed, setting the stage for successful execution. As described in the Introduction to this book, the CD included on the inside back cover contains a Kaizen Event Tools file, which includes two key planning tools: the *Kaizen Event Charter* and the *Planning Checklist* (Tab 1 and 2 in the file). As noted in the CD Instructions for Use that follow the book's Introduction, the Kaizen Event Tools file is an Excel-based toolset that is organized into the three phases of a Kaizen Event with color-coded tabs that indicate the phase in which the tools are used: Planning (blue tabs), Execution (yellow tabs), and Follow-up (purple tabs). Before reading on, *review the CD Instructions for Use*, which includes important information about the tools' functionality. Print a copy of the *Kaizen Event Charter* and *Planning Checklist* to refer to while reading this chapter and the rest of Part II, which describes the process for completing the Kaizen Event Charter and the relationship between the charter and the Planning Checklist.

## KAIZEN EVENT CHARTER

The Kaizen Event Charter, shown on Figure 3-1, is a planning tool that communicates:

- The process the Kaizen Team will be making improvements to;
- Why improvement is needed;
- The measurable results the Kaizen Team will strive to achieve;
- The boundaries within which the team will operate;
- The obstacles the team may encounter (anticipating obstacles and planning countermeasures shortens the time needed to resolve problems that may arise during the Event);
- The people who will be involved, where they should be, and when;
- When the team will hold key briefings and training sessions.

Notice that the charter is organized into left and right sections. The left section contains *strategic* information concerning the *what and why* aspects of improvement—what will be accomplished, why it's needed (what problem you're trying to solve), and the boundaries within which the improvements will occur. The right section addresses the *logistics* of *who*, *when*, and *where* regarding event activities. The final improvement element—*how* exactly the improvement will be made—is determined by the Kaizen Team during the Event itself.

The Kaizen Event Charter is also a vehicle for communicating to the Kaizen Team and the entire organization:

- *Accountability and responsibility*. The charter establishes who's accountable for the various aspects of the Event, including leadership oversight, facilitation, and logistics support (described further in Chapters 4–9).
- *Event scope*. The charter is a scoping tool that defines boundaries to keep teams from becoming victims of "scope creep" or "kaizen creep." Without laser focus, teams often take on too much and end up accomplishing little. As stated, Kaizen Events are

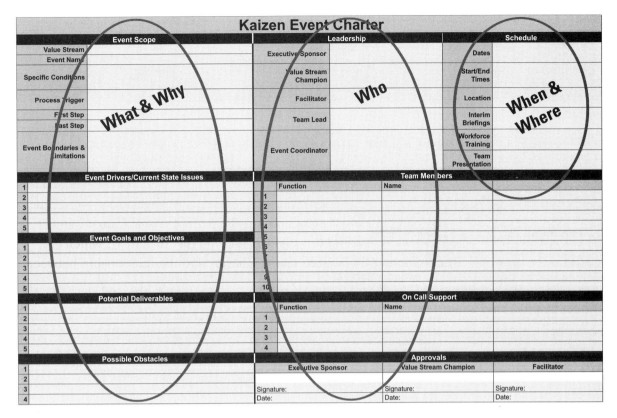

**Figure 3-1.** Kaizen Event Charter Sections

about *implementation*. Simply planning for change won't do. Clearly communicating event scope creates organization-wide alignment regarding purpose and anticipated outcomes.

- *Logistics.* The charter also specifies who needs to be where and when. This information needs to be communicated far enough in advance of the Event to allow the involved parties to schedule their time accordingly.

As illustrated in Figure 3-2, Chapters 4-8 include details for completing the various sections of the charter, but a charter development overview is provided in this chapter.

Creating the charter is typically an iterative process. To gain buy-in regarding event scope and objectives, and to identify potential oversights, the event leaders should distribute an initial draft of the charter to as broad an audience and as early in the planning process as possible. After a designated event leader incorporates the feedback, he or she should redistribute the charter. This critical communication step gives the stakeholders a voice, reduces the risk of overlooking a key issue that could affect event outcomes, and clears the way for a productive event. Team composition, for example, goes through several iterations as event scope and objectives, which drive team formation decisions, are fine-tuned. For this reason, event leaders should distribute the initial draft of the charter *three to five weeks* prior to the Event to the organization's full leadership team (for large organizations, division or regional leadership may suffice) and all levels of management in the areas that will be impacted by the improvement. Some organizations also distribute the charter to

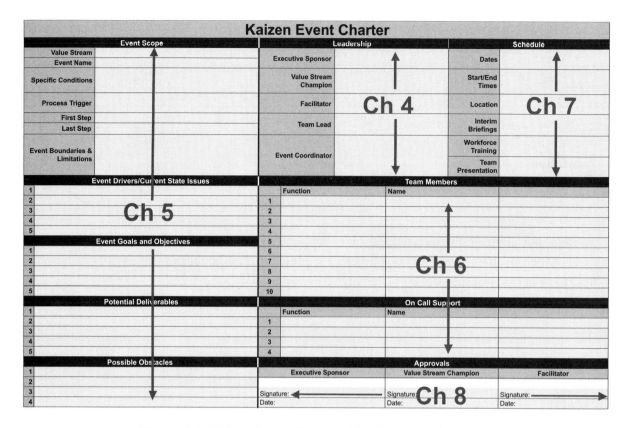

**Figure 3-2.** Kaizen Event Charter with Chapter Designations

the prospective team members and on-call candidates, while others prefer to wait until the team is finalized to share details about the Event.

The charter should also be distributed to departments upstream or downstream from the process being improved and relevant support areas, such as IT, regulatory, finance, etc., even if at first glance they don't seem like they'll be impacted by or involved in the improvement process. That way, if event leaders overlook a particular department or work team when that area's leadership reviews the initial charter draft and they discover the oversight, the event leaders can adjust team composition with ample notice. This adjustment can provide critical voices in designing improvements that could otherwise impact event outcomes and/or sustainability of the changes. The charter should be finalized and redistributed *two to three weeks* prior to the Event to allow adequate time for those involved to schedule their time and obtain coverage during the event.

## PLANNING CHECKLIST

The *Planning Checklist* contains suggested pre-event activities and completion deadlines to ensure a smooth start to the Event and reduce the risk of obstacles arising during the Event's critical work time. Figure 3-3 shows a partial view of the Planning Checklist, which is located on Tab 2 of the Kaizen Event Tools file on the CD.

Note that within the Planning Checklist structure and data entry requirements, planning tasks are grouped based on their typical timing in the planning process (four weeks prior, three weeks prior, etc.). Once you enter an event start date in the upper portion of the checklist, the due dates for all activities automatically calculate and auto-populate the corresponding cells. The CD Instructions for Use goes into greater detail about the auto-populate functionality.

Each time frame section contains additional cells to add activities that are unique to each organization. Enter the name of the person accountable for each task in the owner column cells. The comments column houses relevant notes about specific tasks that event leadership may need to document or track, issues that the Kaizen Team needs to follow up on, or "not applicable" if that item does not apply for the specific event. Once a task is 100 percent complete, left click on the corresponding checkbox (second column) and a checkmark will appear. Much of the content in Chapters 4–9 centers around the tasks listed in the Planning Checklist's activity column.

## Kaizen Event Planning Checklist

| Executive Sponsor | | | | Event Name | |
| Value Stream Champion | | | | Event Start Date | |
| Facilitator | | | | Coordinator | |

| | ☑ | Activity | Due Date | Owner | Comments |
|---|---|---|---|---|---|
| **4 Weeks Prior** | | | | | |
| 1 | ☐ | If event will involve 5S activities, select and reserve "sort" dispositioning area. | | | |
| 2 | ☐ | Determine Event budget (supplies, food, resources, etc.). | | | |
| 3 | ☐ | Identify supplies and equipment needed. If event will include 5S activities, include cleaning and organization supplies. | | | |
| 4 | ☐ | Distribute initial draft of Kaizen Event Charter. | | | |
| 5 | ☐ | Send meeting notices to team members, on-call resources, leadership, prospective trainees, etc. re: event, interim briefing(s), final presentation and workforce training. *RSVP required.* Include draft of Kaizen Charter. Copy direct supervisors. | | | |
| 6 | ☐ | Create initial draft of Kaizen Event Charter. | | | |
| 7 | ☐ | | | | |
| 8 | ☐ | | | | |
| 9 | ☐ | | | | |
| 10 | ☐ | | | | |
| **3 Weeks Prior** | | | | | |
| 11 | ☐ | Finalize Kaizen Event charter and gain approval. | | | |
| 12 | ☐ | Distribute approved Kaizen Event charter. | | | |
| 13 | ☐ | Review Event scope and objectives *with facilitator* to determine the current state data and metrics that need to be collected (e.g. volumes, performance metrics, service levels, survey results, etc.), and assign accountability. | | | |

**Figure 3-3.** Planning Checklist (partial view)

One of the event leaders needs to "own" the Planning Checklist. Ownership includes tracking progress, keeping the checklist up-to-date, distributing or reviewing it with the event leaders at least once weekly, and seeking appropriate help if any aspect of planning falls behind schedule. The checklist owner should be internal to the organization. When using an outside facilitator, the Event coordinator, team lead, or value stream champion should manage the checklist. The executive sponsor doesn't typically have tactical-level responsibilities in the Kaizen Event planning process.

Managing the planning process is vital to Kaizen Event success. Falling behind schedule directly impacts Kaizen Event execution and can create unnecessary organizational "angst" leading up to the Event, which colors people's perceptions before the Event even has a chance to prove itself. If you fall behind in the planning process, the executive sponsor and/or value stream champion should intervene immediately and resolve whatever issues are delaying progress. In many cases, missing a due date by one day can create an obstacle that may not be amenable to corrective action, creating an uphill battle as the team strives to achieve established event objectives.

## GETTING STARTED

To get started, the event leaders should hold an initial planning session to begin developing the charter and agree who will be accountable for the various event planning activities, as outlined in Chapter 4. It's not as critical as to who specifically does what; what matters is that the event leaders establish clear ownership for all planning activities. From that point on, team leaders may opt for a structured planning process in which all event leaders meet on a weekly basis, or a more fluid planning process, with e-mail, phone, and face-to-face meetings scheduled on an as-needed basis. When opting for the fluid approach, event leaders should establish weekly contact to track progress. Many organizations find they benefit from a more structured approach when planning early events, relaxing the process as they become more skilled.

External facilitators, if being utilized, should be involved throughout the planning process. In early Kaizen Events, skilled facilitators provide necessary direction and guidance regarding all aspects of scoping, team formation and overall event planning. Weekly telephone calls with the internal leadership team help assure the Event is being properly planned and that any organizational obstacles to success are being appropriately dealt with.

Chapter 4 delves into each event leader's role more deeply, including information regarding how to select a skilled facilitator.

# CHAPTER 4

# EVENT LEADERSHIP

As mentioned in Chapter 3, planning and executing Kaizen Events is usually accomplished through a team of individuals who play five key roles: executive sponsor, value stream champion, facilitator, team lead, and event coordinator. As shown in Figure 4-1, the names of these leaders are entered in the Leadership section in the top center portion of the Event Charter.

| Leadership | |
|---|---|
| Executive Sponsor | |
| Value Stream Champion | |
| Facilitator | |
| Team Lead | |
| Event Coordinator | |

**Figure 4-1.** Kaizen Event Charter—Leadership Section

The *executive sponsor* is typically a senior leader, such as vice president, general manager, administrator, or "C-suite" leader (CEO, COO, CIO, CMO, etc.), who provides senior leadership direction and support for the Event from pre-event planning through post-event follow-up. The executive sponsor typically has ultimate authority over the area(s) in which the improvement will occur.

The *value stream champion* is usually a vice president, director, or middle manager who's close enough to the process being improved to provide direction regarding event scope, objectives, and team composition, but who also has the authority to approve policy-related changes or improvements that may have legal, financial, or regulatory impact. In smaller organizations, the executive sponsor and value stream champion may be the same person. The executive sponsor and value stream champion are often involved in creating the current and future state value stream maps that precede a Kaizen Event.

The *facilitator's* primary role is leading the Event itself, but he or she is also heavily engaged in planning, including charter development, team formation and event logistics, and post-event activities such as monitoring follow-up tasks and process performance. The quality of the facilitator is a leading indicator of event success, which is why the facilitator must possess a broad range of skills, discussed later in the chapter.

A *team lead* can be helpful, especially when the organization is using an external facilitator for an event. The team lead serves on the Kaizen Event Team, and is also the facilitator's internal "advisor" and "go-to person" when obstacles arise that require intervention by the value stream champion or executive sponsor. Ideally, the team lead is the team member who's most knowledgeable about the process, people, and organizational culture. If the value stream champion is serving on the team, he or she often serves as the team lead. Events led by a seasoned internal facilitator don't always require a team lead. The decision of whether or not to use a team lead needs to be weighed and remains an individual judgment call.

The *Event coordinator* leads the logistics of the Event such as reserving the room, ordering food, and assuring all necessary equipment and supplies are available and in working order. Chapter 8 describes how the coordinator may also be involved in the communication effort. Additional responsibilities may include preparing recognition certificates and awards, and organizing pre-event training for Kaizen Team members.

Table 4-1 provides additional details regarding the roles and responsibilities of these five event leaders in the Kaizen Event planning process, as well as their ongoing roles during the Event execution and follow-up phases.

If the organization has staff dedicated to continuous improvement or achieving operational excellence, those people often receive training to serve as Kaizen Event facilitators. They also often serve as event coordinators. If the improvement target is a CI process itself, a senior CI employee might be the value stream champion. Unless an organization has a VP or higher-level person dedicated to performance improvement, the executive sponsor would not typically reside in the CI department.

Because of the pivotal role the facilitator plays, the rest of this chapter addresses the necessary traits and skills for a Kaizen Event facilitator, when to use an external facilitator, how to select a facilitator who will produce substantive results, and how to develop skilled internal facilitators from within your workforce.

## FACILITATOR ROLES

As Table 4-1 shows, a Kaizen Event facilitator (*sensei* in Japanese) is a guide. He or she serves as the team's teacher and mentor. Through the process of a Kaizen Event, the facilitator teaches team members how to think lean, identify waste, apply specific tools, and sustain their gains. In Kaizen Events, the facilitator *truly facilitates*. Arguably, the facilitator's greatest value lies in the questions he or she asks, and how he or she guides the team members to discover *on their own* the solutions that will best solve the process problems they've discovered. The facilitator keeps the team on track from a time perspective, helps maintain momentum, and assists the team in overcoming obstacles. But that's not to say this teacher/mentor is necessary soft in playing this role. Effective Kaizen Event facilitators can be quite direct, an approach that is often needed to challenge long-standing paradigms and achieve rapid improvement. When we asked skilled facilitators what one single trait they feel

**Table 4-1.** Event Leaders' Roles and Responsibilities

| | | | EVENT LEADERSHIP ROLES AND RESPONSIBILITIES | | | |
|---|---|---|---|---|---|---|
| | | | | **Specific Responsibilities** | | |
| **Kaizen Event Role** | **Characteristics** | **Typical Level Within the Organization** | **Overall Role** | **Pre-event Planning** | **Event Execution** | **Post-event Follow-up** |
| **Executive Sponsor** | Senior leader within the organization who is ultimately accountable for event outcomes and who has a high degree of authority over policy and the organization's strategic direction. | Vice President, General Manager, Chief Operating Officer, General Manager, Managing Partner, or the equivalent. In a smaller organization, the executive sponsor might be the President or Chief Executive Officer. | Provide support throughout the process; address high-level policy, regulatory or financial issues; assist the value stream champion and facilitator in removing obstacles to the team's success. | Provide direction re: event scope, objectives, and boundaries. Approve the Event Charter. | Assist the VSC with negotiating interdepartmental differences of opinion at the leadership level. Respond to team requests re: policy, regulatory considerations, etc. Respond to VSC's requests for assistance. Attend all interim briefings and the final presentation. | Hold the VSC accountable for measurable improvement of the target process. Share results with senior leadership team and relevant external stakeholders. |
| **Value Stream Champion (VSC)** | In function-based organizational structures, the person in a middle management or senior leadership role who oversees the primary functional area involved in the improvement effort. In organizations structured with a lean perspective, the VSC is the leader who carries responsibility for an entire value stream (often referred to as a value stream manager). | Usually a manager or director-level leader. In smaller organizations, the same person may hold the executive sponsor and VSC roles. | Assist with event planning. Provide support throughout the process. The VSC may or may not serve on the team, depending on the involvement target. Hold team accountable for results and follow-up activities. | Assist with establishing event scope, objectives, and boundaries. Provide direction re: team formation. Ensure the Planning Checklist elements are completed according to the schedule. | If not on the team, be fully accessible and provide support throughout the Event. Respond to team's requests, engaging executive sponsor as needed. Attend all interim briefings and the final presentation. Respond to team lead and/or facilitator's request for assistance. | Monitor the team's progress re: the 30-day list and the 30-day audit. Monitor process on an ongoing basis via measurement, report results broadly, and provide direction re: further improvement activities. |

(Continued on next page)

**Table 4-1.** (continued)

| | | EVENT LEADERSHIP ROLES AND RESPONSIBILITIES | | | |
|---|---|---|---|---|---|
| | | | | **Specific Responsibilities** | |
| **Kaizen Event Role** | **Characteristics** | **Typical Level Within the Organization** | **Overall Role** | **Pre-event Planning** | **Event Execution** | **Post-event Follow-up** |
| **Facilitator—Internal** | A person with significant experience facilitating mapping and Kaizen Events and applying the full range of continuous improvement and lean-specific principles and tools. | Trained lean facilitators, industrial engineers, continuous improvement specialists. | Lead the entire Kaizen Event process (planning, executing and follow-up phases). | Lead planning activities, delegate tasks as needed, manage Checklist, form team, communicate event. Create and approve the Event Charter. | Establish daily agenda. Assign tasks. Assist team with applying lean principles and tools. Monitor progress. Mediate disagreements. | Distribute 30-Day List and parking lot issues. Lead post-event: team meetings. Lead (or delegate) 30- and 60-day audits. Ensure sustainability plan is completed and distributed. Ensure VSC is transitioning responsibility for managing and monitoring the improved process to area managers. |
| **Facilitator—External** | | Experienced lean practitioners and consultants who have proven track records in effective facilitation and generating aggressive results. | Provide assistance to internal staff with planning and follow-up; lead the Kaizen Event itself. | Provide guidance to internal resources re: the above. Ensure checklist tasks are being completed on time. Approve Event Charter. | Prepare team for interim briefings and final presentation. Seek assistance from team lead and/or value stream champion as needed. | |
| **Team Lead** | This role isn't always necessary. It's helpful when: 1) the event's being externally facilitated or 2) The process being improved requires a subject matter expert that's the facilitator's "go to" person for assistance, direction, issues that arise. etc. This role is not needed if the value stream champion is a team member. | Any level of employee. Key characteristic is someone who knows the process best from a tactical perspective but also has an understanding of organizational strategy and can balance operational needs with financial, regulatory, and customer needs. | Assist facilitator during the event as needed. | Assist with event planning if requested by value stream champion. | Assist facilitator when process steps are unclear. Access the value stream champion for assistance if the facilitator is focused on another activity. Serve as the tie breaker when differences of opinion arise regarding current state. | Attend follow-up meetings for first 30 days. Assist with 30-day audit. Assist with monitoring process performance on ongoing basis and identifying additional improvement opportunities. Possibly serve as standard work owner. |
| **Coordinator** | Someone who is organized and good with details. | Administrative assistant or coordinator. Role can be held by facilitator or team lead but the responsibilities are fairly administrative. | Planning and executing event logistics, including follow-up meetings and 30-day audit. | Schedule meeting rooms. Order food. Send event communications. Create recognition certificates and/or obtain recognition gifts. Ensure all supplies and A/V needs are being met. | Ensure all event logistics are in place and working well. Trouble shoot as needed. | Send post-event communications. |

is most important in performing in their role, 90 percent said "thick skin." Facilitators consistently encounter resistance to change, which requires the development of effective conflict management skills. Serving as a Kaizen Event facilitator is not for everyone. So, what traits and skills are needed for an effective facilitator? Let's start by reviewing the five key roles a Kaizen Event facilitator plays:

1. *Event planner.* As an event planner, the facilitator provides guidance with developing the Event Charter, scoping the Event, establishing measurable objectives, forming a high-performing team, and determining what information or resources need to be gathered prior to the Event.

2. *Project manager.* Kaizen Events are short-term projects that require quick execution. During event execution, the facilitator is at once managing the Event scope (to prevent scope creep), the team (to maximize results), and the schedule (to assure event objectives are met or exceeded). Additional project management responsibilities include overseeing the event budget, if one has been established, and managing the overall change process to assure the improvements are fully implemented and will be sustained.

3. *Teacher.* This is arguably the facilitator's most important role. While achieving rapid results is an important Kaizen Event outcome, developing the individual team members has longer lasting, deeper organizational benefits. The facilitator teaches the team how to think and analyze differently, apply root cause analysis and improvement tools to reduce waste and create flow, and create a continuous-improvement environment.

4. *Motivator.* Implementing change is hard work. Analyzing the current state is often tedious and designing improvements can require a fair amount of "selling." For this reason, the facilitator must continually motivate the team to keep them energized and driving toward results. The facilitator provides encouragement, acknowledges incremental successes, and assures the team that they are making progress if they begin to doubt the process.

5. *Mediator.* When concerns or overt disagreements arise, the facilitator must mediate to help the parties reach consensus. In addition, if internal or external obstacles arise that the team is unsuccessful in removing on their own, the facilitator intervenes, often achieving mediation success by redirecting the parties' focus to their shared goals—maximizing customer value and achieving Event objectives.

The Kaizen Event facilitator's role is to help the team succeed. Successful Kaizen Events require strong facilitators who are effective in each of the five roles previously listed, deliver results, and create positive, high-energy team environments. And they need to be skilled in recognizing when specific improvement tools are needed and how best to help the team apply them. For these reasons, Kaizen Event facilitators need specialized training over and above typical facilitator skills development. They must possess a well-developed combination of technical and psychological skills to deal with process-design issues and team dynamics. Let's explore these necessary traits in further detail.

## FACILITATOR TRAITS

Kaizen Event facilitators need a broad range of traits to lead Events and effectively manage the complexities inherent in designing and implementing rapid improvements. No one person typically possesses all of these traits when he or she begins facilitating. Even seasoned facilitators have areas they must continually develop in their personal and professional quest for improvement. Many of the following traits are "hard-wired" into an individual—they're inborn traits that are tough to develop—whereas others, with strong desire, can be developed easily. No facilitator is perfect.

The following list will help you identify the strongest candidates for development as internal facilitators and/or select an external facilitator who has the greatest chance of producing agressive results, while creating a positive environment for rapid change that spreads throughout the organization:

- Technical Skills
    - Able to apply the full range of lean principles and tools
    - Adept at performing root cause analysis
    - Strong project, time management, and organization skills
    - Effective team building
    - Effective at communicating with all levels of workers, from frontline workers to senior executives
    - Strong listening skills
    - Understands organizational dynamics
    - Understands human psychology and the change process
- Authority
    - Has organization-backed designation as a change agent
    - Seen as a strong-influence leader among peer group and up and down the organization
    - Confident and trustworthy
    - Comfortable removing obstacles; doesn't fear conflict
- Personality
    - Challenging, yet supportive
    - Can tolerate and effectively resolve conflict
    - Energetic, positive, and uses humor regularly
    - Compassionate and able to walk easily in others' shoes
    - Creative, innovative, visionary
    - Honest; integrity drives all action
    - Analytical, detail oriented
    - Task oriented
    - Quick study; thinks fast on one's feet

- Innate curiosity about how things operate
- Comfortable with the unknown
- Balanced ego; willing to give others credit for their ideas; comfortable leading team to solutions rather than telling them what to do
- Passion for continuous improvement
- Objectivity
  - No attachment to outcome
  - No agenda coming into the event, other than to achieve the event objectives (*Note*: for this reason, internal facilitators should not facilitate Events that directly affect their own work area.)

## DEVELOPING INTERNAL FACILITATORS

To become self-sustaining as quickly as possible, an organization's ultimate goal should be to develop a team of internal lean facilitators to lead lean activities, such as value stream mapping and Kaizen Events. While there are several methods for developing internal facilitators, whenever possible, organizations should do so under the guidance of a seasoned lean facilitator.

Developing highly skilled facilitators requires many years, because the bulk of their development occurs outside the classroom, during real-world Kaizen Events. However, a company doesn't have to invest years in developing someone before he or she is ready to facilitate an event. Lean thinking embraces the wisdom that we learn best through doing. And fast-moving Kaizen Events, with their varied challenges and obstacles, provide a ripe opportunity for "green" facilitators to apply their fledging skills and learn from their mistakes. They will see circumstances and events unfold that classroom education can only address in theory. Because every event is unique—team dynamics vary widely, and each process has a unique set of challenges and opportunities—even seasoned facilitators sharpen their skills further with each event they facilitate. In fact, an important part of the development of an expert facilitator is the process of reflecting on one's performance and considering ways to avoid trouble spots in future events. The fifth step in the lean journey as defined by Womack is to continually seek perfection. That applies as much to professional and personal development as it does to organizational performance and process design.

While "baptism by fire" as previously described is a necessary part of a facilitator's development, he or she should begin with classroom education and training, and then progress through escalating responsibility for Kaizen Event facilitation. To avoid an event disaster or destroying the novice facilitator's confidence, the following six-step developmental path should be incorporated into his or her training:

1. Obtain classroom training and *demonstrate competence regarding lean principles and core tools*. Competency with all tools takes years to develop, but it starts with a minimum of 40 hours of classroom education. Ideally, the curriculum contains a balance between theory and practice, and includes many hands-on activities to maximize the learning that results from a "learn-do" model.

2. Obtain detailed training about *planning and executing Kaizen Events*, with heavy emphasis on *facilitation techniques*. A minimum of 20 classroom hours is typically required to provide a solid foundation.

3. Serve on Kaizen Teams to experience the process from a team member's perspective. If possible, the facilitator-in-training should serve as a fully engaged participant (process stakeholder) at least once for an improvement that directly impacts his/her work area. This experience will sensitize the facilitator-in-training to the difficulties team members can have when their process is targeted for improvement. (An adage that's useful to remember is: "It's uplifting to kaizen; it can be traumatizing to be kaizened.") If possible, he/she should also serve as the *outside eyes* on a kaizen team to experience the improvement effort from an outsider's perspective and study the facilitation process itself.

4. Pair with a skilled facilitator, and assist in planning and executing a Kaizen Event and conducting post-event follow-up. At this stage, the facilitator-in-development serves as the *assistant to the lead facilitator* and plays an entry-level role in facilitating during the Event.

5. Serve as the *lead facilitator* for an Event with primary responsibility for planning, execution, and follow-up and with backup available as needed. At this stage, it's best if a seasoned Kaizen Event facilitator is present to provide support during the Event, should it become necessary. The seasoned facilitator serves as the "assistant" to the lead facilitator, continuing to offer suggestions and leading lessons-learned discussions at the end of each day to provide "real-time" development. While a second facilitator at any stage of development could arguably provide objective feedback to the primary facilitator, if both facilitators are green, the feedback may not be as insightful and relevant as a seasoned facilitator could provide.

6. *Facilitate on one's own.* Mistakes will be made, but the facilitator will develop the confidence to adapt during the Event and learn from his or her mistakes. *Note*: If the organization can manage the resources, it's *highly* preferable to have two facilitators lead each Kaizen Event. This is true on an ongoing basis, even after the facilitators have reached a reasonable level of competency. When two facilitators are present, teams typically generate more dramatic results and experience deeper learning, and the facilitators generally develop faster.

Following these six steps will ensure a natural progression in the facilitator's development and avoid the organization-wide problems that can develop from prematurely placing unseasoned facilitators in a complex leadership role. Depending on how seasoned and confident the facilitators-in-training are, they may need to perform each of the previously mentioned steps multiple times before they become full-fledged Kaizen Event facilitators.

During the development process and throughout their roles as champions for change, the facilitators should hold regular "community of practice" sessions to provide a forum for discussing best practices, sharing the frustrations that sometimes accompany rapid improvement, providing ongoing education, and providing a formal vehicle for giving feedback to organizational leadership about Kaizen Event strategy, leadership support, and event challenges. These community-of-practice sessions should also include continuing education regarding specific lean tools, conflict management techniques, development of high-performing teams, etc. Developing a formal mentor program that pairs facilitators with complementary skill sets is another way to accelerate facilitator development.

If an organization plans to develop a team of internal facilitators, it might want to opt for a formalized in-house facilitator certification program, with required education, training, and demonstration of skills and measurable results.

## IDENTIFYING PROSPECTIVE FACILITATORS

The three primary ways for identifying potential facilitators across an organization are:

- Ask for volunteers.
- Ask leadership and key staff whom they would recommend, given the facilitator's varied roles and responsibilities, preferable traits, and time commitment needed.
- Recruit people you think would be strong facilitators (based on their level of engagement on past Kaizen Teams, their passion for improvement, and their ability to manage projects and teams).

An organization may want to include a combination of all three methods. If a person is identified through all three approaches, he/she is likely an ideal candidate. If no one's name appears on all three lists, or someone doesn't stand out as a likely candidate, then leadership must decide whether to recruit from the outside or to work harder at developing its internal resources. No two organizations are the same. Sometimes, people volunteer who are ill suited for the role and sometimes leadership blocks the strongest candidates because they're "too valuable to give up any of their time." Occasionally, candidates buck recruiting efforts because, to the surprise of the recruiter, they lack the necessary confidence for the role. A straightforward method is to conduct a formal interview process before finalizing the candidate list and initiating the first round of training and development. An interesting organizational strategy is worth noting—some organizations are beginning to require service as a rapid improvement facilitator as a condition for advancement into leadership roles.

Regardless of an individual's reason for wanting to serve as a facilitator or the organization's selection method, expect at least one of the following things to occur during the development process:

- Some candidates will decide they don't possess the necessary traits or have the time available to serve as effective facilitators and will decline further involvement.
- The organization will recognize that a candidate lacks the appropriate time, interest, and/or traits to facilitate effectively, and leadership gracefully suggests that his or her skills are best suited for a different responsibility.
- Some candidates who appear to lack the necessary traits initially, but have a high drive will, when given the opportunity, develop into strong facilitators.

- New candidates will surface. Through the course of being exposed to lean principles and rapid improvement, additional staff members may become passionate for this type of improvement and seek development as facilitators.

The facilitator pool will be in constant flux. Expect only a third of initial candidates to become full-fledged facilitators. And, as people are promoted or leave the company, facilitators will need to be added to the pool. Moreover, the organization will need to adjust the number of facilitators it has available as it increases the number of value streams being improved. One note of caution: It's best that the facilitators are giving opportunities to facilitate as close in time to their training as possible. Organizations often develop too many facilitators for the volume of improvement activities they are engaged in, creating excessive gaps between training and practice, and destroying the high degree of motivation that newly appointed facilitators typically possess.

A final consideration is whether to staff continuous-improvement activities with part-time facilitators with operational responsibilities, or full-time dedicated facilitators. If an organization selects the dual-role approach, it needs to be careful not to overburden the facilitators. Kaizen Events will suffer and possibly even fail if the facilitators don't have adequate time to plan for event execution and oversee follow-up activities. Another problem is that, when faced with choosing to address an operational fire or plan a Kaizen Event that's two or three weeks out, the facilitator will most likely choose the immediate problem, which is the very type of organizational behavior Kaizen Events are attempting to change in the first place. It takes a fair amount of leadership commitment and organizational discipline to give part-time facilitators the focused time they need to run successful events.

## Using External Facilitators Appropriately

Many organizations benefit by using external facilitators in the beginning of their lean journey—or when they are moving their lean journey into their office areas—when there's typically a high degree of organizational resistance to rapid improvement. Even organizations with mature continuous-improvement programs and well-developed internal facilitators sometimes benefit from outside support. Any of the following situations signal the need for an external facilitator:

- An internal facilitator is unlikely to risk challenging the status quo to the degree necessary.
- The Kaizen Team contains a high number of executives, making it uncomfortable for an internal facilitator to challenge a team of senior staff.
- The improvement gains being sought are more aggressive or complicated than what internal facilitators have experience with.
- The target process requires an objective perspective from a seasoned practitioner who has no attachment to the outcome.
- Internal facilitators lack experience applying the particular lean tools needed to make the improvement.

- The Event may be especially contentious, e.g., management is at a stalemate about what direction to go in, or the working relationships between two or more of the involved areas is extremely poor.
- The organization has reached a plateau on its lean journey and needs fresh eyes to infuse new energy into the improvement process.
- The organization is skilled in applying lean in one area (manufacturing, for example) but not in another (e.g., office processes).

An organization can expect to pay from $1,500 to $3,500 or higher per day, per external facilitator (2007 rates). Facilitators typically set their fees based on their experience and skill level, as well as their reputation for success and the tangible results they typically generate. If an organization is serious about using this powerful improvement tool, it should select the best external facilitator that it can afford. The dividends will include not only successful Kaizen Events, but seasoned practitioners will accelerate the development and confidence of your internal facilitators, which will ultimately make you less reliant on outside facilitators. While not all high-priced consultants are equally skilled as facilitators, it's a sure bet that the lower-priced ones are not as experienced.

This chapter has assisted readers in understanding the different roles that event leaders play and the process for selecting and developing appropriate facilitators. The next chapter addresses scoping—establishing measurable objectives and the "fence posts" within which rapid improvement will occur.

# CHAPTER 5

# SCOPING THE EVENT

To set the stage for a successful event, it's critical to define exactly what the Kaizen Team is being asked to accomplish. Equally important is communicating to the team and the organization what parameters the team will be operating within: The Event scope.

Scoping is as much art as science and has two elements: objectives and time. Ideally, you want to schedule just enough time for the team to accomplish the Event objectives—no more and no less. An alternative approach is to scope the Event to fit a specified time period. The first approach is the preferred scoping method, but if team members' schedules or meeting room availability stands in the way, it is better to align the Event objectives with the available time than to delay holding Kaizen Events.

"Rome wasn't built in a day" is a proverb to keep in mind when establishing event objectives. Many organizations try to take on too much during a single event. The most successful events have beginning and ending *fence posts* that are broad enough to generate significant results, but narrow enough for the team to analyze the current state thoroughly and implement the improvements fully.

The left side of the Kaizen Event Charter includes several key elements in defining the Event: the scope itself, current state process performance issues and opportunities for improvement, objectives for the improvement process, projected team outputs, and potential obstacles to improvement (Figure 5-1). The following is a guide to completing the charter.

## Event Scope

1. *Value stream*—Specify the value stream (or value stream segment, for complex value streams) the team will be focused on improving (e.g., purchasing process, emergency department patient flow, new client implementation, DNA test processing, engineering change notice process).

2. *Event name*—The Event should be referred to by a name that's easily recognized. Some organizations number their events (e.g., KE1, KE2, etc.). Others refer to the Events by the value stream. The more descriptive the Event name, the better.

3. *Specific conditions*—Since processes often vary depending on specific conditions or circumstances, this cell includes essential scope-narrowing information. For example, the Event may focus on one geographic area, one customer group, one type of medical condition, or a specific market segment. Or it could exclude particular circumstances (e.g., a particular time of the year, a particular sales region, or a certain value for purchase orders) that, for any number of reasons, should not be considered when

| Event Scope | |
|---|---|
| Value Stream | |
| Event Name | |
| Specific Conditions | |
| Process Trigger | |
| First Step | |
| Last Step | |
| Event Boundaries & Limitations | |

| Event Drivers / Current State Issues | |
|---|---|
| 1 | |
| 2 | |
| 3 | |
| 4 | |
| 5 | |

| Event Goals and Objectives | |
|---|---|
| 1 | |
| 2 | |
| 3 | |
| 4 | |
| 5 | |

| Potential Deliverables | |
|---|---|
| 1 | |
| 2 | |
| 3 | |
| 4 | |
| 5 | |

| Possible Obstacles | |
|---|---|
| 1 | |
| 2 | |
| 3 | |
| 4 | |

**Figure 5-1.** Kaizen Event Charter—Left Side

making improvements. If the value stream being improved includes multiple service/product lines, the specific conditions cell should specify which line the Kaizen Event will focus on (or will be excluded).

4. *Process trigger*—The process trigger is the activity that triggers the action in the first step (beginning fence post) to occur. How do the people who perform the first step know to begin work? The process trigger is often the receipt of something (e g , an order, requisition, telephone call, e-mail, etc.). With scheduled activities, the calendar or a formal schedule is often the trigger. In service industries such as healthcare, food service and retail sales, the trigger could be a person arriving.

5. *First step*—This is the first activity (the beginning fence post) within the range of process steps the Kaizen Team will focus on.

6. *Last step*—This is the final activity (the ending fence post) within the range of process steps the Kaizen Team will focus on.

7. *Event boundaries and limitations*—This section houses any process elements the team is *not* authorized to alter. This cell is critical for granting the Kaizen Team "freedom with boundaries." They are authorized to make improvements within the established fence posts, specific conditions, and any predetermined limitations that have been established. For example, altering an IT system may be off limits if a new system is about to be implemented, or changing the scope of work for a particular job function that's being reconfigured may be restricted. If the Event involves 5S activities (workplace organization and visual management), a particular physical area may be off limits. Leadership may determine that a particular company policy may not be challenged. If the team is being asked to pilot the improvement, the pilot area should be clearly defined in this cell.

## Event Drivers/Current State Issues

Here, the event leaders list up to five reasons why the organization is holding the Event, which typically address the current performance issues that are impacting the value stream. Other drivers may include anticipated market demands, business growth, or changing customer requirements. Information in this section should establish a sense of urgency or "burning platform" for making the improvement.

## Event Goals and Objectives

After the event leaders have identified the current state drivers, they must define the Event goals and objectives to provide further focus. While the event leaders may consult with the supervisors and managers of the work areas that will be impacted by the improvement, it's important that the Event goals align with value stream goals and objectives. Note: Defining the Event objectives, as well as the other scoping activities described in this chapter, must be completed *prior to* determining team composition (discussed in Chapter 6).

Goals and objectives are not the same. Ideally, you want to establish objectives, which are *measurable*, such as:

- Reduce lead time from 4 to 2.5 days
- Improve patient satisfaction scores from 85 percent to 92 percent
- Improve output quality from 50 percent to 85 percent

If current state metrics are not fully known when creating the Event Charter, the objectives could be stated in terms of the desired magnitude of the improvement: reduce lead time by 60 percent, improve quality by 80 percent, or reduce abandoned calls by 25 percent. The key is in establishing a target by which the team can measure their success.

Goals, on the other hand, are statements of intent that do not contain numbers: reduce lead time, improve quality, improve productivity, free capacity, reduce telephone hold times, etc. Goals generally precede objectives, but are less effective for driving team performance because they are not specific enough to effectively measure progress. However, event leaders may want to include goals, such as, standardize the process, organize the workplace, define key performance indicators and a monitoring process, etc. The key is to be as specific as possible, keeping the need for measurement in mind. Establishing objectives takes practice; organizations get better and better at it the more Kaizen Events they run.

### Potential Deliverables

This section houses information regarding the "product(s)" the Kaizen Team is projected to produce during the Event. While it's difficult to predict this upfront (and not always necessary to do so), it can help leadership understand why the team is being sequestered for multiple days when they better understand the anticipated output from the Event. The information, if known up front, also helps the Kaizen Team better understand what they'll be doing with their time. But event leaders walk a fine line here. They need to provide information without telling the team exactly how they'll make improvements. That's the team's job.

### Possible Obstacles

When it comes to project management, the best surprise is no surprise. This adage is especially appropriate for Kaizen Events, which are structured as rapidly executed mini-projects. To reduce the possibility of a "showstopper" that slows or stops the team during the Event, potential obstacles should be identified upfront and a game plan put into place so that, if the obstacle occurs, the team can resolve it quickly. Obstacles could include unscheduled regulatory audits that would pull key members from the team, equipment downtime, or encountering significant resistance to change. If the obstacle is very likely to occur, you may want to reschedule the Kaizen Event. But if the possibility is slim, it's best to move forward with solutions in mind should the obstacle be realized.

After the scope and objectives have been defined, the Event schedule of activities should be established, the subject of the next section.

## EVENT SCOPE AND SCHEDULE

Determining event scope is not a straightforward activity, and there are no magic formulas. When scoping, the event leaders possess relevant information such as event drivers, current state performance, and the desired performance, but they will not know exactly how the team will achieve the desired results. That's the team's job, and it occurs during the Event. So this important aspect of event planning requires educated guesswork, based on experience. Therefore, the event leaders must obtain as much upfront information as possible, and determine scope and time frames based on the following organizational and event variables:

1. *Event objectives*. How aggressive are the Event objectives? If the goal is to reduce lead time by 75 percent, the team may need a day or two to determine how to accomplish this, followed by another day or two for implementation. If you seek to reduce the number of handoffs in approving a particular document, the team may not need as much time.

A word of caution about establishing objectives: On the one hand, narrowly focused and 100 percent achievable objectives can provide tremendous satisfaction to a team in terms of accomplishment. They declare, "We met our goal!" and their enthusiasm becomes contagious across the organization, helping to garner the interest in, and momentum for, future rapid improvement efforts. On the other hand, scoping the Event slightly outside of what most teams can accomplish often generates more dramatic results because teams strive to "do it all." It all depends upon the organization's readiness, culture, and need for change, whether the scope should be more conservative or whether the Event leaders should set *stretch objectives* that carry higher risk, but may yield greater rewards. When choosing the more aggressive approach, expectations need to be clearly established. If the team fails to fully achieve the objectives, their results still reflect substantial progress on the road to continuous improvement, and their efforts must still be applauded.

2. *Current state understanding.* The amount of time event teams need to fully understand the current state before designing specific improvements can vary widely. For example, imagine that one of the Event objectives is to improve the output quality for a particular process step. If the reasons for poor quality and the necessary improvements have already been identified, the team may be able to accomplish the objectives in a day or two. But if they need to perform root cause analyses to identify the fundamental reason(s) for the quality problems—and if the future state design will require a fair amount of input and buy-in from upstream suppliers and downstream customers—they will need more time to accomplish the Event objectives.

   Another consideration is whether or not the team will need to perform micro-level process mapping to fully understand the current state. While value stream maps provide macro-level strategic direction regarding improvements, a micro-level map is often needed to identify root causes for waste and properly define tactical-level improvements. As discussed in Chapter 12, the Metrics-Based Process Map (MBPM) can be invaluable for designing and implementing improvements, and typically requires one to two days *during the Event* to construct maps that reflect both the current and desired future state.

3. *Process complexity.* Process complexity is a function of: 1) how cross-functional the process is; 2) how many individual steps, IT systems, and external suppliers or contractors are involved; and 3) the nature of the work itself. Complex processes require more time to fully understand, design, and implement desired improvements. If the team has limited time available and the target process is complex, you will likely need to narrow the scope by moving the beginning and ending fence posts closer together. Additional Kaizen Events can be used to broaden the improvement by including process steps before and after the initial improvement focus area.

4. *Complexity of projected solutions.* The complexity of the projected solutions is another factor when scoping and scheduling an event. In most Kaizen Events, the team creates standard work of some sort (e.g., visual job aids, standard operating procedures, checklists, cheat sheets, and flowcharts) to document the new process. Team

members also need a fair amount of time to obtain input from involved parties to define and design the standards, test them, finalize them, and finally train the affected workforce on the standard work "rules" and any new job aids the team has developed. Other solutions may take even longer, such as designing new data storage options to eliminate redundant data entry. Developing visuals for the workplace may be quick, whereas designing a pull system might take a full day in and of itself. A word of caution: The Event leaders need to predict how long the Kaizen Team will need to fully implement improvements without telling the team how; specifically, they should solve the current state problems that have been identified. That's *the team's* job. So event leaders walk a fine line here. And the more aggressive the Event objectives, the more aggressive the solutions may be.

5. *Organizational culture and experience with Kaizen Events.* How flexible and open is the organization? If the organization or the area that owns the target process is highly resistant to change, the Kaizen Team will need more time to obtain input and buy-in for their proposed improvements. Are you planning the organization's first Kaizen Event or the twentieth? Is leadership driven to make improvements or do leaders feel threatened by the prospect of change? Answers to these questions give insight into how rapidly the team will accomplish event objectives.

6. *Lean principles and Kaizen Event overview.* To generate understanding about the change process and begin establishing buy-in, the Kaizen Team and the workers in the areas targeted for improvement need to receive training about lean principles and Kaizen Events, including, at a minimum, the following topics:
   - The concepts of customer value and flow
   - The eight wastes
   - Benefits of standard work and the various forms standard work may take
   - What Kaizen Events are
   - The role of the Kaizen Team in designing and implementing improvements
   - What to expect during and after the Event

   Ideally, this training is provided one week prior to the Event. However, if you're using an external facilitator for the Event and are relying on the facilitator to deliver the training, it may be scheduled for the first few hours of the first day.

7. *Workforce training.* Scheduling adequate time for the workforce to learn the new process is an essential element in successful Kaizen Events. The number of workers who require training, and the extent of this training require careful thought. A Kaizen Event cannot be considered a success unless the process is performing significantly better the next day or shift after the Event concludes. Full implementation requires workforce awareness and training—delivered *during* the Event. Chapters 7 and 16 cover this vital step in greater detail.

8. *Pilots versus full rollouts.* One last scoping consideration concerns how broadly the team will implement an improvement across the organization. Some improvements can and should be rolled out across an entire organization at once. But complex

improvements, or those that will affect a large portion of the workforce in a defined area, often benefit from implementing the improvement first in one department or geographic area, or with one product type or customer group. Pilots allow for smoother implementation in two ways: 1) they reduce the "organizational noise" and negative impressions about Kaizen Events that can result from an overly aggressive rollout, and 2) even though the Kaizen Team tests the improvements during the Event, process workers often make new discoveries after the new process has been rolled out. It's often best to make these discoveries in an area with smaller impact rather than exposing the entire organization to a process adjustment right away.

The Kaizen Team will need more time during the Event for a full organizational rollout. Whichever approach is selected, the rollout plan should be determined during the Kaizen Event planning phase. If a pilot is selected, set aggressive time frames for evaluating the pilot. Also, identify resources and target dates for rolling the improvement out to the rest of the organization.

Most Kaizen Events in office, service, and technical environments need a minimum of two full days and many require four to five days to gain significant ground. If process-level mapping is likely, allow one to two days for mapping and an additional two to three days for improvement design and implementation. The natural human tendency is to fill the allotted time we're given to accomplish a task. So time requirements for making changes must be limited, but not to the point where this constraint results in no improvement being made. Creating sustainable change takes time. The challenge is to match the time requirements with event objectives; with practice, this determination becomes easier. And time requirements will change over time. The more skilled an organization becomes in holding Kaizen Events, the less time it will take the teams to generate productive results.

For those who have never planned a Kaizen Event, it may feel uncomfortable planning for something in which you don't know exactly what will happen. But keep in mind that discovery is an important element of Kaizen Events, and it applies to the planning stage as well. With time and experience, event leaders will grow increasingly skilled in establishing the parameters within which the Kaizen Team will operate and the time frames for doing so.

The next chapter addresses arguably the most important planning activity—forming the Kaizen Team.

# CHAPTER 6

# KAIZEN TEAM FORMATION

Forming a high-performing Kaizen Team is a strategic activity, which requires a fair amount of forethought and planning. Ultimately, the team must meet seemingly conflicting quality and quantity criteria. Without all the necessary expertise, the team will be handicapped from the beginning, impacting results. But progress will be slow if the team has too many "cooks in the kitchen."

Team formation is an iterative process, driven by two key considerations: 1) Which *functions* need to be represented, and 2) *Who* should represent these functions? The Event scope defines the functions—the *process stakeholders* who will be directly impacted by an improvement—that must be included. Choosing individuals to represent those functions is based on a wide variety of considerations, discussed in the next section. But before detailing the process of selecting specific team members, overall team structure must be considered.

## KAIZEN TEAM STRUCTURE

Kaizen Event Teams must be structured to achieve two desired outcomes: shorter-term performance improvement results, and longer-term workforce development and cultural transformation. As discussed in Chapter 2, workforce involvement and teamwork are critical elements in creating a continuous-improvement culture. And the team must include the proper mix of individuals who can deliver rapid results. Proper Kaizen Event Team structure ensures that the team will complete an event successfully and lays the foundation for employees to learn and apply lean principles in real time. The following guidelines will help build an effective team:

- *Minimal leadership/management representation.* Kaizen Events are tactical-level activities used to implement the strategic directives established by leadership (typically through value stream mapping). As a result, at least 50 percent of the Kaizen Team needs to be comprised of the employees who actually perform the work being improved. The balance of the team typically includes internal and external customers and suppliers, subject matter experts, representatives from support departments, and outside eyes.

    While it's critical that leadership participate on Kaizen Teams to gain hands-on experience with rapid improvement (which provides development and fuels ongoing support for the approach), the best ways for providing this experience are: 1) hold Kaizen Events for leadership-level processes, such as creating annual budgets, tracking key performance indicators, strategic planning, and hiring staff, or 2) have leadership serve as the outside eyes on a team improving a process outside the leader's

59

umbrella of authority. In the latter approach, it's critical that these leaders are willing to function as equals on the team—where *rank has no privilege*. If the leader has a strong personality, discuss roles with this person up front to set the stage for the egalitarian climate that Kaizen Events require.

- *Six to eight people ideally; no more than ten.* When it comes to high-performing work teams, more is not always better. More than ten people on a Kaizen Team slow progress considerably. Small work groups are essential for rapid decision making and full implementation of the improvements by the end of the Event. If an event requires more than ten people, revisit the scope and eliminate any redundant representation on the team.

  Why are so many people required to improve seemingly "simple" processes, such as the purchase order generation process, patient registration, or month-end closings? When one person or one department makes an improvement without consulting anyone else, or when consultants or managers dictate change, results are often ineffective. A fundamental tenet of the lean philosophy—and an essential element in creating sustainable change—is the "inclusion factor" in designing and implementing improvements. Obtaining the perspective of upstream suppliers and downstream customers nearly always makes for a better process. Another tenet is that *the workers know best*. The people closest to the work have the most experience with the process and are, therefore, in the best position to evaluate the current state and define improvements. These individuals possess the detailed knowledge and experience necessary for designing effective improvements with staying power.

  Lean thinking also recognizes that "command and control" management simply does not work, and that people resist change unless they are actively involved in the change process. Kaizen Events provide the opportunity to put this basic human psychology into practice.

  The Kaizen Team should comprise people who *currently* perform the work being evaluated, and not those who previously performed the work (even if it was as recent as a month prior to the Event) or those who say they know how the work is done. Since requirements and practices change frequently, avoid the risk of using old information to shape decisions that could result in suboptimal processes by adhering to this important team requirement.

- *Cross-functional composition.* In office, service, and technical environments, rarely is only one department represented on a Kaizen Team and occasionally more than five functional areas are represented. As addressed in Chapter 2, in addition to the process workers themselves, representatives from areas upstream and downstream from the target area, subject matter experts, and outside eyes should be included. Depending on the Event scope and objectives, external contractors, suppliers, and/or customers may also be involved. To design and implement the most effective improvements, the Kaizen Team must understand all of the relevant inputs and outputs in the process. In office, service, and technical environments—which often operate in functional silos—most workers do not possess sufficient knowledge about the steps that lead into and out of the work that they do. As a result, no one person fully understands the process. A sufficient variety of perspectives provide a truer picture of the current state—including variations in input and output information and material—and aids in designing and implementing the best sustainable solutions.

Team members should be chosen with care, considering both the need for varying perspectives as well as the limitation of having only ten seats available. The three essential perspectives that must be included on the team are: process stakeholders, subject matter experts, and outside eyes, described below.

## Process Stakeholders

A stakeholder is anyone with an interest or involvement with the process being improved. This category covers a broad spectrum but typically includes:

- Those performing the process
- Internal customers who receive output from the target area
- Internal suppliers who provide input into the target area
- External customers and suppliers/contractors

Stakeholders can also include subject matter experts (defined in the next section) who play an active role in the process, as well as union representatives, shareholders, and board members where applicable.

## Subject Matter Experts

Subject matter experts (SMEs) are individuals who possess specialized knowledge about particular issues. While SMEs may play an integral role in the process itself, they often reside in support areas, such as regulatory, information technology, legal, safety, quality, finance, marketing, human resources, facilities, and engineering, to name a few. An SME is necessary on a team if the required expertise or perspective does not reside among the process stakeholders on the team. Administrative support qualifies as an SME if no one on the team possesses the skills that may be needed to create standard work, job aids, and monitoring systems (e.g., creating Excel-based tracking systems, modifying forms, inserting photographs in Word-based standard work documents, etc.).

Predicting SME needs upfront can be challenging. For this reason, SMEs may be placed "on-call," but this role requires that they will have time-limited involvement and will be *immediately available* when the team needs them. But be careful here. You want to avoid a situation in which the Kaizen Team suddenly discovers it needs an on-call SME for the remainder of the Event, which can alter team dynamics and create scheduling challenges. Adding a new member when the team has transitioned from the "forming" stage into "storming" or "norming" (discussed further in Chapter 11) can be disruptive. And, assuming the team has spent hours or days analyzing the current state, getting a new member up to speed often requires significant rework. To minimize this risk, spend some extra time during the team formation stage talking with the process workers to gain a clear understanding about the SME requirements, who within the organization possesses the identified knowledge or skills, and whether the SME should be a full-time team member or placed on call.

For scheduling purposes, some organizations avoid potential disruption that slows the team's progress by placing all relevant support services (e.g., IT, regulatory, facilities, human resources, finance, etc.) on-call during events, but this approach may not work for every organization.

### Outside Eyes

Outside eyes refer to objective parties who have no attachment to the outcome of an improvement activity. The most dramatic innovations are often envisioned by people outside the established "community," rather than from those closest to a process. Outside eyes often ask questions and see opportunities that process workers themselves wouldn't think to ask about or suggest. They're able to ask "why" and "what if" more freely than colleagues who may be handicapped by "that's the way we've always done it" thinking. Having outside eyes on a Kaizen Team creates an effective means for challenging legacy processes and long-standing paradigms. This practice often results in strikingly innovative solutions.

If an organization is developing internal facilitators, the facilitators-in-training may serve as the outside eyes on Kaizen Teams who are focused on an improvement area foreign to the particular facilitator-in-training. This role will provide much-needed exposure to the Events he or she will eventually lead, without expanding team size. As previously mentioned, having leaders serve as outside eyes on a Kaizen Team—assuming they're fully prepared for the egalitarian role they'll play—is an effective way to provide leaders with exposure to the process. Some organizations also find it beneficial to fill the outside eyes seat for one event with a team member for a future event, providing continuity from event to event.

## EFFECTIVE TEAM MEMBER TRAITS

In addition to varying perspectives, effective Kaizen Teams also comprise individuals who possess specific personality traits. While a wide range of traits is helpful, such as the ability to listen, strong analytical skills, and open-mindedness, three key traits prove vital. Repeatedly, teams tend to generate the best results when each member is: 1) action oriented, 2) detail oriented, and 3) influential.

- *Action oriented.* While people who work more deliberately than others should not be categorically excluded from Kaizen Teams, they may struggle with the quick pace of Kaizen Events. Most of the team should be characterized as "doers." If one of the essential team members operates in a more introverted or deliberate fashion, an upfront discussion with him or her might minimize the frustration that may develop when the team wants/needs to move more quickly than this person is comfortable with.

- *Detail oriented.* Possessing a high tolerance for details is a helpful trait in Kaizen Event Team members. People who are more visionary than tactical may have difficulty with the often tedious nature of analyzing the current state, designing effective improvements, and executing change.

- *Influential.* Since each team member represents the "voice" of his or her functional peers, he or she should be influential among peers and/or across the organization. If the peer group doesn't respect the team member, this person may have difficulty "selling" the improvement to his or her colleagues, or worse, encounter overt resistance from peers. It's also helpful if leadership also respects the team members. In larger organizations, leadership won't necessarily know the Kaizen Team members. But in smaller organizations, it hurts both implementation and sustainability if leadership doesn't respect or trust a team member leading a particular improvement or recommending a specific policy change.

Event leaders often wonder whether they should include individuals who have been branded as chronic complainers. Including them, if they meet the previously mentioned traits, allows them to adopt a more constructive approach to communicating their concerns and suggesting solutions. In addition, they are often vital resources for understanding the current state, and they are typically enthusiastic ambassadors for change. Their "bad behavior," as perceived by others, is often a result of repeated attempts to address problems and share improvement ideas that are never implemented. When given a structured venue for analyzing the root causes of waste in a process, and a proper forum for implementing improvements, chronic complainers frequently turn into some of the strongest lean advocates the organization has—and *the transformation from negative complainer to positive champion for change often occurs overnight.*

## DEFINING THE FUNCTIONS TO BE REPRESENTED ON THE TEAM

After discussing team membership at a high level, it's time to begin actually forming the Kaizen Team. The exact process for selecting team members can and does vary from organization to organization, but one constant proves true and is critical for event success: *Kaizen Teams are stronger when the Event facilitator plays an active role in directing team formation and selecting team members.* While it's sometimes appropriate to ask for volunteers or have management "nominate" team members, a seasoned facilitator's recommendations regarding team composition should be taken into serious account. It takes a fair amount of experience to form the most effective Kaizen Teams.

The Team Formation Worksheet that appears as Tab 3 on the Kaizen Event Tools file on the CD provides help with this vital step. Figure 6-1 contains a portion of the first page of the worksheet and Figure 6-2 shows the second page. As with all of the tools that follow the Kaizen Event Charter, the header will auto-populate with information from the Charter.

The first two columns house the *functional departments* in your organization and the specific *work groups* that may exist within those departments. For example, accounts receivable and accounts payable work groups may exist within a finance department. Clinical laboratories are often divided into testing areas, such as hematology, microbiology, and blood banking. A

## Kaizen Event
## Team Formation Worksheet

| Executive Sponsor | | Event Name | |
|---|---|---|---|
| Value Stream Champion | | Event Dates | |
| Facilitator | | First Step | |
| | | Last Step | |

| | Department | Work Group | Role in Target Process | | | | |
|---|---|---|---|---|---|---|---|
| | | | Upstream Suppliers | Process Workers | Downstream Customers | Subject Matter Experts | No Involvement or Impact |
| 1 | | | ☐ | ☐ | ☐ | ☐ | ☐ |
| 2 | | | ☐ | ☐ | ☐ | ☐ | ☐ |
| 3 | | | ☐ | ☐ | ☐ | ☐ | ☐ |
| 4 | | | ☐ | ☐ | ☐ | ☐ | ☐ |
| 5 | | | ☐ | ☐ | ☐ | ☐ | ☐ |
| 6 | | | ☐ | ☐ | ☐ | ☐ | ☐ |
| 7 | | | ☐ | ☐ | ☐ | ☐ | ☐ |
| 8 | | | ☐ | ☐ | ☐ | ☐ | ☐ |

**Figure 6-1.** Team Formation Worksheet—Page One (partial view)

sales department may be arranged by geographic region, product type, or customer classification. As described in the CD Instructions for Use, you may complete these two columns once and save the Kaizen Event Tools as an organization-specific template, which you may need to revise from time to time as departments or work groups are created or eliminated in your organization. As you use the Kaizen Event Tool file for new Kaizen Events, start with the modified template and immediately save it with a new file name. As a reminder, the file name you select will appear in the tool's footer.

For each Kaizen Event, once the event leaders have established the starting and ending steps (the fence posts) for the process segment that the team will focus on, they can complete the right portion of page one of the Team Formation Worksheet's first page: Role in Target Process. Here, they place a checkmark to denote the role the particular department and/or work group plays in the target process, if any, which helps define the process stakeholders—those who are essential team candidates. Check "No Involvement or Impact" if the department and/or work group will not be affected in any way by the process being improved and, as a result, this group cannot provide insight, perspective, or information that would create a more thorough understanding of the current state or a better designed improvement. It's helpful to review the Event drivers and/or future state value stream map when defining the process stakeholders.

## SELECTING SPECIFIC TEAM MEMBERS

In the *Essential Team Candidates* section on the second page of the Team Formation Worksheet, enter the names of up to eight functional areas you feel should be represented on the team (based on the discoveries you've documented on page 1). Next, enter the names of individuals in those areas who are knowledgeable about the process being improved and

# Kaizen Event
# Team Formation Worksheet

| Executive Sponsor | | Event Name | |
|---|---|---|---|
| Value Stream Champion | | Event Dates | |
| Facilitator | | First Step | |
| | | Last Step | |

**Essential Team Candidates**

| | Function | Names | |
|---|---|---|---|
| 1 | | | |
| 2 | | | |
| 3 | | | |
| 4 | | | |
| 5 | | | |
| 6 | | | |
| 7 | | | |
| 8 | | | |

**Additional Team Candidates**

| | Role | Names | |
|---|---|---|---|
| 1 | External Customer(s) | | |
| 2 | External Supplier(s)/Contractor(s) | | |
| 3 | Subject Matter Experts | | |
| 4 | Union Representatives | | |
| 5 | Outside Eyes | | |

**On-Call Support Candidates**

| | Function | Names | |
|---|---|---|---|
| 1 | | | |
| 2 | | | |
| 3 | | | |
| 4 | | | |
| 5 | | | |
| 6 | | | |

**Figure 6-2.** Team Formation Worksheet—Page Two

would likely be effective Kaizen Team members. (*Note*: As described below, prospective team members are considered "candidates" until their immediate supervisors have approved their participation and the team members themselves have agreed to serve on the team.)

If the event leaders do not know who could/should represent a particular functional area, they should meet with area management to solicit ideas. But, to assure the manager suggests *appropriate* team members, event leaders may need to do a fair amount of educating—including the Event scope and objectives, why representation is needed, and traits of Kaizen Team members.

The next step is to consider *Additional Team Candidates*, the middle section on page 2 of the Team Formation Worksheet. Candidates include external customers, external suppliers and contractors, subject matter experts, union representatives, and outside eyes. You can enter up to four candidates in each category. Remember that outside eyes could also include internal facilitators-in-training and/or leadership (as long as they can be 100 percent objective in analyzing and improving a process).

The final step at this stage of team formation is considering the need for *On-Call Support*. As described earlier, "on-call" status is reserved for people who truly don't need to serve on the team full time and can be *immediately available* to the team as issues arise. Enter up to four candidates for up to five functional areas.

The next steps vary in the order in which they occur, which is why forming the team is an iterative process. The event leaders need to meet with every candidate's immediate supervisor to check on the person's availability, as well as obtain the supervisor's approval to free this individual from daily duties for the duration of the Event. The next step is to talk with the prospective member, to make sure the person is willing to participate. Candidates are sometimes eliminated at this point because they've scheduled time off that the immediate supervisor wasn't aware of, or they don't want to participate for any number of reasons. If someone's absolutely essential for a successful event, the Event should be rescheduled rather than moving forward without the necessary experience and perspectives on the team.

Lobbying for team members is often part of the team formation process. The event leaders may need to "sell" the immediate supervisor on why his or her staff member's participation is vital for event success. Or, depending on the candidate's rank, they may need to lobby the candidate him or herself. In both cases, the discussions need to be face-to-face or by telephone, not e-mail. And, in both cases, a fair amount of education may be necessary. The prospective team member and immediate supervisor both need to understand (at least at a high level):

- The current state issues driving the need for the Kaizen Event.
- The scope and objectives for the Event.
- Why the person's involvement is vital for achieving the desired results.
- What the department will gain from having a representative on the team.
- What the person will gain from participating.
- The dates and times for the Event.
- The "rules" around a Kaizen Event (e.g., full-time participation, no interruptions, etc.), discussed in detail in Chapter 11.

Without the full buy-in and support from both the candidate and his or her immediate supervisor, you risk having accessibility problems during the Event—or last minute changes to the team, which can create logistics problems.

Table 6-1 lists a few of the reasons immediate supervisors sometimes give when unwilling to relinquish their staff for an event, with suggestions for countering their concerns. You may need to rephrase this blunt language to fit your organizational culture and the particular manager to whom you're "selling."

**Table 6-1.** Responses to Supervisor Concerns Relinquishing Workers

| Concerns | Suggested Responses |
|---|---|
| He/she's too busy with day-to-day work. | I understand, but we need to improve the process so we can better handle our daily work and that takes focus.<br><br>We shouldn't ever be too busy to make improvements.<br><br>Our leadership has determined that continuous improvement is our #1 priority (use this one only if it's true). |
| We're "one deep" in this department. I don't have backup for this person. | How do you handle the work when he/she is ill? Does he/she ever take a vacation? What if he/she suddenly resigned with no notice?<br><br>Being "one deep" is a problem that needs to be addressed. But we can't avoid making improvements because our staffing doesn't allow for it. |
| I need him/her for a higher priority project. | Have your director/VP talk with the executive sponsor for this Event and see if he/she wants to reprioritize projects or not. |
| I can't give you so-and-so (for any of the above reasons), but I can give you so-and-so. | See the paragraph below for how to deal with this. |

If a direct supervisor or manager suggests "a trade" ("I can't give you so-and-so, but I can give you so-and-so"), the Event planners—the facilitator in particular—need to evaluate whether the suggested person will represent the functional area well or whether to lobby harder for the first choice. You may run into a manager who is only willing to give up one of the department's weaker performers. But the people you want on your Kaizen Team—especially for your first few events—are the department's top performers or, at a minimum, middle performers. Later, you can include some of the organization's weaker performers, which aids in their growth and development. If you can't reach consensus with the supervisor, you may need to escalate your request to the next leadership level (through the value stream champion or executive sponsor). The limited number of seats on the Kaizen Team requires that each team member be strategically selected for his/her expertise and ability to produce team-based results, *so never accept someone on the team who you feel is not likely to contribute to the team's success.*

Once you've narrowed down your candidates and have begun to finalize the Kaizen Team, you're ready to complete the *Team Members* section of the Kaizen Event Charter.

## COMPLETING THE EVENT CHARTER

When the team has been finalized, complete the *Team Members* and *On-Call Support* sections of the Event Charter (Figure 6-3), by entering the function or role each individual is representing (name of department, outside eyes, external customer, etc.). The third column houses user-defined information. Some organizations use this column to list contact information or departmental charge codes, while others list the names of supervisors or managers who have authorized the team member's participation in the Event. When you enter a heading for this column (e.g., contact information, approving supervisor, etc.), the yellow cell will convert to gray automatically, but remains unlocked and editable.

| Team Members | | |
|---|---|---|
| | Function | Name |
| 1 | | |
| 2 | | |
| 3 | | |
| 4 | | |
| 5 | | |
| 6 | | |
| 7 | | |
| 8 | | |
| 9 | | |
| 10 | | |
| On-Call Support | | |
| | Function | Name |
| 1 | | |
| 2 | | |
| 3 | | |
| 4 | | |

**Figure 6-3.** Kaizen Event Charter—Team Members and On-Call Support Sections

As a result of the draft charter's initial distribution and feedback from affected areas, team composition may need to be modified to accommodate adjustments to the Event scope and/or objectives. This is another reason why team formation is an iterative process. But, by the time the charter is finalized (at least three weeks prior to the Event), the team needs to be finalized as well.

With the team formed, you're ready to address the logistical aspects of a Kaizen Event, such as selecting an appropriate location, gathering supplies, and planning for the team's technology needs.

# CHAPTER 7

# EVENT LOGISTICS

After accomplishing the "heavy lifting" of the Kaizen Event planning process—establishing scope, setting objectives, and forming the team—it is time to turn your attention to the logistics component. Where will you hold the Event? When will it start and end? Will you provide food? What supplies will be necessary? How many interim briefings will be held? How will you recognize the team for their efforts? You will also need to consider smaller details, such as whether you will use table tents or some other means to identify team members and whether you will need an icebreaker to help team members get to know one another.

While any of the event leaders can complete the logistical activities, the Event coordinator often carries the greatest responsibility. The Planning Checklist (Tab 2 on the Kaizen Event Tools file on the CD), described in Chapter 3, lists a wide range of pre-event activities and the time frames for completion. Ownership for the various logistical activities should be established early in the planning process.

As shown in Figure 7-1, the upper right section of the Event Charter contains scheduling details that are selected based on the discussion below.

| Schedule | |
|---|---|
| **Dates** | |
| **Start & End Times** | |
| **Location** | |
| **Interim Briefings** | |
| **Workforce Training** | |
| **Team Presentation** | |

**Figure 7-1.** Kaizen Event Charter—Schedule Section

## SELECTING DATES

Chapter 5 addressed how to determine the Event time frames based on the scope of the improvement effort. This section discusses the specific schedule for the Event. *The most successful Kaizen Events are held for full days and on consecutive days.* Organizations are sometimes tempted to schedule events for half days or on nonconsecutive days to create more consistent coverage in key departments or to allow team members to work on other projects. This is not recommended because each time the team's concentration is broken, a fair amount of "setup" time is required to get back into the flow of things. Following an interruption, the team members must spend valuable time reviewing where they were when they left off, why they made key decisions, etc. The longer the break in momentum, the longer the team members will need to return to the place where they left off, so they can move forward. This "mental rework"—a form of waste—is minimized when the Event is held on consecutive full days. As discussed in Chapter 2, *focus* is one of the key reasons why Kaizen Events generate such impressive results. Proper event scheduling maximizes the team's ability to focus and generate strong returns on the organization's investment.

Another key scheduling consideration is assuring that essential team members are available on the selected dates. If an essential team member is not available for any portion of the dates selected, and an appropriate alternate team member with equivalent experience and perspective is not available, the Event should be rescheduled. Too many organizations move forward without essential team members, which typically results in suboptimal outcomes. Pre-planned vacations, family time, and conferences are all valid reasons for rescheduling the Event, whereas conflicting priorities may not be. Engage the team member's immediate supervisor or senior leadership in a discussion about the potential impact of a team member's absence, including the possibility of event cancellation. As mentioned in Chapter 6, having a conversation with the team member's direct supervisor and, in many cases, the team member him or herself before you distribute the Event Charter, can avoid rework later.

For organizations with staff who travel frequently, Kaizen Events need to be viewed as high priority activities, or it may become impossible to secure an effective Kaizen Team. In most cases, business travel can and should be rescheduled. This is another reason why planning four to six weeks in advance of the Event is essential. You should also consider key leadership's availability for interim briefings and final presentations, especially in the early stages of holding Kaizen Events in office and service environments. In these early events, leadership is often more actively engaged than down the road when leadership has granted greater authority to the workforce for designing and implementing improvements.

## SELECTING START AND END TIMES

To avoid rework and maximize team dynamics, the Kaizen Team needs to begin and end each day together, which can pose challenges for organizations with flexible work schedules. Some organizations address this issue by creating a policy that all Kaizen Events are held from 8 a.m. to 5 p.m., no matter what the typical work schedule is for individual team members. Team members are expected to work from eight to five on those days. Other organizations survey Kaizen Team members and select daily start and end times that correspond with the latest arrival and the earliest departure times—e.g., 9 a.m. to 4 p.m.

The team needs *seven to eight full hours of work time*, a 30- to 60-minute lunch break, and at least one break in the morning and afternoon. As previously mentioned, team momentum is an important element of Kaizen Events. If an event is scheduled for less than eight hours, it produces shorter "stints of momentum" and productivity losses due to the mental setup periods required to get back into the flow, impacting team progress. If you must schedule your event for less than eight hours of work time (to accommodate flextime schedules, for example), make sure you adjust your objectives accordingly. It's unfair to expect teams to produce aggressive results with insufficient time.

Some lean practitioners promote holding Kaizen Events for longer than eight hours per day. This is not recommended for Kaizen Events in office, service, and technical environments. Analyzing and making improvements in data-intensive areas often requires a higher degree of concentration than making improvements to manufacturing processes. Also, because office and service sector Kaizen Teams are typically more cross-functional—and less experienced in challenging the status quo and making change through structured, rapid improvement—these Kaizen Events are often more emotional than those held in their manufacturing counterparts. Finally, Kaizen Events in nonmanufacturing environments often require that the team members challenge long-standing corporate policies, which can be more draining than designing visual job aids, moving equipment, and creating manufacturing cells. To avoid the productivity and creativity losses that occur when people work beyond the point of diminishing returns, eight hours is the recommended work time.

## SELECTING A LOCATION—"KAIZEN CENTRAL"

Though a seemingly simple decision, choosing the appropriate room in which to conduct the Kaizen Event—*Kaizen Central*—can be challenging, especially if the organization does not have dedicated space for its continuous-improvement activities and/or has limited conference room availability. In organizations with heavy meeting room use, attempting to reserve a room four weeks before the Event can already be too late.

Ideally, larger organizations that are fully committed to the lean journey have dedicated space for its various continuous-improvement activities. These "war rooms," as they are sometimes called, provide space for continuous-improvement meetings, training sessions, mapping activities, and Kaizen Events, as well as wall space to hang value stream and process-level maps and storage for dedicated equipment and supplies. When dedicated space is not available, Kaizen Central needs to be established in conference/meeting rooms that meet the criteria discussed in the next section.

### On-Site Location

Kaizen Events should be held on-site. This requirement often surprises event leaders who think that a sequestered team would perform better off site due to fewer interruptions. But off-site locations can be problematic because they:

- Limit the team's ability to conduct "*gemba walks*," a Japanese term that means "the actual place" and, in lean terminology has been expanded to mean "going to the place to see the actual situation for understanding." It's common for the Kaizen Team to "go to gemba" to see the work environment and observe the process in action when analyzing the current state and/or designing the desired future state.

- Limit access to coworkers, on-call support, subject matter experts, etc., with whom the team may need to consult during the Event.

- Limit access to the organization's information systems, data, work samples, etc., which are often required during the Event.

- Require transportation (one of the eight wastes) to and from the off-site location for interim briefings and the team presentation, which cuts into productive work time and reduces the likelihood of strong participation from those who must travel.

- Most importantly, it is nearly impossible to implement an improvement remotely. Implementation includes workforce training, replacing old versions of procedures and forms with newly created standard work and, in some cases, physically moving equipment and office furniture. Remember that Kaizen Events are not merely planning activities. They are action-oriented implementation activities. *If the team has not fully implemented improvements by the end of the Event, you have not held a true Kaizen Event.*

In addition, there are positive cultural reasons for holding events on site. First, it visually demonstrates leadership's commitment to using the concept of focus and cross-functional teamwork to implement improvements. When workers walk by Kaizen Central, they are reminded that making improvements is the Kaizen Team's singular priority during the Event, and that working on multiple projects simultaneously, which produces slower results, has been replaced with the focused attention that yields dramatic, rapid results. In addition, when employees see Kaizen Teams sequestered on site, their curiosity is aroused about "what's going on in there." While not knowing what's going on behind closed doors can prove anxiety-provoking, there's also power in it—and a message: *the culture is changing.*

Finally, placing a sequestered team physically on site and forcing coworkers to leave team members alone begins to create the organizational discipline required to move from an environment that tolerates excessive work loads, inconsistent priorities, and impossible demands to a flow-based culture that reaps the rewards produced by focused attention. Holding Kaizen Events on site creates a visual, real-time, physical presence to the organization's commitment to continuous improvement and cultural transformation.

## Ample Size and Wall Space

The room needs to be large enough to accommodate the Kaizen Team members when they are working together as a single team and adequate space for dedicated work areas for two to four breakout work groups. These dedicated work areas can range from four corners of the room to four corners of a large conference table. Naturally, the larger the space, the better. Working in cramped quarters can impact team dynamics and productivity.

If Kaizen Central cannot accommodate the larger groups that will attend interim briefings, workforce training, and the team presentation, the Event planners will need to reserve a second location for these sessions. But, as previously mentioned, make sure the second location is physically close to the kaizen room to avoid wasted time and suboptimal attendance due to meeting location issues.

Also, if the Kaizen Event includes 5S activities (sort, set-in-order, shine, standardize, and sustain), you'll need to secure a sorting area adjacent to the area being organized that's large enough to accommodate the projected volume of material and equipment that will be sorted.

Kaizen Central must also have adequate wall space for mapping activities and to hang flip chart pages listing the daily schedule, work plans, to-do lists, improvement ideas, parking lot lists, 30-day lists, etc. (More about these lists in Part III, Kaizen Event Execution). Large white boards can be beneficial, but flip charts are essential.

## Technology Ready

Kaizen Events in office and service environments typically require a fair amount of equipment and technology, as listed on the Planning Checklist and the Supplies Checklist (Tab 4 on Kaizen Event Tools), discussed later in this chapter:

- *Two to four computers* with access to the Internet; company intranet, e-mail, shared drives, and all software applications related to the process being improved; and Microsoft Office (including full versions of all programs).

- Convenient access to at least one *printer*. Ideally, the printer is located inside Kaizen Central and is dedicated to the Kaizen Team. If a dedicated printer is not available, a designated printer should be identified that's nearby. If the team has to walk a fair distance to a printer, it can rob them of valuable work time. In addition, the workers who use the equipment need to understand that the Kaizen Team has priority. Since color is often used to create effective visuals, a color printer works best.

- *An LCD projector* is needed for the training that's delivered during the Kaizen Event, projecting standard work drafts, and reviewing data entry screens and software applications that are relevant to the process.

- *A speakerphone*, placed in the center of the room, is essential.

- *A fax machine* should be available nearby—all-in-one printers that include fax and scanning capabilities are ideal.

- If audiovisuals will be used, a *DVD or VHS* player is required. If computers are being used to show training DVDs, *external speakers* are needed as most computer speakers don't project loudly enough for a roomful of people.

Properly functioning hardware and software is a frequent obstacle that slows Kaizen Teams. To avoid unproductive downtime, engage your IT and/or facilities staff early in the planning process to make sure everything is available and working properly when the Event kicks off. Someone who knows how to troubleshoot the equipment should be on call throughout the Event. *Teams should not be required to contact IT help desks during the Event.* A dedicated IT support resource with cell phone access is essential.

From a technology perspective, planning for a Kaizen Event is contingency-based, because it's difficult to determine the exact equipment and software requirements the team will have until they're in the middle of the Event and don't have the time to wait for setup. IT departments should be educated about this aspect of events so they don't become frustrated if a Kaizen Team doesn't use all of the computers they set up or they only use the printer once. Being prepared for anything and everything up front avoids the significant delays that can occur during an event once IT needs are fully realized.

As indicated on the Planning Checklist, it's critical that the room be set up and all equipment and software tested thoroughly the day before the Kaizen Event. If user IDs and passwords are required, they should be included in the testing. *All of the team members should be able to log into the computers—not just one designated person.* All equipment should include written work instructions that include details such as:

- Do you need to dial "9" when making an outside phone call?
- Do you need to use the area code when making a local call?
- What's the room's telephone number and/or extension (for people who need to return the team's calls)?
- What password(s), if any, are needed to access various system components/software applications?
- What's the printer code or network address?

The Supplies Checklist includes additional technology-related requirements, such as staff telephone and e-mail directories and the like.

## SCHEDULING THE INTERIM BRIEFING(S)

Interim briefings (described fully in Chapter 10) are effective tools for:

- Communicating to leadership the improvements that the team is implementing.
- Providing an opportunity for leadership to surface issues and areas of concern that the team may have missed.
- Enabling team members to raise issues they need help with and obtain leadership help in removing any obstacles they are encountering.
- Assuring the team that they have leadership's continued support.
- Reducing the risk of unsustainable improvements due to post-implementation disagreement.

Due to the unpredictable nature of Kaizen Events, the Event planners should schedule the interim briefings for the last hour of every day and hold them at least every other day, usually for the last hour of the team's work day. A differentiation is made here between *scheduling* and *holding* because, on any given day, the team may or may not need to hold an interim briefing. Much of the Kaizen Event process is discovery-based, so there is a fair amount of "not knowing what you don't know" that enters into event planning and execution. But to ensure that relevant leadership is available if the team needs to hold a briefing, it's easiest to schedule them for every day and cancel them with a few hours advance notice if they are not needed.

For example, for 8 to 5 p.m. events, the team should make a decision no later than 2 p.m. Someone (preferably outside the team), notifies the key leadership involved, or the entire leadership team if an open invitation was issued. During the upfront scheduling process, event leaders typically remind those attending the briefings to check their e-mail and/or shared calendars at 2:15 p.m. or later to see if the briefing is being held that day or not. In today's fast-paced world, most people appreciate the unexpected window created in their schedule when meetings are cancelled. The Kaizen Team should also place a sign outside Kaizen Central and/or the room where the briefings are scheduled to indicate whether the briefing will be held.

## WORKFORCE TRAINING

This proves one of the most challenging logistical issues and the most difficult scheduling need to predict up front. To properly schedule the location(s) and time frame(s) for training the workforce how to perform the new process, it helps to know who will need to be trained and what the nature of the content will be. But, like interim briefings, these determinations are made real time during the Event and are part of the discovery aspects of a Kaizen Event. So event leaders must plan a tentative schedule that ensures workforce availability, but doesn't include a precise training schedule that the Kaizen Team is locked into.

Two considerations will help establish the tentative training schedule that's included on the Kaizen Charter. The first consideration is *who* will need to be trained on the improvements. Related questions include: Where are they physically located? How large is the group? The second consideration is *how* the training will be conducted. Does it need to be in person or could a conference call or some sort of electronic training be as effective? Answers to both of these questions lead to the final considerations: *when* and *where*?

The time allotment and locations for training are often communicated as "tentative" because the training requirements cannot be accurately determined until the improvements are being designed. Some organizations prefer to place "TBD" (to be determined) in the training schedule cell on the Charter, but it's best to communicate an approximate schedule based on event objectives and the projected deliverables, in order to put the potential trainees on notice from a scheduling perspective. The easiest way to do this in office and service environments is to notify the anticipated trainees to hold a window open—generally late morning to early afternoon on the last day of the Event. Let them know that a final decision will be made 24 hours before the scheduled training activities. Chapter 10 (Event Structure) and Chapter 16 (Implementing Improvements) go into more detail about the training process. As you hold more and more Kaizen Events and your organization grows more comfortable with the unpredictable aspects of Kaizen Events, this scheduling task will become easier.

## THE TEAM PRESENTATION

The team presentation (discussed fully in Chapter 17) is usually scheduled for the last hour of the last day of the Kaizen Event. If the improvement included physical modifications to a work area, hold the presentation in or close to the improved area. For physical improvements, some teams include a "process walk" during the presentation, whereas others prefer holding a celebratory open house immediately following the presentation so leadership can experience the improvements first hand. Before and after photos may also be shown during the presentation.

If the team implemented nonphysical improvements (e.g., new process design, standard work, and job aids), hold the final presentation in Kaizen Central or a larger meeting room if the Kaizen Event room will not accommodate the group size.

After you enter the schedule details on the Kaizen Charter, it's ready for its initial distribution, which is discussed in Chapter 8. While the charter circulates, the Event coordinator can move on and finalize other logistical details, as outlined in the next section.

## FOOD

People bond when breaking bread together. Many of the most creative solutions to long-standing problems in politics, religion, business, and personal relationships have been resolved over a meal, which provides an ideal environment for establishing common ground, holding productive discussions, and reaching consensus. No matter if you provide coffee and muffins, a boxed lunch or a four-course dinner, Kaizen Teams function best when the organization provides food and beverages. It's a small price to pay for the effort they're putting into making rapid improvements.

As mentioned earlier in the chapter, at least a 30-minute break should be allotted for lunch—not a working lunch, but a *true break* with minimal discussion about the Event. To stir conversation and build team cohesiveness, the facilitator and/or team lead can mention nonwork topics such as current movies, upcoming holidays, or the previous night's sporting event. Kaizen Events are fast and intense, and require an enormous amount of energy. To avoid burnout, encourage the team to refuel and recharge over a shared meal, strengthening relationships in the process. An additional reason to provide lunch in particular is that it prevents delays in starting the afternoon session that can occur if team members go out for lunch and are late in returning.

Many office and service environments prefer allotting an hour lunch break so team members can check voice mail, respond to e-mails, and check the status of work they've left behind. In other events, the opposite is true: The team wants to work through lunch. For the reasons previously stated, a forced break is necessary to maintain a high degree of productivity. The question is low long should it be and should the team be required to eat together. While it's best that team members stay fully sequestered for the entire day and focus solely on the Kaizen Event, it's not always practical. In this case, encourage team members to eat together for the first 30 minutes, then use the other 30 minutes for catch-up work. Realize that there's a significant risk in having team members go to their offices and/or workstations during a Kaizen Event. Coworkers often pull the team member into a work situation that requires more energy and time than the team member has available. And, once the team member gets drawn into work issues that fall outside the Kaizen Event, he or she may use valuable time and energy on the "mental changeover" necessary to focus on the Kaizen Event once again. In addition to the distraction that can result from returning to one's work area, the team's start time is at risk as well. In all cases, the team needs to reconvene promptly at the designated time. Tardiness is not acceptable.

## SUPPLIES

A Supplies Checklist is provided on Tab 4 of the Kaizen Event Tools CD file, which lists the range of supplies the Kaizen Team may need (a partial view is shown in Figure 7-2). The checklist also includes six user-defined cells to include organization- or event-specific supplies. If you anticipate 5S activities, you'll need to add cleaning, labeling, and organization supplies to the list. Not all of these supplies are needed for every event. You will have to choose based on the Event scope, objectives, and likely deliverables. Place a checkmark in the N/A column for supplies not applicable for your specific event. When using an external facilitator for your event, check with him or her to confirm which of the items he or she will need.

You should confirm that you have all the necessary supplies the day prior to the Event start date. It's essential that you have everything you need right in Kaizen Central so the team doesn't have to look for or wait for supplies. It's best to house frequently used supplies in a portable carrying case or dedicated storage area, which is restocked following each Kaizen Event.

## TEAM RECOGNITION

In most Kaizen Events, team members work harder and more intensely than they ever have. They move quickly, work with a larger cross-functional team than usual, analyze intensely, and roll up their sleeves to implement everything by the end of the Event. And they do all of this, knowing full well that work is piling up in their absence. Organizations have many choices about how to best reward team members for their effort, for example:

- Certificates of achievement
- Hand-written thank you notes (from the executive sponsor or value stream champion)
- Gift cards (e.g., coffeehouses, movie theaters, bookstores, etc.)
- T-shirts, sweatshirts, or polo shirts with company logo or continuous-improvement program slogan
- Cash bonus
- Team dinner
- Feature articles in company newsletters
- Posting results throughout the company

| | ☑ | N/A* | Description |
|---|---|---|---|
| | **Kaizen Event**<br>**Supplies Checklist** |
| | **Facilitator** | | **Event Name** | |
| | **Coordinator** | | **Event Dates** | |
| 1 | | | Batteries for all battery-operated devices (extra sets recommended) |
| 2 | | | Binder clips or paper clips |
| 3 | | | Calculator |
| 4 | | | Card stock in various colors (if needed) |
| 5 | | | Digital camera (with USB cable or memory card/reader) |
| 6 | | | DVD and/or VHS player with monitor and speakers |
| 7 | | | Flip chart pads and stands (at least 2) |
| 8 | | | Handouts for participants (kickoff info, charter, training material, etc.) |
| 9 | | | Kaizen Team t-shirts (if being provided) |
| 10 | | | Label maker and label stock (if needed) |
| 11 | | | Laminator and laminate sheets (if needed) |
| 12 | | | Laptop or PC for training and presentations |
| 13 | | | Laptops or PCs for team use—2 to 4 based on group size each with access to MS Office, Internet, e-mail, intranet, shared drives, and internal applications |
| 14 | | | LCD projector |
| 15 | | | Markers, flip chart—various colors |
| 16 | | | Markers, Sharpie |
| 17 | | | Markers, white board |
| 18 | | | Masking tape |
| 19 | | | Name tents (if preferred) |
| 20 | | | Paper (36" wide plotter/butcher paper) |
| 21 | | | Pencil sharpener (if pencils being provided) |
| 22 | | | Pencils and/or pens |
| 23 | | | Post-it notes (4" x 6" and smaller sizes)—various colors |
| 24 | | | PowerPoint kick-off material loaded on laptop and memory stick for backup |
| 25 | | | Printer (color preferred) |
| 26 | | | Recognition certificates |
| 27 | | | Recognition gifts for team members (i.e. gift cards, movie tickets, shirts, etc.) |
| 28 | | | Rolling tape measure or pedometer (if needed) |
| 29 | | | Scissors |
| 30 | | | Speakerphone |
| 31 | | | Staff telephone directory or easy access to electronic copy |
| 32 | | | Stapler |
| 33 | | | White board eraser |
| 34 | | | Yardstick (for metrics-based process mapping) |
| 35 | | | |
| 36 | | | |
| 37 | | | |
| 38 | | | |
| 39 | | | |
| 40 | | | |

*N/A = not applicable

**Figure 7-2.** Supplies Checklist

Most important, leadership should provide verbal recognition for a job well done. This seemingly simple act goes a long way with team members. As described more fully in Chapter 17 (Event Wrap-up), leaders should verbally acknowledge the team during the team presentation. The event leaders should determine its team recognition approach early on in the planning process to leave sufficient lead time to obtain and/or create the rewards.

Now that the various logistical elements of a Kaizen Event have been covered, the next chapter addresses communication, another key element for success.

# CHAPTER 8

# PRE-EVENT COMMUNICATION

When asked what they wish they had done differently in their office- and service-based Kaizen Events, organizations nearly always mention better communication before, during, and after the Event. They report feeling frustrated because, though they entered an event thinking they communicated adequately and engaged all the necessary parties, they experienced disruptions along the way because "someone didn't know or understand something they should have." And, while clear, complete, and timely information is vital in all types of relationships during all types of activities, it is especially critical before, during, and after rapidly paced activities, such as Kaizen Events. This chapter addresses pre-event communication. Sections III and IV include recommended communication during and after the Event. During the pre-event planning process, communication serves several purposes:

- *To explain how the activity is relevant to today's business needs.* What problems will it solve? How does it tie to overall organizational vision and strategy? Why is rapid improvement needed rather than continuing with the way the organization has traditionally made improvements?

- *To form the strongest Kaizen Team possible.* If the right people are in the same place at the same time, innovation is more likely, decisions can be made quickly, and sustainable improvements can be designed and implemented with unprecedented speed.

- *To "legitimize" the team, and demonstrate that team members have leadership's full support and have been granted the authority to make change.* If the workforce doesn't sense leadership is fully behind the team, it will view the Event as a waste of time and spread cynicism across the organization.

- *To set the stage so the team can start quickly and maintain momentum throughout the Event with no delays.* While you can't completely eliminate the risk of delays during the Event, you greatly reduce the odds through clear, complete, and timely communication.

- *To assure the correct people attend key activities that occur during the Event.* These activities include interim briefings, the team presentation, and workforce training sessions. Ample notice and information—especially *why* the person should attend— maximizes the desired level of participation.

- *To minimize rumors and reduce anxiety.* Without adequate information, people will often "fill in the blanks" with their own prejudices, past experiences, and perceptions. In distrustful environments, this can lead to misinformation that requires unnecessary confusion and rework to undo. The workforce often meets new types of improvement approaches with skepticism, often believing that a new improvement approach signals layoffs. Minimize the risk with timely and clear communication upfront, preferably from a respected senior leader.

## COMMUNICATION CONSIDERATIONS

Every organizational culture is different and has unique communication needs. In fact, over time, an organization's communication needs around Kaizen Events will change. In the beginning, you will need to explain far more about lean, what Kaizen Events are, and why particular team members are required, than you will down the road. And even within one organization, the communication needs may vary. A manufacturer just starting to hold Kaizen Events in its office and service areas, needs to be especially diligent in conveying clear, concise, and timely information to a much broader cross-section of the organization. As your company holds more Kaizen Events and matures as a lean organization, the organization will grow to understand why waste must be eliminated, what a Kaizen Event is all about, and what roles various employees need to play. At this point, you may be able to scale back on the level of education and details you provide.

The Event Charter forms the backbone of your communication strategy and drives the following decisions that shape how and when you communicate and to whom:

### Are you conveying information or seeking input?

If you are simply *conveying information*, a one-way information transfer device such as e-mail will suffice. If, however, you *seek input or buy-in*, a real-time, two-way conversation is required, either in person or by telephone.

### How much information?

Ideally, you should deliver just enough information—no more and no less than what is required. The fundamental lean tenet of expending minimum effort and resources to achieve optimal outcomes applies to communication as well. But a word of caution here: To avoid communication difficulties that arise when the delivering party feels they've communicated the right amount of information and the recipient feels they needed more information earlier in the process, carefully consider the content needs of the recipient before deciding how to proceed. Some people have a "high need to know" and will never feel they have received adequate information. Others become impatient with what they view as irrelevant information, whereas the first group may view those "irrelevant" details as vital for understanding. While you can't please everyone, you can take steps toward exceptional communication by thinking strategically.

In determining *what* information is needed, use the time-honored strategy of walking in the other person's shoes. Think about what *you* would want to know—and when you'd want to know it. And include WHY in every communication—no matter what information is being conveyed and who the recipient is.

When determining *how much* information to communicate, an effective communicator will have his or her pulse on the organization and will accurately determine how much information is needed in the early days of holding Kaizen Events—as well as knowing the point when everyone in the organization understands the process and his or her role in Kaizen Events and communication can be scaled back. When you begin holding Kaizen Events in office and service environments, both leadership and the workforce benefit by understanding how team members are selected, how fast change will occur, and how they will be impacted. It's important to answer the often unspoken questions of, "What's in it for me?" and "Am I going to be hurt by this?" Later on, they will understand the process and won't need such detailed information up front.

### When does the recipient need to know?

If the recipient is supposed to take action but is given an inadequate response time, the quality of the response will suffer and will produce frustration, which could spawn poor communication—the very thing you're trying to avoid. On the other hand, if relevant details are still being gathered, you might consider waiting until you can communicate more complete information. This is another area that requires strategic thought. You don't want to delay relevant communication simply because you don't have all the information, but you don't want to overload communication channels with bits and pieces of information on which no one can take appropriate action. Just-in-time communication is a worthy ideal to strive for—just make sure your definition of timeliness matches that of the recipient's.

### What do you want from the recipient?

This vital piece of information needs to be expressly stated, and it is surprisingly absent from many otherwise thorough communication efforts. Be clear about what you need, from whom, and by when. If no action is required, clearly state that the communication is informational only.

## COMMUNICATION WORKSHEET

As shown in Figure 8-1, the Communication Worksheet included on the Kaizen Event Tools file (Tab 5) will help you consider the range of communication needs before, during, and after Kaizen Events. As suggested in the CD Instructions for Use, you may want to create a new Kaizen Events Tools template in which your organization's functional departments are pre-loaded into the Communication Worksheet (you may want to copy and paste the department list from the Team Formation Worksheet) and save the file as an organization-specific template. For each Kaizen Event, you can save the file with an event-specific name.

The *Level of Engagement* section is a shaping tool to help determine the communication needs for each functional department, which depend on each department's level of involvement with the specific improvement being designed and implemented. *The E-mail/Meeting Notice Content* section helps determine which departments need to receive e-mails and/or meeting notices for the specific activities before, during, and after the Event.

**Figure 8-1.** Communication Worksheet—Page One (partial view)

As shown in Figure 8-2, page two of the Communication Worksheet provides space to list the names of the actual recipients for the various types of communication, including telephone calls, which allows you to list the specific individuals within a functional department who should be communicated with.

If you use the Communication Worksheet as a guide, you're less likely to miss critical communication steps, and your communication will be higher quality.

## COMMUNICATION DETAILS

Table 8-1 includes key communication steps that should occur during the planning phase of most Kaizen Events, especially when holding your first few Kaizen Events. The table includes who, what, when, how, and why. While you may choose to combine some of these

*(continued on page 89)*

| Kaizen Event Communication Worksheet | | |
|---|---|---|
| **Executive Sponsor** | | **Event Name** |
| **Value Stream Champion** | | **Event Dates** |
| **Facilitator** | | **Coordinator** |
| **Team Lead** | | |
| ✓ **Communication Type** | | **Recipient Names** |
| ☐ Notification e-mail to leadership | | |
| ☐ Phone call to Kaizen Team members' direct supervisors | | |
| ☐ Informational email to Kaizen Team members' direct supervisors | | |
| ☐ Invitation and informational e-mail to Kaizen Event Team and on-call support | | |
| ☐ Pre-event lean/kaizen overview training notice | | |
| ☐ Interim briefing–required attendance notice | | |
| ☐ Interim briefing–courtesy invitation | | |
| ☐ Final presentation–required attendance notice | | |
| ☐ Final presentation–courtesy invitation | | |
| ☐ Notification to those who will be impacted by improvements | | |
| ☐ Organization-wide event announcement | | |
| ☐ Event report (post-event) | | |
| ☐ Audit results (post-event) | | |
| ☐ | | |
| ☐ | | |
| ☐ | | |

**Figure 8-2.** Communication Worksheet Page Two

**Table 8-1.** Pre-Event Key Communication Activities

| | PRE-EVENT KEY COMMUNICATION ACTIVITIES | | | |
|---|---|---|---|---|
| **Activity** | **Initiator** | **Recipient** | **Preferred Mode** | **Time frame** | **Key Points** |
| Obtain approval for requested Kaizen Team member and/or on-call support. | Facilitator and/or value stream champion. | Direct supervisors of desired team members and/or on-call support. | Conversation | 4 weeks prior | • Briefly educate re: Lean and Kaizen Events (if person is unfamiliar with the approach).<br>• Explain why the particular team member is needed (review Event scope and objectives).<br>• Acknowledge that taking someone from his/her normal work can be painful, but that significant, measurable improvements will result.<br>• Remind them to secure coverage for team members as they are 100% committed to the event (review Event schedule).<br>• Remind them that on-call support must be accessible directly by the team and immediately available.<br>• Ask them to attend the team presentation (and interim briefings, if relevant). |
| Seek team members and/or on-call support to represent functional areas for which no specific person has been identified. Obtain approval for their participation. | Task owner listed on Planning Checklist. | Relevant supervisors and/or managers. | Conversation | 4 weeks prior | • Briefly educate re: Lean and Kaizen Events (if person is unfamiliar with the approach).<br>• Explain why functional representation and/or on-call support is needed (review Event Charter scope and objectives).<br>• Remind them to secure backup for team members as they are 100% committed during the event (review event schedule).<br>• Remind them that on-call support must be immediately accessible directly by the team.<br>• Ask them to attend the team presentation (and interim briefings, if relevant). |

**Table 8-1.** (*continued*)

(Continued on next page)

| Activity | Initiator | Recipient | Preferred Mode | Time frame | Key Points |
|---|---|---|---|---|---|
| Talk with team members and on-call support to obtain their buy-in for participating on the Kaizen Team. | Direct supervisors. | Team members and on-call support. | Conversation | 4 weeks prior | • Briefly educate re: Lean and Kaizen Events (if person is unfamiliar with the approach).<br>• Explain why they were selected and why their participation is vital to event success.<br>• Mention they will receive more details from one of the event leaders.<br>• Tell them the plan for providing backup coverage (since they are 100% committed to the event). |
| Talk with team members, on-call support, and workers in the area targeted for improvement to generate momentum for upcoming Event. | Facilitator and/or value stream champion. | Team members and on-call support. | Conversation | 4 weeks prior | • Briefly educate re: Lean and Kaizen Events. Briefly explain event structure: current state analysis, brainstorming improvement options, designing a future state, interim briefings, expectations from leadership, and expectations of team members.<br>• Explain why their participation is vital to event success (Note: you may want to explain the process for forming the team and selecting on-call support, including why they were specifically selected).<br>• Review event scope, objectives, and schedule.<br>• Tell them when pre-event training will occur and how long it will last.<br>• Remind them that they are 100% committed to the event, so backup coverage should be secured, if needed. |
| Distribute initial draft of Kaizen Charter (redistribute as needed when modified during this iterative process). | Task owner listed on Planning Checklist. | Senior leadership and management of areas within event fence posts, as well as those upstream and downstream and those who supervise team members and/or on-call support. | E-mail | 4 weeks prior | • Briefly review Kaizen Event purpose and projected outcomes.<br>• Explain the role of the charter and request input. Highlight event scope, objectives, and schedule.<br>• Ask for feedback/input by a certain date. |

**PRE-EVENT KEY COMMUNICATION ACTIVITIES**

**Table 8-1.** (*continued*)

| | PRE-EVENT KEY COMMUNICATION ACTIVITIES | | | | |
|---|---|---|---|---|---|
| **Activity** | **Initiator** | **Recipient** | **Preferred Mode** | **Time frame** | **Key Points** |
| Explain how the workforce will be trained on the improvements. | Task owner listed on Planning Checklist. | Supervisors and direct workforce in affected areas. | E-mail or conversation with supervisors. | 4 weeks prior | • Explain that you can't schedule actual start and end times yet, but that training will occur in a certain window (usually a 3–4 hour block of time on the final day of the event).<br>• Explain that exact times will be determined 24 hours before training occurs.<br>• If a large group will be trained, solicit input re: training logistics (e.g., where, how many sessions, etc.). |
| Distribute final charter (PDF version)—can be attached to meeting notices listed below. | Task owner listed on Planning Checklist. | Same as recipients as for initial draft of charter plus entire senior leadership team. | • E-mail.<br>• Physical posting in the areas that will be impacted and on common CI posting boards.<br>• Electronic posting on company intranet, if used. | 3 weeks prior | • Ask for full support during the planning process and the event itself.<br>• Generate enthusiasm for the event.<br>• Give reminder that team is 100% committed and team members may not be disturbed during the hours the event is in session. |
| Send formal meeting notices to those attending various event activities. Attach final charter. | Task owner listed on Planning Checklist. | • Pre-event training—Team, on-call support and those in areas that will be impacted by the improvement.<br>• The event itself—Team and on-call support.<br>• Interim briefings—Relevant leadership.<br>• Workforce training—Supervisors of areas that will receive training on the final day of the Event.<br>• Final presentation—Senior leadership, direct supervisors of team members and on-call support, management in target, upstream and downstream areas. | E-mail or Outlook meeting notices. | 3 weeks prior | • Require a response.<br>• Follow-up with team, on-call support and interim briefing attendees if you don't receive a response.<br>• For interim briefing meeting notices: Explain the purpose of interim briefings—to gain buy-in, to reduce risk of failure or nonsustainable improvements, to build team confidence in the direction they're taking. Explain their role at the briefing—to probe, to make sure proposed improvements are aligned with regulatory and organizational requirements and market conditions—but they cannot veto the team. And explain that the briefings may or may not be held, depending on the team's needs that day. Decision will be made no later than two hours prior to the scheduled start and e-mail or telephone notification will be made. |

activities, it's critical that the communication occurs within the time frame listed. If you skip steps or miss critical timing, you may experience unnecessary resistance and frustration. The Pre-event Key Communication Activities table includes:

- A description of the activity and the purpose (notification vs. soliciting input, for example).

- The person initiating the communication and the parties receiving information or engaged in conversation.

- The preferred mode of communication—whether one-way communication can be used for efficiency purposes or whether two-way communication is best to assure high-quality communication. You may always substitute two-way communication via conversation by phone or in person for e-mail but e-mail should never be used when a conversation is required.

- How far before the Event should the communication occur? It never hurts to have a longer planning cycle (five or six weeks instead of four, for example) but it almost always hurts to have less time to properly plan the Event, which requires a fair amount of communication with a broad cross-section of the organization for the team to achieve significant results.

- Key points to be communicated or discussed—as mentioned earlier, the content of your communication will change as your organization matures and turns to Kaizen Events more and more frequently to rapidly implement sustainable improvements. The key points on Table 8-1 are designed for a fairly unseasoned organization.

Throughout the Event planning process, keep the four elements of effective communication in mind: complete, clear, concise, and timely. Make sure that all of the vital information is included; that it's clearly, accurately, and concisely conveyed; and it's delivered to the right people at the right time. With e-mail, it's often helpful to use visuals to assist in communicating by bolding, using italics, color-coding to highlight key details, dates, or expectations.

## SPECIAL CONSIDERATIONS

While there may be no way to completely eliminate the anxiety inherent with change, proper communication is essential if you want to minimize it. Especially when Kaizen Events are new to the organization, Kaizen Team members and others across the organization often wonder: Am I going to lose my job? What are they going to change? Is my job going to change?

The best way to minimize anxiety is through education and communication. As previously mentioned, organizations need to offer lean overviews to the workforce before holding Kaizen Events, so the workforce understands basic lean principles, and how rapid improvements can be made. In addition to heightening awareness about customer-defined value and waste, the overview should address the organization's continuous improvement plans and how the workforce will benefit. It's best when a senior leader makes a clear statement up front about why the organization is choosing the lean approach for improving the company's service to its customers and calm any fears about job loss due to lean improvements. Lean thinkers strongly advise against using lean to make job cuts, as this will immediately undermine the lean effort, dooming it to failure from the get-go. The lean thinking rule of thumb is that staff will only lose their employment for two reasons: 1) poor performance, or 2) market downturns. Freed capacity in the form of reduced process time should be used to absorb additional growth, perform more value-added work, reduce overtime, and support continuous-improvement activities.

It is important to communicate clearly that, barring the previously mentioned two conditions, using Kaizen Events to make rapid improvements may mean that an employee's job may change, but it doesn't mean he or she will lose a paycheck. This way, everyone knows up front that making improvements may affect how the work is done, but it won't affect anyone's livelihood. In most cases, people whose jobs change as a result of a Kaizen Event are eventually much happier in the new role. This is because most employees, once they get past "that's the way we've always done it" thinking, are relieved to let go of non-value-added work that doesn't matter to the customer. Most employees want to provide value and become motivated when they are better able to do so.

Another special consideration is how you communicate to the entire organization that a Kaizen Event is occurring. Should you send the Event Charter to everyone? Probably not. Some organizations distribute the Event Charter to supervisors and above and encourage them to share the information at a staff meeting. Other organizations post the Event Charter electronically on the company intranet and physically on continuous-improvement communication boards placed throughout the organization. Still others publish a monthly Kaizen schedule that provides basic details about upcoming Kaizen Events (including key contacts) and refers employees to a shared drive to view the Charter and additional Event details. If you post the Charter on a shared drive, make sure that you've designated one and only one of the event leaders as the owner of that Event Charter, so that only one or two people are authorized to edit it. Broadly communicate ownership for the Event Charter (usually the facilitator, value stream champion, or team lead), so everyone knows whom to contact with questions or concerns.

As shown in Figure 8-3, the Charter includes an approval section for those organizations that want to formalize leadership's commitment to the process. If you plan on using the approval section, make sure it's completed before you distribute and/or post the Charter.

Finally, if unions are represented within your organization, they should be involved from the get-go. Union leadership needs to understand how a lean enterprise, and Kaizen Events specifically, benefit the workforce by granting them greater control over their work and authority for making improvements. Failing to engage unions early in the planning process at

| Approvals | | |
|---|---|---|
| **Executive Sponsor** | **Value Stream Champion** | **Facilitator** |
| | | |
| Signature: | Signature: | Signature: |
| Date: | Date: | Date: |

**Figure 8-3.** Kaizen Event Charter—Approval Section

both strategic and tactical levels creates avoidable fear and misunderstandings. When they become active participants in event planning and understand how Kaizen Events will *improve* the work environment and job security for their constituents, they often become the organization's greatest ally in implementing improvements.

Simultaneous to communicating the final details about the Event, the event leaders make and/or oversee the final preparations for the Event: gathering relevant performance data and process materials, and delivering pre-event training, the subject of our next chapter.

# CHAPTER 9

# FINAL PREPARATIONS

The Planning Checklist (Tab 2 of the Kaizen Event Tools file on the CD) includes a wide range of activities that must be completed prior to the event kickoff. This chapter focuses on the data, information, and training the team will need to successfully analyze the current state, design the future state, and prepare for their role as change agents. These activities are essential for minimizing delays during the event.

## PROCESS PERFORMANCE DATA

Accurate data is vital for identifying non-value-adding (NVA) activities, designing improved lean processes that meet customer needs, and providing a baseline from which to measure improvements. Since many service and office environments don't have measurements in place that provide this necessary data, a critical step in preparing for a Kaizen Event is determining the team's likely data requirements, and obtaining this essential information *before* the event begins. In most cases, either the team lead or the value stream champion gathers this data, as directed by the event facilitator. Common data requirements include:

- *Current and forecasted work volume* (customer demand). How many orders or requests does the first step in the target process experience per day, week, or month? Make sure you segment the data so it applies to the specific conditions defined on the Kaizen Event Charter. It's helpful to know the total demand, as well as the demand for the defined conditions.

- *Order frequency.* How often do orders arrive at the first step of the target process? Do they arrive in batches? Is the customer demand level, or is it heavier during certain hours, days, or weeks? What are the volume and frequency ranges for incoming orders?

- *Current performance.* How long does it take for the "thing" passing through the process—e.g., information, material, or people—to move from the initial order or request for service through the final step (typically delivery to the customer)? What level of quality are your internal and external customers currently experiencing? *Note*: Some "things" remain stationery and the process occurs around them (e.g., people receiving service at a single location, stationery equipment, etc.).

- *Market Expectations.* What are your industry's standards in terms of quality and delivery expectations? How well do you currently perform compared with your competition?

- *Staffing.* How many people currently perform the activities that comprise each process step? What percentage of their workday do these activities consume? (*Note*: Assessing the degree of multitasking provides helpful information in designing the future state.) Are external contractors/suppliers involved? If so, how many are there and how are they performing? How much of the internal staff's time is spent managing these outside resources?

- *Customer and workforce satisfaction.* If *recent* survey results are available, how satisfied are your customers (whether internal or external) and workforce? It's helpful to obtain detailed information that would indicate what improvements would lead to exceeding customer expectations and becoming an employer of choice from the workforce's perspective. If recent information is not available, conduct a quick, informal survey before the event. It can be as simple as creating five questions that can be assessed with a five-point Likert Scale and distributing it to a department to complete anonymously. If you have easy access to your customers, you could do the same for a representative sample. Kaizen Teams are hampered when they don't have a clear picture of how their customers and workforce view the organization and/or target process. While statistically sound data is desirable, informal surveys can often provide the necessary baseline data from which to make and measure improvements.

Two words of caution here: First, as organizations begin to measure their processes and gather baseline data for Kaizen Events, it is tempting for the event leaders and/or management who oversee the process areas slated for improvement to begin designing change. In many cases, necessary improvements become painfully obvious once data is collected. While it's helpful to capture improvement ideas, they need to be exactly that—*ideas*. The Kaizen Team needs to consider all ideas and add a few of its own before deciding how the work should be done. And, for the greatest effectiveness, team members need to go through that discovery and decision process in the same place, at the same time—*during the Kaizen Event.*

Second, when making decisions, there's often a fine line between too little and too much information. Without adequate current state data, improvement teams run the risk of designing changes that are suboptimal at best and counterproductive at worst. Yet, you don't want the event leaders or management in the areas targeted for improvement to spend valuable time gathering irrelevant data that will not significantly help in assessing the current state and designing a future state. There's a fine line here: You need enough data to make good decisions, but not so much that the organization incurs unnecessary expense. Again, the lean tenet applies to data gathering and analysis: expend the minimum effort and resources to achieve optimal outcomes.

You need to assess how much data is required to make informed, effective decisions. The types of improvements typically implemented during a Kaizen Event, while directly related to an organization's performance, don't typically require months of operational research or gathering extremely precise data. In fact, too much data can cloud a team's judgment. However, teams often face the opposite problem: not enough data, not even coarse data. One way to counter this is for the event leaders to have workers within the targeted process area track relevant data on well-designed checksheets for a week or two leading up to an event, to record the frequency of specific activities or issues. This information will help the Kaizen

Team understand the current state. Maintaining a simple checksheet (discussed in Chapter 13) for a couple of weeks will not place excessive burden on the workforce. Typically, it is not necessary to create Excel spreadsheets or PowerPoint presentations to display the findings—handwritten data is usually sufficient.

As a last resort, if data is not available and/or cannot be gathered quickly enough, obtain anecdotal data from the workers. Reliable anecdotal data, while subjective, can be just as valuable as objective measurements if the people providing the data are experienced and feel safe telling the truth, no matter how "ugly" the truth may be. Make it clear why you are asking these questions so they feel safe that their answers will not be judged, nor will someone dole out "consequences" for revealing the true current state situation.

The bottom line is this: While detailed data is valuable to Kaizen Teams, many highly effective and efficient improvements can be made with "directionally correct" data. For example, unless you are comparing performance with an established baseline, it doesn't matter whether the output quality of a particular process step is 20 percent or 30 percent. Either figure represents unacceptable quality and the need for improvement. When designing the future state, that's often all you need to know.

## ADDITIONAL RELEVANT INFORMATION

Depending on the target process and the event objectives, a wide range of additional materials may be helpful as the Kaizen Team progresses on its improvement journey including:

- Written policies and procedures
- Process tracking tools
- Current job aids, work tools, flowcharts, etc.
- Relevant regulations, accreditation standards, or audit requirements
- Organization charts
- Blueprints or drawings of work space (if physical improvements may be considered)
- Performance reports (turnaround times, volume of work completed per unit of time, volume of work currently waiting in queue, etc.)
- Competitive analyses, market trends, benchmark reports, etc.

The team should be told at the beginning of the event that, while these materials will be helpful in designing the future state, they should *not* refer to them during the current state analysis. When teams refer to this type of information during current state analysis, they often fall into the trap of talking about how the process *should* be performed, rather than how it *is* performed. At the end of the current state analysis, this information may be consulted to make sure the team hasn't missed any key process steps or relevant conditions, but the team needs to discover the true current state *as it exists in reality*, not on paper.

In summary, to anticipate the data and information the Kaizen Team may need during the event, return to the event scope and objectives, and potential deliverables. If the data are not currently available, determine if you can easily obtain it before the event. Even data gathered for only a day or two can be helpful, especially if a large volume of work passes through the process. The Kaizen Teams will be in a much better position to make quick decisions and implement a greater number of improvements if they begin with solid data.

## LEAN OVERVIEW

As mentioned earlier in this book, it is essential that the organization's leadership, workforce, and Kaizen Teams receive training on the lean basics, and it's particularly important to offer lean overviews prior to holding Kaizen Events. Teams that enter the event with a fair to moderate understanding of lean principles, familiarity with lean terminology, and exposure to some of the more common lean tools, such as value stream mapping, Kaizen Events, visual workplace, 5S, and standard work typically produce greater results. Team members don't need to receive extensive training, but they do need the foundation to be able to progress quickly without requiring time-intensive explanations—or worse, needing to be sold on lean principles. Targeted training on specific tools is provided during the event itself as the need arises.

The optimal time to hold the lean overview session is *no more than one week prior to the event*. If you can't pull the Kaizen Team together prior to the event because, for example, team members are traveling from out-of-the-area for the event—or you're relying on an external facilitator and don't want to bring him or her on site for a separate training session—you can include a lean overview during the event kickoff (Chapter 11 covers the event kickoff). However, understand that if you use the event kickoff time for a lean overview, this reduces the team's available work time and should be taken this into account when scoping the event.

Also, to ensure a successful Kaizen Event, it's highly beneficial if the workers in the areas that will experience the greatest change also understand key lean principles and what outcomes they can expect from the Kaizen Event. Likewise, all on-call support should receive this training as well.

At a minimum, you should structure the lean overview as a one-hour session for workers who will be affected by the improvements and a two-hour session for the Kaizen Team and on-call support. The overview should include the following topics:

- Key lean principles (including customer-defined value, value stream, flow, pull, perfection)
- Value-adding vs. non-value-adding activities
- The eight wastes
- Lean enterprise benefits
- Kaizen Event overview
    - Event characteristics, structure, and typical results
    - Roles and responsibilities for team members, on-call support and the facilitator(s)

- The team's level of authority and the "Kaizen Commandments"—the rules by which they agree to operate
- Relevant current and future state value stream maps and implementation plan
- Event Charter for their event
- Basic lean tools—standard work, visual workplace/5S, and one-piece flow

This chapter concludes Part II on event planning. Now that the Charter is set, the team is formed, and you've communicated and planned all details concerning the event, it's time to hold the event itself—the D in the macro-level PDCA cycle—covered in Part III of this book. Chapter 10 provides an overview of the typical event structure and the stages of team development that you'll experience during the event. Chapters 11 to 17 cover the details concerning event execution from the kickoff to the final presentation and event wrap-up.

# PART III

# Kaizen Event Execution

# CHAPTER 10

# EVENT STRUCTURE

Kaizen Events vary widely in their shape and form. You can convene Kaizen Teams for four hours, five days or anything in between. You can focus on one functional department, reach across an entire organization, or extend even further to include external customers, suppliers, or contractors. The key is tying the event to a value stream map or some other type of strategic plan to avoid "drive-by kaizens."

Regardless of their scope and objectives, the following six steps are common to all Kaizen Events and will be described fully in Part III. Table 10-1 lists the steps, their location in Part II, and how each step fits into the micro PDCA cycle that frames a Kaizen Event.

**Table 10-1.** Kaizen Event Execution

| Phase | Description Location | Phase in Micro PDCA Cycle |
|---|---|---|
| 1. Event Kickoff | Chapter 11 | P |
| 2. Current State Analysis | Chapter 12 & 13 | P |
| 3. Future State Design | Chapter 14 & 15 | P & D |
| 4. Improvement Testing | Chapter 15 | D & C |
| 5. Improvement Implementation | Chapter 16 | C & A |
| 6. Event Wrap-up | Chapter 17 | A |

Of these six essential elements, the one that is typically the most challenging to accomplish is step #5—actual implementation. If the event scope is too broad, the team won't have enough time to fully design the improvement, create training materials, and provide workforce training on the improvement—which is required to meet the primary objective of a Kaizen Event: an *implemented* improvement. In Monday through Friday operations, if the Kaizen Event ends on a Friday, the workers should perform the process differently on Monday. In a 24-hour operation, if the event concludes at 4:30 p.m., the work should be being performed differently at 4:31 p.m. This vital step is fully addressed in Chapter 16, Implementing Improvements.

## APPROXIMATE EVENT AGENDA

One of the facilitator's responsibilities is establishing an approximate schedule for the event. This agenda provides a benchmark for the Kaizen Team to assess its progress and provides direction for what may otherwise be a disorienting experience for team members who've never served on a Kaizen Team. The rough schedule also helps the facilitator assess his or her own progress as the team's guide. But since a Kaizen Event is as much about discovery as it is accomplishing actual work tasks, it's difficult to set a firm agenda up front. The agenda provides structure and a point from which the team can benchmark their progress. Since one can't firmly predict how long the analysis or design process will take, the team shouldn't be held to an exact schedule.

Since Kaizen Events can vary widely in length and the type of targeted improvement, a sample agenda for a five-day Kaizen Event can be found in Figure 10-1, which would only be required for the most complex improvements. If your organization is holding shorter, more narrowly scoped events, compress this sample agenda to fit the event. For example, you may not need to create a micro-level process map, or you may need to hold only one interim briefing. No matter how long or short the Kaizen Event, include time frames on your agenda to provide additional structure. For example, on a particular day, the team may be given four hours, from one to five p.m. to create standard work for the new process. You may also find it helpful to break apart some of the longer activities into smaller chunks with assigned time frames—e.g., 45 minutes to debate an issue, one hour to create a draft document, one hour to review it and run it by colleagues for input, 30 minutes to finalize it.

## INTERIM BRIEFINGS

Interim briefings are progress reports held at the end of every day or two during the Kaizen Event with the Kaizen Team and relevant leadership. Interim briefings, essential for rapid progress, provide an opportunity for:

- The team to update leadership about key *current state findings as well as future state design considerations.*
- The team to conduct a reality check, which gives them confidence that they are on the correct path and haven't missed relevant considerations.
- Leadership to confirm that, in redesigning the process, the team has taken into account relevant financial, regulatory, safety, or customer relationship requirements and that the improvements do not conflict with the organization's strategic direction.
- Leadership to *challenge the team's thinking* to ensure that they've explored relevant options.
- Leadership to provide *buy-in and endorsement* of proposed improvements. (*Note*: leadership does not *approve* improvements. Once the team has fully explored any concerns that leadership has raised, leadership must honor their commitment to accept the team's decisions and selected improvements. It's the facilitator's job to make sure the team fully explores any issues the leadership raises and report findings back to leadership, typically during the next interim briefing.)
- The team to request a *policy change* that a planned improvement hinges on. Ideally, the required discussion and analysis can occur real time, and a decision can be rendered by the end of the interim briefing, so the team can move forward the next

| SAMPLE FIVE-DAY KAIZEN EVENT AGENDA | | | | |
|---|---|---|---|---|
| **Day 1** | **Day 2** | **Day 3** | **Day 4** | **Day 5** |
| Event kickoff | Discuss event progress | Design improvements | Continue designing and testing | Train affected workers |
| Leadership kickoff | Perform "check-in" with team | Create standard work | new standard work | Create Sustainability Plan |
| Facilitator introduction | Provide training re: relevant | Begin testing standard work | Obtain workforce input/buy-in | Finalize 30-Day List |
| Day one agenda review | tools | Obtain stakeholder input | Finalize standard work | Complete Kaizen Report |
| Team introductions and ice | Design future state | Hold interim briefing (probably) | Prepare training materials | As required, document Event |
| breaker | Brainstorm for improvement | | Hold interim briefing (if | information electronically (e.g., |
| Event charter review | ideas | | necessary) | improvement ideas, mapping, |
| Lean overview | Select and prioritize | | | parking lot, etc.) |
| Kaizen event overview | improvement ideas | | | Prepare for team presentation |
| Current and future state | Create future state process- | | | Hold team presentation and |
| VSM review | level map | | | celebration |
| Create current state process- | Hold interim briefing (definitely) | | | |
| level map (or other current | | | | |
| state analyses to identify | | | | |
| waste) | | | | |
| Hold interim briefing (if far | | | | |
| enough along) | | | | |

**Figure 10-1.** Sample Kaizen Event Agenda for a Complex Improvement

morning. If leaders legitimately need more time to think and/or receive input from people who are not present at the briefing, they should commit to as quick a turnaround time as possible for their decision. If a decision cannot be made quickly, the issue should be placed on a parking lot list, deemed out of scope, and the event objectives and deliverables adjusted accordingly.

These aspects of the interim briefing help leadership gain trust in the team, and they also facilitate the transition of authority for making improvements to the staff closest to the work. Conversely, team members gain confidence that they are designing improvements with "staying power," because they have received leadership support along the way. The interim briefings also provide the opportunity for leadership to challenge the team's thinking to ensure that team members have considered all aspects of the particular improvement they plan to implement as well as the full spectrum of alternatives.

Policy decisions are typically strategic and rightfully within the leadership's domain. That authority *should not* be delegated to the team unless the leaders with the authority to change policy are also Kaizen Team members or they have clearly delegated this authority to the team. But if an improvement doesn't impact a company policy, is within the boundaries established prior to the Event, and doesn't create a legal, financial, regulatory, safety, or customer retention risk, *leadership must give the team full authority to make the change.* Other than the issues previously stated, leadership does not have veto power over the team. This is why the interim briefings are vital for event success. If leadership doesn't stay abreast of the team's progress, it may miss the opportunity to raise a valid concern, and the team risks unknowingly implementing an unsustainable improvement. There's nothing less motivating to a Kaizen Team and to an entire organization than to sequester up to ten people for up to five days only to learn after an improvement has been fully implemented that the improvement has placed the organization at risk.

Clearly, the content for interim briefings varies from day to day. In addition to policy discussions, they can revolve around the current state findings, future state design, or implementation issues, to name a few topics. Briefings held following current state analysis are typically more informational as the team presents, "Here's what we learned." The information presented by the team at this briefing is sometimes shocking to leadership. Often leaders do not truly understand the current process and why problems exist, nor should they necessarily be expected to. But the interim briefing following the team's current state analysis may raise concerns and leadership anxiety and can also incite questions. The facilitator and the team need to assure leadership that the future state design will likely address many of its concerns and resolve many of the current state issues discovered.

Once the Kaizen Team determines the future state design, the team presents, "Here's what we are planning to do and why." A skilled facilitator will ask probing questions to assess leadership's support for the team's recommendations. Full leadership buy-in is one of the key elements in sustaining improvements. Early in this briefing, it is helpful to establish a ground rule that no one should leave the room in silent disagreement. This is the time for leaders to express their concerns and, though not authorized to veto the team's decisions during these briefings, they should be encouraged to ask:

- "What if…?"
- "How will we handle…?"
- "What about…?"
- "Have you considered…?"

In the design and testing phase of the event, the briefings serve yet another purpose. Here the team asks:

- "Have we forgotten anything?"
- "Is this the best way to depict the new process?"
- And … "Here's our plan for training the workforce how to perform the new process."

For your first few Kaizen Events, your interim briefings may go over an hour because your leadership and the team are experiencing a learning curve as they adapt to their new roles in a structured, rapid-improvement environment. The facilitator should keep an eye on the clock and keep the briefing moving along. Remember that the briefings are generally held at the end of the day. If more time is needed to resolve all pending issues, the facilitator may excuse team members and attendees who have transportation restrictions, child care issues, or other commitments, and continue the briefing with those capable of meeting beyond the scheduled time. This is another reason why your facilitator must possess strong time and people management skills, as discussed in Chapter 4. With maturity, trust, and experience, you may be able to limit the briefings to 30 minutes.

As previously mentioned, the event planners typically schedule interim briefings for the last hour of every day. By 2:00 p.m. each day, Kaizen Team members make a decision whether or not they need an interim briefing, and one delegate notifies the invitees of the decision (usually via e-mail but, in some organizations, voice mail is more effective). The team should also place a sign on the Kaizen Central door stating the status of the briefing. Organizations aren't typically used to this type of scheduling, so it may take some getting used to, but it avoids the scheduling problem of the team needing a briefing and the risk that relevant leadership won't be available. The five-day sample agenda in Figure 10-1 includes a descriptor, next to each of the interim briefing listings, that addresses the likelihood of a briefing being held on any given day.

One final tip: It's best if the team members know exactly who will attend the briefings so they can prepare accordingly. For this reason, the organization should require its leadership to RSVP for the interim briefings and establish expectations up front that—barring a true emergency—if a leader commits to attending an interim briefing, he or she needs to show up. Showing up sends a strong and positive message to the team about leadership's commitment.

# EVENT EXECUTION

The Kaizen Event Tools file on the CD contains several tools to help track and record progress throughout the event, and it archives activities electronically. Guided by the sample daily agenda previously discussed, the facilitator should track the team's progress by following the Execution Checklist as seen in Figure 10-2 and found on Tab 6 of the Kaizen Event Tools.

| | | | **Kaizen Event Execution Checklist** | | |
|---|---|---|---|---|---|
| | Value Stream Champion | | | Event Name | |
| | Facilitator | | | Event Dates | |
| | ✓ | N/A* | **Description** | | |
| 1 | ☐ | ☐ | Conduct Event kickoff / review Event Charter with team. | | |
| 2 | ☐ | ☐ | Conduct ice breaker / team introduction(s). | | |
| 3 | ☐ | ☐ | Deliver Lean and Kaizen Event overview training  (if not delivered prior to event), review Event Charter. | | |
| 4 | ☐ | ☐ | Document current state (before) conditions (MBPM, relevant metrics, spaghetti diagram, photos, etc.). | | |
| 5 | ☐ | ☐ | Summarize / analyze current state metrics. | | |
| 6 | ☐ | ☐ | Brainstorm session re: possible improvements. | | |
| 7 | ☐ | ☐ | Prioritize improvements. | | |
| 8 | ☐ | ☐ | Create standard work, checklists, visual aids, etc., to document the new process. | | |
| 9 | ☐ | ☐ | Prepare for interim briefings. | | |
| 10 | ☐ | ☐ | End of each day—Prepare agenda for following day. | | |
| 11 | ☐ | ☐ | Identify who will need to be trained on new process and schedule training (to be held during the event). | | |
| 12 | ☐ | ☐ | Create and document future state / "after" conditions and calculate projected percent improvement. | | |
| 13 | ☐ | ☐ | Deliver training to those who perform or are affected by improved process. | | |
| 14 | ☐ | ☐ | Create 30-Day List, assign owners and deadlines for completion. | | |
| 15 | ☐ | ☐ | Create Sustainability Plan. | | |
| 16 | ☐ | ☐ | Complete Kaizen Event Report. | | |
| 17 | ☐ | ☐ | Assign ownership for tasks on "Post-Event Activities" list. | | |
| 18 | ☐ | ☐ | Schedule weekly follow-up meetings (for first four weeks following the Event). | | |
| 19 | ☐ | ☐ | Schedule 30-day audit. | | |
| 20 | ☐ | ☐ | Take team photos. | | |
| 21 | ☐ | ☐ | Prepare and deliver final presentation. | | |
| 22 | ☐ | ☐ | Recognize participants via certificates, shirts, gift cards, handshake from leadership, etc. | | |
| 23 | ☐ | ☐ | | | |
| 24 | ☐ | ☐ | | | |
| 25 | ☐ | ☐ | | | |

* N/A = not applicable

**Figure 10-2.** Execution Checklist

In addition, the facilitator should maintain two lists throughout the event: a list of the team's improvement ideas and a "parking lot" for issues that arise but fall outside the scope of the event and/or need heavy leadership involvement to resolve. Tabs 7 and 11 on the Kaizen Event Tools file includes templates for creating electronic versions of these lists, but recording these lists on flip charts and posting them throughout the room so they are visible to the team is recommended. (This is another reason why it's important to have ample wall space in your Kaizen Central room.) By the end of the event, additional flip chart pages containing data, findings, drawings, results, etc., will likely be posted throughout Kaizen Central and will form the foundation of the team's final presentation, discussed in Chapter 17.

Now that you've been introduced to a high-level view of the event structure, let's explore the initial activity on the first day of the event: the event kickoff.

# CHAPTER 11

# EVENT KICKOFF

For the Kaizen Team, the first day of a Kaizen Event often feels similar to the first day at a new job. The team members may not all know one another, and some may be anxious about their role. A strong kickoff helps allay concerns, and sets the team in a positive direction that enables them to achieve aggressive results. A successful kickoff includes the following components:

- Leadership Welcome
- Facilitator Introduction
- Day One Agenda Review
- Team Introductions and Icebreaker (if needed)
- Key Lean Principles (if overview training was not conducted prior to the event)
- Kaizen Event Overview
- Review Relevant Value Stream Maps (both current and future states) and the Future State Implementation Plan
- Kaizen Charter Review

## LEADERSHIP WELCOME

Especially when an organization is holding its first few Kaizen Events, it's critical for the team to receive a clear message from a respected leader in the organization about the organization's commitment to the change process and the team's role and authority in making improvements. As the organization matures and rapid improvement becomes a part of the culture, the need for leadership presence during the kickoff lessens. But for early events, if leadership doesn't physically and verbally demonstrate its support for the event and its confidence in the team's ability to implement rapid improvements, the team will doubt its role and authority to make change, slowing their progress.

At a minimum, the event's executive sponsor and/or value stream champion should be present to kick off the event. In small to mid-sized organizations, it's helpful if the CEO, president, or general manager joins the executive sponsor and/or value stream champion at the event kickoff. But even in larger organizations, you may want to invite the CEO or president to say a few words at the kickoff—especially for the first few Kaizen Events. Hearing from the most senior leader in the organization can leave an indelible mark in team members' minds around the importance of the event. The more that teams witness leadership's support—and the higher the leader demonstrating the support is in the organization—the more energized the team becomes.

Leaders often ask what they should say during the kickoff. The best advice for them: Speak from the heart. Otherwise, the team members will perceive a "disconnect" between the leader's actions and words, and conclude that leadership is not fully supportive of the event, which may impact their will to succeed and may create unnecessary anxiety. Second, keep it brief—no more than 10 minutes (five minutes per person if two leaders speak). Content for the leadership welcome typically includes topics, such as:

- The *compelling need for change* (e.g., industry trends, market conditions, projected growth, etc.). The leader needs to instill a sense of urgency without creating fear, which can paralyze otherwise high-performing teams.

- Specific *current state issues* that drove the need for the Event, and how event objectives are tied to value stream performance.

- *Leadership's expectations* (tied to event objectives and overall corporate strategy). The leader should make it clear that the leadership team expects a redesigned process fully implemented by the end of the event, even if it's only a small piece of a larger process.

- What *level of authority* the team has. The leader should address the difference between strategy and tactics and mention that, while leadership has established the objectives and boundaries for the event (strategic decisions), the team is completely free to make improvements within those boundaries (tactical execution). The team should understand that leadership may challenge the team's thinking during the event but ultimately will accept the team's recommendations. The leader should remind the team that leadership will entertain suggestions for altering company policies during the interim briefings, but that leadership must approve all policy changes before they are put into practice. This is one area in which the team does not have free reign.

- Reminder that they need to follow the *"rules" for the event* (discussed in detail later in the chapter). The leader might hit on key rules, such as silencing cell phones and Blackberry-like devices; no interruptions (maintain 100 percent focus); and the need for punctuality, open-mindedness, and innovative thinking.

There's a noticeable difference in the team's energy and final results for Kaizen Events when no leader is present at the kickoff. If, for example, the executive sponsor is not present (or at least participates by telephone), it sends a message to the team that, "While I'm sponsoring this event, it's not important enough for me to show up." Especially in organizations that have tried many different improvement approaches, skeptical Kaizen Team members study leadership and process both spoken and unspoken messages to get a sense whether "this too shall pass" or the organization is serious this time. They judge how much support and authority the organization will truly give them based on leadership action and words. Leaders need to demonstrate their support by making it a priority to attend the event kickoff. For the greatest effectiveness, Kaizen Events should be viewed as the organization's—*and the leadership team's*—top priority for the duration of the event. Otherwise, improvement will always take a back seat to daily firefighting.

At the conclusion of the leadership welcome, the leader turns the event over to the facilitator and leaves the room, providing a clear signal to the team members that they are now leading the change process.

## FACILITATOR INTRODUCTION

Whether internal or external to the organization, the facilitator's introduction should include his or her name, background, experience, and approach for facilitating Kaizen Events. He or she should also briefly explain the facilitator's role, and how he or she will guide them to success. Remember that, at this point, team members may still be somewhat anxious about their role. They may fear they're not up to the task, that leadership won't support them, or that their colleagues will be angry with them over their improvement choices. It's the facilitator's job to reinforce the messages delivered during the leadership welcome, further allay concerns, generate energy, and communicate his or her confidence in the team's ability to succeed. It helps to share what type of results other high-performing teams have been able to achieve. By establishing credibility and demonstrating competence within the first few minutes after taking the floor, the facilitator builds the team members' confidence in themselves and in the facilitator's ability to guide them through any challenges that may arise. Following the general introduction, the facilitator proceeds with the following activities.

### Agenda for Day One

The facilitator should present an approximate agenda for the day, including time frames for each of the activities scheduled and the objectives that should be reached by day's end. The schedule will depend on the type of current state analysis tools being used and the complexity of the process in question. Process-level mapping, if needed, typically occupies all of the first day and sometimes much of the second day (more about this in Chapter 12). The sample agenda provided in Chapter 10 can be modified to fit the scope, objectives, and time frames for your event. A skilled facilitator can typically set an estimated schedule he or she can share with the team to monitor progress throughout the day.

### Team Introductions and Icebreaker

Each Kaizen Team member should introduce him or herself with, at a minimum, his or her name and role in the process being improved. It's also often helpful to have the team members describe their continuous-improvement experience and expectations from the event. If the team includes several people who have never worked together, or have worked by phone but have never met in person, you might want to include a quick icebreaker (15 minutes maximum) to start the process of team-building and reduce anxiety. You can find icebreaker ideas in meeting management and training books, as well as on the Internet.

As noted on the Supplies Checklist, you may want to use name tents to help the facilitator and fellow team members get to know one another more quickly. You can either preprint them with your company logo and the person's name, or have each team member write his or her name and the function he or she represents or the role this person is playing on the Kaizen Team (e.g., outside eyes). You may want to include inspirational sayings, a summary of lean principles, or event reminders on the reverse side of the name tent.

## Kaizen Event Charter Review

Next, the facilitator leads the team as they review the Kaizen Charter. Even if the team reviewed the charter during a lean overview training session held prior to the Kaizen Event, the facilitator should give a 10-minute refresher, highlighting the event drivers, objectives, and boundaries.

## Lean Principles and Tools (Overview or Refresher)

Depending on the team members' familiarity with lean principles and tools, they need at least a 30-minute refresher to set the stage for their work ahead. Even experienced teams need to be reminded about the philosophical foundation behind the approach and tools they will apply. If you are using an external facilitator, and the team has not received a lean overview one week prior to the Kaizen Event, the overview will take one to two hours. This is why pre-event training is preferred; a two-hour training session during the event cuts into valuable work time that the team could be using to analyze the process so it can begin making improvements.

Chapter 9 includes a list of topics typically included in the overview. If the team members are experienced lean thinkers, a refresher lasting about 30 minutes is needed that covers basic lean principles, the eight wastes and the basic improvement tools, such as standard work, batch reduction, and visual controls. More advanced tools are introduced during the event on an as-needed basis.

## Kaizen Event Overview

The lean overview or refresher will naturally lead into the Kaizen Event overview, which should include:

- Typical event structure.
- Roles and responsibilities (for facilitator, team members, leadership, etc.).
- The "Kaizen Commandments"—Table 11-1 lists these rules of engagement for how the team will operate. The CD accompanying this book contains an electronic version of Table 11-1 that the facilitator may want to distribute to the team. The rules can also be enlarged and posted in Kaizen Central. Event results are typically in direct proportion to the degree to which the team agrees to and abides by these ground rules, which are vital for maintaining an effective work environment on an extremely fast-paced schedule. It bears repeating: *Kaizen Events are a special breed of results-based activities that require 100 percent commitment and 100 percent focus.* To achieve this, you need a disciplined environment for the rapid decisions and work output that are characteristic of this improvement approach.

Teams unfamiliar with Kaizen Events may initially scoff at the notion of "rules," especially if the organization lacks discipline and/or has a workforce that resists structure. But Kaizen Teams typically grow to appreciate the discipline and ask for more of it. Once they

**Table 11-1.** Kaizen Commandments

| KAIZEN COMMANDMENTS | | |
|---|---|---|
| | **Commandment** | **Explanation** |
| **BEHAVIOR ORIENTED** | | |
| 1 | The team starts and ends the day together. | There's no time for rework when someone misses a portion of the day. |
| 2 | Being on time is critical. | Again, there's no time for the rework of informing team members what they've missed, and it's not fair to the team or the process to repeat information that's already been discussed.<br><br>This includes the start of the day and after all breaks.<br><br>If someone has an unexpected emergency that will require them to be late, they need to communicate with the team lead or facilitator. |
| 3 | Cell phones, Blackberries, and other communication devices must be turned *off or placed on 100% silent (no vibration) mode*. | Silent/vibration mode still distracts the owner and adjacent team members.<br><br>There will be breaks during which you can check your e-mail and voice mail. Or, you can do it before or after the scheduled time for the Event. |
| 4 | No interruptions. | Unless there is a medical or physical emergency.<br><br>Backup coverage must be prearranged.<br><br>The company manages the workload without you when you're ill or on vacation, so it can handle issues without you for this limited period of time. |
| 5 | Team stays in the room. | Except for restroom breaks, to directly observe some aspect of the improvement target, or to deliver training—and the facilitator has been notified. |
| 6 | Avoid scope creep; keep focused on event objectives and work within predetermined event boundaries. | You won't accomplish the event objectives if you allow the event to expand beyond the established fence posts.<br><br>You need the time to "go deep" rather than going broad. |
| **COMMUNICATION ORIENTED** | | |
| 7 | Finger pointing has no place. Kaizen Central is a blame-free zone. | Stay forward looking. Unless there are valid reasons to look in the past to determine why an activity/process was put into place, operate by this principle: "The past is the past." It doesn't matter why the current state exists—it is what it is. What matters is that the team understands current customer requirements, identifies current issues, and makes improvements from that point.<br><br>History is useful from a lessons-learned perspective, but a Kaizen Event is not the venue for this. The focus in Kaizen Events is moving forward, not looking back.<br><br>The goal is to extend this rule to the broader organization, day in and day out as soon as possible. Blame is not a useful tool—people will not admit mistakes if a supportive corrective action environment doesn't exist. |

*(Continued on next page)*

**Table 11-1.** (*continued*)

| | KAIZEN COMMANDMENTS | |
|---|---|---|
| | **Commandment** | **Explanation** |
| | **COMMUNICATION ORIENTED,** *continued* | |
| 8 | No veto power from outside the team. | The team is fully authorized to make changes within the predefined boundaries. |
| | | Leadership may establish the improvement strategy (the "what"), but the team determines "how." |
| | | Leadership is authorized to challenge the team members' thinking and make sure they've considered all improvement options and the full impact of selected improvements, but leadership may not dictate nor veto specific improvements unless they would negatively impact organizational performance, regulatory standing, or customer relationships. |
| 9 | No silent objectors. | No one should ever leave the room in silent disagreement. |
| 10 | One conversation at a time. | Sidebar conversations are distracting to the facilitator and fellow team members. |
| | | Listening is an art and another discipline-building tool. Listening is vital to effective problem solving. It's easy to get excited and all start talking at once, but the facilitator must remind the team that everyone has a right to be heard. |
| 11 | What's said in the room, stays in the room. | Re: personalities, sensitive or confidential organizational information, trade secrets, etc. |
| | | The current state of a process may include some "ugly truths" that the team needs to explore and resolve, which are not details that would benefit others by knowing. |
| 12 | It's okay (and encouraged) to disagree; it's not okay to be disagreeable. | Team members are obligated to share their knowledge and insight freely, but they must do it in a professional, positive, supportive, nonthreatening manner. |
| | | Team members must respect each other, but it's okay (and encouraged) to respectfully disagree. |
| | **MINDSET/PHILOSOPHY ORIENTED** | |
| 13 | Rank has no privilege. | Kaizen Events require level playing fields. Everyone on the team is of equal rank, no matter what their individual job titles and rank are outside of the room. |
| | | *Note:* If leadership is on the team, they need to be prepared for this reality up front. They need to be members of the team, not *leading or directing* the team. You want nonleadership team members to think and respond independently, not based on what they believe their leadership wants them to do. |
| 14 | Think "creativity before capital." | Use your creativity to make improvements with your existing resources: people, software, equipment, budget, etc. |
| | | Only spend money (for people or things) if a "no cost" option does not exist and then limit funds spent during a Kaizen Event. The budget for the event is established on the boundaries/limitations section of the Kaizen Charter. |

**Table 11-1.** (*continued*)

| KAIZEN COMMANDMENTS | | |
|---|---|---|
| | **Commandment** | **Explanation** |
| **MINDSET/PHILOSOPHY ORIENTED,** *continued* | | |
| 15 | Ask "Why?" and "What if?" and "How could we?" | These questions need to be asked frequently during the event. |
| 16 | Think "yes, if …" instead of "no, because …" | Team members need to break out of their usual mindsets and explore all options.<br>"No, because …" thinking can create a self-fulfilling prophesy. Language matters. |
| 17 | Eliminate "can't" from your vocabulary. | You *can* do anything. It's just a matter of whether it's the right thing to do, whether it's the best use of time and resources, and whether it meets improvement and organizational objectives. |
| 18 | Seek the wisdom of ten rather than the knowledge of one. | While one person may know specific process steps better than most, the collective wisdom of a team often results in more innovative and lasting improvements. |
| 19 | All ideas are worthy of consideration. | When brainstorming, avoid rejecting an idea until the brainstorming phase has ended, and the team has moved into the evaluation phase. Outside of formal brainstorming sessions, document ALL ideas expressed and evaluate them either in real time or during an evaluation session. Do not reject a team member's idea outright unless you've moved into an evaluation period. |
| 20 | Keep an open mind. | The best improvement ideas often fall outside of organization "norms" and established ways of operating. |
| 21 | Improvements implemented today are better than planning to implement in the future. | Incremental improvement is action based and keeps us from getting analysis paralysis. |
| 22 | Abandon departmental/functional/siloed thinking. | Think "customer" and "value stream." |
| 23 | Stay focused on customer-defined value. | Process improvements aren't "personal" and shouldn't be viewed as such. It's not about "us." It's about your customers and what they value. |
| 24 | Focus on how the results are achieved, not just the results. | A Kaizen Event is both a problem-solving technique and a learning activity.<br>You are learning new ways to solve organizational problems, and it will take practice before you become highly skilled in this new approach. |

experience how much more effective they are with clearly defined boundaries and rules of engagement, they prefer the structure. And Kaizen Teams' positive reactions to the level of organization and discipline inherent in Kaizen Events is often the most important first step in transforming the existing culture into a lean organization.

Effective facilitators review these rules thoroughly and work to assure the entire team understands why they are necessary. You may want to distribute these rules to team members in advance of the event to aid in setting their expectations.

**Value Stream Maps and Implementation Plan Review**

If your Kaizen Event is tied directly to a specific value stream improvement, the final activity during the kickoff portion of the event is reviewing the current and future state value stream maps and the implementation plan to provide context for the Kaizen Event. Through this process, team members learn how the improvements made during the Event impact the delivery of customer value. And team members build faith in the likely sustainability of their hard work by seeing how their efforts fit into an overall strategic plan.

If team members attended a lean overview class just prior to the event, they may have already been exposed to the current and future state value stream maps. But they still benefit by briefly reviewing the maps once again in the early stages of the event to firmly establish the need to create flow and drive the point home that suboptimizing a particular functional area is not the goal of a Kaizen Event.

## STAGES OF TEAM DEVELOPMENT

The facilitator's portion of the kickoff also lays the groundwork for leading the team through the five typical stages of team development as defined by Bruce Tuckman: Forming—Storming—Norming—Performing.[1] (See Figure 11-1.) Tuckman later added a fifth and final stage—Adjourning, which is also sometimes referred to as mourning. A skilled facilitator understands how team dynamics shift during each of these phases, and knows how to adjust his or her role to accommodate the team's needs in each phase. The remainder of Part III discusses each of these phases in greater detail.

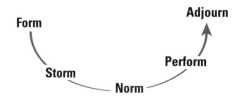

**Figure 11-1.** Stages in Team Development

Throughout the event, a skilled facilitator is acutely aware of where the team is in terms of these stages, which shapes his or her facilitation strategy while leading discussions, resolving conflicts, and encouraging decisions and actions. It's also helpful for the facilitator to assess where the team is at the end of each day, to shape his or her kickoff strategy for the next morning. Sometimes facilitators validate their observations with the team members and encourage discussions about where they are, but much of the time facilitators use their observations to silently monitor team progress and shape their leadership strategy.

By the end of the event kickoff, the team members should clearly understand what their mission is and how they're expected to accomplish it. They are usually eager to dive in and begin the process of change, which begins with current state analysis, the subject of our next chapter.

---

1. Tuckman, Bruce. "Developmental Sequence in Small Groups," *Psychological Bulletin*, 1965.

# CHAPTER 12

# DOCUMENTING THE CURRENT STATE

Effective process improvement is similar to a well-planned trip. You need to know more than simply the starting point and destination for the journey. You need to know the specific route you will take to get there. But if you are not clear about the current state, you may select a path that leads you off course, slowing or blocking entirely your ability to reach your destination.

Establishing a clear understanding of the current state is also vital because, while individual Kaizen Team members may be experts about the process steps they perform on a daily basis, typically no one on the team—in fact, no one in the entire organization—understands the complete process targeted for improvement. It's difficult to design an improved state if the Kaizen Team doesn't fully understand the true customer requirements, the quality of existing inputs and outputs, and the downstream impact of design decisions they may make regarding upstream process steps.

The heightened awareness that team members gain during current state analysis is valuable both for the specific improvement effort they're focused on, and the longer-term organizational gains realized by developing a more informed workforce. That deeper knowledge results in faster problem solving, better decisions, and a more fulfilled workforce because each team member better understands his or her role in providing customer value. The primary reasons for documenting the current state are:

- Identify all functions and individuals who are engaged in the process.

- Build a common understanding about process flow, customer requirements, performance issues, and the presence of waste.

- Document current process performance related to lead time, process time, and quality, providing the means to prioritize waste elimination and a baseline against which improvements can be measured.

- Make better decisions while designing the future state.

## CURRENT STATE DOCUMENTATION AND ANALYSIS OPTIONS

The type of current state information you need is largely dependent on what problem you're trying to solve. At a process level, a wide variety of documentation and analysis tools exist including:

- Process flow diagrams

- Spaghetti diagrams

- Photographs and videotape
- Performance metrics
- Written procedures, decision trees, cheat sheets, and other job aids
- Survey and audit findings (e.g., customer satisfaction, workforce satisfaction, operations audits, regulatory audits, etc.)

Choose your documentation tools wisely. While every improvement effort should include baseline measurements and a review of relevant survey results, photographs are not always needed. If the team needs to create visual controls for the workplace and implement 5S, the current state is documented by performing a 5S audit, taking "before" pictures, and obtaining pre-improvement measurements such as people movement, staff morale, and/or time wasted looking for information and material.

If team members need to standardize the order in which documents appear in a customer package, but they don't need to improve the process for creating the documents, their current state documentation may consist of reviewing an appropriate number of packages to assess the variation in how the customer packages are currently organized. From this information, coupled with a clear definition of customer requirements, a single best practice can be designed and adopted. Videotaping, commonly used when analyzing processes that involve manual handling and motion, would be irrelevant for this improvement.

Experienced lean practitioners are familiar with spaghetti diagrams, another tool that can be helpful when documenting and analyzing the current state. The spaghetti diagram (Figure 12-1) is a visual rendering of the physical paths taken by material, information, or people as it/they travel through all the steps required to transform a requirement into a deliverable. The

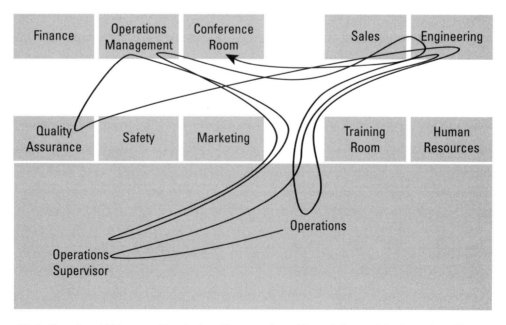

**Figure 12-1.** Spaghetti Diagram Depicting Current State Travel for an Engineering Change Notice

spaghetti diagram is so called because the finished diagram often looks similar to a plate of spaghetti. The visual depiction of the physical movement inherent in a process that is otherwise difficult to see is valuable in understanding why flow has been difficult to achieve and provides a baseline from which to make improvements, such as physical rearrangement and co-location. Ideally, the post-improvement spaghetti diagram depicts a simplified process with reduced travel, which improves flow.

If, however, the team is chartered with streamlining a process, documenting the current state is a more involved process. To date, no single tool has provided a visual means for documenting and analyzing a process at a tactical level, while integrating time and quality performance metrics. The remainder of this chapter introduces you to a tool developed by the authors of this book that serves this purpose: the *Metrics-Based Process Map*.

## METRICS-BASED PROCESS MAP (MBPM)

While your Kaizen Event is likely driven by a future state value stream map (VSM), a more detailed current state analysis is often required to design improvements at the tactical level. That is, for many processes under consideration for improvement, the team will need to create a process-level map. The VSM provides a high level strategic plan for making improvements to an entire value stream. A process-level map enables deeper analysis in a more narrowly defined portion of the value stream and defines executable, tactical improvements. The *Metrics-Based Process Map* (MBPM), which allows you to "get into the weeds" and "peel back the layers of the onion" to reveal deeper problems, combines the strongest elements of two existing analytical tools:

- The swim-lane structure of traditional function-based process maps, which provides the means to visualize handoffs.

- The time and quality metrics of today's value stream maps to help us quantify process performance and make it easier to see waste.

As you see in Figure 12-2, the MBPM is not a process flow diagram. While flow diagrams are valuable training and standard work tools, they lack metrics and, therefore, are not the most effective tools for identifying disconnects, bottlenecks, delays, and quality problems. Without metrics, teams may focus on irrelevant solutions that don't ultimately impact the two components to operational excellence—quality and speed. If you don't have a baseline of how a process is performing, how can you measure your improvements? In today's return-on-investment environment—and in the interest of demonstrating a Kaizen Team's results—improved processes can't just *feel* better. They need to be *measurably* better, and the team can't assess if processes truly are "better" unless it has an effective tool by which to monitor performance.

Here's another way to look at it. As described in Chapter 1, the VSM reveals delays in the timeline that contribute to long lead times, but not necessarily the specific reasons for the extended lead time such as rework loops, multiple approvals, excessive review, redundant data entry, interruptions, multitasking, etc. The Kaizen Team must understand why the waste

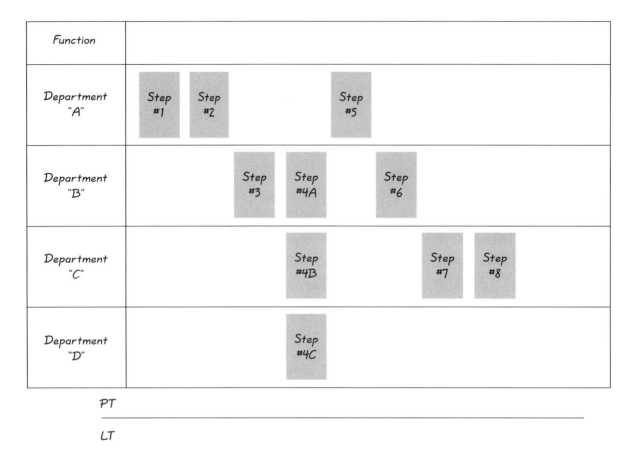

| Function | | | | |
|---|---|---|---|---|
| Department "A" | Step #1 Step #2 | | Step #5 | |
| Department "B" | | Step #3 Step #4A | Step #6 | |
| Department "C" | | Step #4B | Step #7 Step #8 | |
| Department "D" | | Step #4C | | |

PT

LT

**Figure 12-2.** MBPM (showing functional labels, swim lanes, Post-it® placement, and timeline)

exists—the fundamental *root cause* or underlying problem that's producing the symptoms of waste the VSM reveals—before they can design a proper tactical solution. So at a macro level, you may know you need to shorten the lead time, but you need micro-level data to determine how to best accomplish that objective. Simply put: *VSM is a strategic tool* that helps leadership determine the general improvements that need to be made, and the *MBPM is a tactical tool* that helps the Kaizen Team identify the root cause behind the waste. Once the team identifies the root cause, it can design and implement effective countermeasures.

How do you decide if you'll need a MBPM? The VSM typically determines whether or not you need to drill down to the micro level and get into the weeds. For example, if your VSM depicts a process riddled with handoffs that are merely reviews, you won't gain significantly more information about the waste by creating an MBPM. In this case, the solution for shortening lead time to the customer and improving quality is obvious: reduce the number of approvals, and mistake proof the process. Implementing this improvement requires the creation of standard work and some cross-training for the people performing the remaining approval steps, but an MBPM isn't needed to make these determinations. However, you *will* find the MBPM to be a useful tool when the VSM:

- Depicts macro-level activities that comprise a series of individual steps performed by one or more persons.
- Reveals opportunities for improvement, but it's not clear what specific problems are leading to prolonged lead times, excessive process times, or poor quality.

The MBPM can also be used as a stand-alone tool outside a Kaizen Event for process analysis and improvement design. But if a process is likely to benefit by using a cross-functional, metrics-based mapping tool, a Kaizen Event is probably the best approach for implementing improvements to that process. And, because of the reasons stated in the next section, this type of micro-mapping needs to be performed *during* the event, not in advance of it.

Depending on the Kaizen Event scope, you will need one to two days to create the current state and future state MBPMs, and prioritize opportunities, and select the improvement(s) to be implemented *during the event*. This micro-level mapping activity is held during the event to assure two key mapping criteria are met:

1. The mapping team should include the *same people* who will be designing and implementing the improved process. This requirement is necessary to ensure that those designing the solutions fully understand the process issues. Because solutions begin revealing themselves as the current state is being documented, it is critical to engage the design and implementation team at this stage of the process. Given the detailed nature of an MBPM, significant rework can be required to get a new pair of eyes up to speed.

2. Since most processes are in constant flux to accommodate shifting business needs, documenting the current state needs to *immediately precede* the future state design. Doing so avoids scheduling challenges, and reduces the mental setup required and rework that occurs when a gap in time exists between current state documentation and future state design.

## CREATING THE MBPM

As you may recall from Chapter 7, the Kaizen Event planning process includes selecting a room with adequate wall space. If possible, remove art and other wall hangings. The Supplies Checklist provided with the Kaizen Event tools, lists a number of items you'll need specifically for mapping, including:

- 36″ wide roll of white paper*
- Scissors
- Masking tape
- Yardstick or other straight edge (for drawing "swim lanes")
- 4″ × 6″ Post-its® in various colors
- Smaller size Post-its® in various colors
- Sharpies (or other black medium-point markers)

- Colored markers
- Calculator

\* Mapping tip: Blueprint shops typically offer lower cost paper (by volume) than office supply stores and are a good paper source if you map frequently.

Before the team arrives, prepare the room for mapping as follows:

1. Estimate the length of 36″ wide paper you'll need, and then add 50 percent more. Cut it accordingly, and affix it to the wall with masking tape (or push pins, if allowed). Mapping tip: consider the facilitator's and team members' heights when hanging the paper.

2. Draw six horizontal "swim lanes" across the paper, each 6″ tall. For complex processes with more than six functional areas involved, you may need to hang two rows of the mapping paper.

3. Draw a vertical line 4″ to 6″ from the left edge of the map to house the swim-lane labels for each functional area involved.

When the team is ready to begin mapping, the facilitator should inform the team members that they are not allowed to consult written procedures, manuals, and process flowcharts until *after* they have created the current state MBPM and then, only to ensure that the team members didn't overlook a relevant process step. Otherwise, they may be tempted to use these written "standardized" documents to depict the current state as it *should be* rather than how it actually *is*—how people actually do the work *today*. The facilitator should also remind the team about the process fence posts that were defined on the Kaizen Event Charter. These will be the first and last steps of the MBPM.

With these preliminary steps completed, the team is now ready to begin mapping. On the left side of the map, the facilitator will list the functional departments that "touch" the process between and including the fence posts—the starting and ending steps within which the process will be mapped (as defined on the Kaizen Event Charter). These functional labels define the swim lanes within which the team will map each functional area's role in the process.

In the upper right corner, the facilitator should write the map's title (e.g., Current State MBPM), the process name, date, and customer demand (volume of work per week, month, or year). The lower right corner typically houses the facilitator and team members' names.

The map will be constructed in three phases—or three passes at reviewing the current state. During the first pass, the team will define how the process currently operates—who passes work and/or information to whom and in what sequence. Here, the team tracks how the data, material, or people being served flow through the process, identifying process inputs and outputs along the way. During the second pass, the team adds key metrics for each process step, including process time (PT), lead time (LT), and percent complete and accurate (%C&A). This chapter will address these first two passes. Chapter 13 addresses the third and final pass—the analysis phase.

## 1st Pass—Identify the Process Steps

The facilitator or the team members themselves document each process step on a 4″ × 6″ Post-it®. Different colors may be used to depict the various functional departments, or to depict different individuals within a given functional "swim lane" who perform the identified tasks. A process step is defined as a single activity or series of minor activities that are typically performed in a continuous time period, producing output that is passed to another individual, team, or department for the next task to occur.

As shown in Figure 12-3, the process steps are documented by briefly describing the activity in the upper portion of the Post-it®, using a verb/noun format—the action followed by the object of that action. For example, describe a data entry activity as "enter data" rather than "data entry." This convention keeps your map action-based.

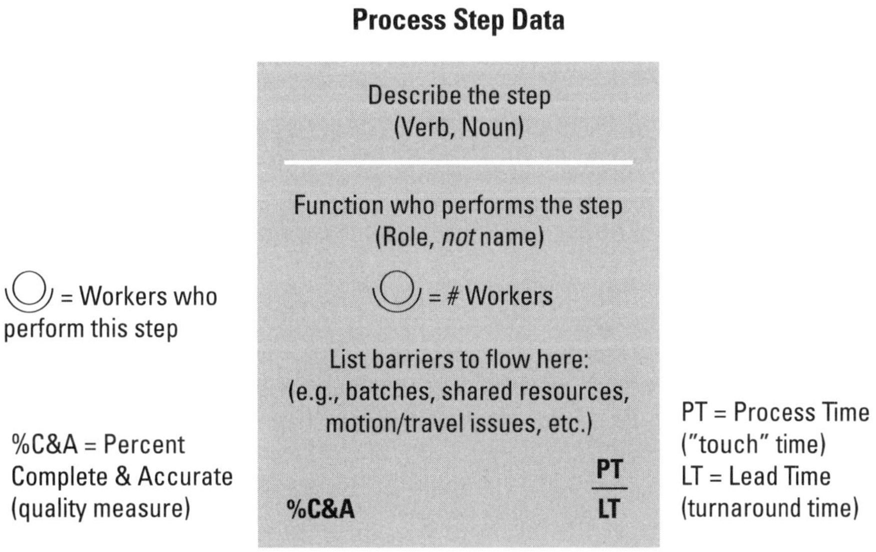

**Process Step Data**

**Figure 12-3.** Post-it® Conventions

Each Post-it® should be placed in the correct swim lane for the function involved, immediately to the right of the preceding action from a timeline perspective. The only Post-its® that should be aligned vertically are those in which the tasks are being performed in parallel. All other steps should be depicted serially, from left to right. Later, a timeline will be added to the bottom of the map.

A separate process step (requiring a separate Post-it®) exists if:

- A physical handoff occurs (work is passed from one person to another).
- A delay exists within the process step.
- Multiple IT systems are accessed.
- A batch is created.
- Separate quality issues are identified for specific process step components.

The following mapping tips will help the team move as quickly as possible through the first pass:

1. Encourage team members to pretend they're *the thing* (the work product) being passed through the process (or experiencing the process from a stationery position, such as a person receiving a service and or equipment being serviced) and view the process from that perspective. The "thing" could be data, information, paperwork, drawings, equipment, and material—or, in the case of healthcare and other service environments, it might be a person. Regardless of whether the thing is moving or stationery, if team members pretend they're the thing ("*be the thing*" is a common reminder), they're less likely to skip process steps.

2. During this first pass in the MBPM process, the facilitator's most common question is: "And then what happens?" The team's typical response is: "It depends." To minimize the "it depends" responses, which slow the mapping process, you may need to further refine the target process beyond the specific conditions defined by the Kaizen Event Charter. At this level of detail, you should map only one or two specific conditions, and then apply the future state map to a broader set of circumstances, adjusting it if necessary to accommodate legitimate variation. For example, the charter may narrow the Kaizen Event focus to a process that's performed only in a particular region for a national company, or a specific time of the year. When creating the MBPM, the team may have to refine the scope further and focus on a particular customer group or type of service being delivered.

3. Regardless of the specific process you end up mapping, create a map that reflects what happens in 80 percent of the circumstances. In some cases, it can be helpful for the team to focus on a recent occurrence as an example. You want to focus on the norm, not the outliers and exceptions. Exceptions often seem more frequent than they really are because they're typically more painful to deal with, so teams often focus on those situations. To avoid slowing the mapping process, the facilitator will need to keep reminding the team to focus on "the 80 percent." That said, if the exceptions are causing the greatest pain and are what need to be addressed, then those exceptions are fair game for improvement and should be clearly identified in the specific conditions section of the Kaizen Event charter.

4. Since this is a time-based map (the clock is ticking continuously from the first to the last step), you'll need to "linearize" the process steps, including those that typically loop. For example, if the thing passing through the system is sent back to an upstream supplier for correction 90 percent of the time, depict each of those steps linearly, placing them sequentially from left to right, on the map. So, in the case of rework, you may need three Post-its® arranged in sequence to depict the rework cycle: 1) initial receipt and review of the work product by the customer, 2) correction of the error by the upstream supplier, and 3) processing of the corrected work product by the customer.

5. While the team members are initially documenting the current state, they will be tempted to begin designing improvements. To keep the team fully focused on

the current state, the facilitator should record improvement suggestions on a flip chart or white board, and guide attention back to the current state as quickly as possible. Don't let the team get distracted and start evaluating ideas at this stage; that comes later.

6. Creating the current state MBPM is eye opening, but it can be tedious work. The facilitator should keep the team members' energy up by regularly applauding members efforts, acknowledging that it's hard work, and assuring them that there will be payoff when they begin designing the future state.

Mapping teams often benefit by performing a "gemba walk" or "going to gemba"— going to where the work is actually performed to observe the process in action. This is particularly helpful for high-volume, repetitive processes that have a relatively short total process time. Walking the process is extremely important during value stream mapping; during MPBM micro-level mapping, you need to decide if it would be beneficial or not. If you aren't sure, err on the side of going to gemba, even if it's visiting a set of cubicles containing computers. Improvement teams typically learn a lot by going to where the work is actually performed. Another option is to "bring gemba" to Kaizen Central. For some processes, workers can demonstrate process steps in a conference room as effectively as they can at gemba, which may be logistically challenging to arrange, or where a mapping team may be disruptive. For example, team members may be able to demonstrate the transactions they perform on a computer connected to an LCD projector.

Also, it's important to realize that, on Day One, the team is typically in the "forming" stage of team development. Members have agreed to a shared objective, but they are still operating somewhat independently. As they get to know one another, they establish the foundation for moving into the next phase, "storming," a necessary part of the improvement effort. Metrics-Based Process Mapping provides an extended period for the forming stage, which allows the team to build relationships, which helps reduce (but rarely eliminates) the tension that can arise during the future state design period. The facilitator may observe a few pockets of "storming" during current state mapping if team members disagree about the true nature of the current state.

Another form of storming can surface if workers react defensively as wasteful activities are uncovered. In these situations, the facilitator can help reduce tension among team members by reminding the participants that the objective is to stay forward looking, not to find fault in or assign blame for the current process. Another form of storming sometimes occurs when team members' perspectives and experiences regarding the current state are widely divergent. In this case, the facilitator can help redirect the team back into the forming stage—or advance them into the norming stage—by asking questions that enable the differing team members to reach a consensus position (often by adopting a median between two extremes). In some cases, documenting the extremes is helpful and relevant. Extended storming should be discouraged during current state mapping.

123

## 2nd Pass—Add the Key Metrics for Each Step

Next, the team adds the three key metrics for analyzing and monitoring a process—lead time (LT), process time (PT), and percent complete and accurate (%C&A), described below. Most of this data is obtained by questioning the relevant process workers. As suggested throughout this book, you should seek "directionally correct" data that's accurate enough to lead to solid conclusions and appropriate decisions regarding prioritization. During this second pass, with its different focus, the team often discovers a few missing steps, which should be added to improve the map's accuracy.

The CD includes a summary sheet that defines the key mapping metrics (Table 12-1). It's helpful to print this and give it to the team either during the lean overview training or during mapping. It's important that the team fully understand the three key metrics—lead time, process time, and percent complete and accurate—before the facilitator leads them into this phase.

As described in Table 12-1, the three key metrics are determined as follows:

*1. Process Time (PT)* is the actual time it takes a worker to perform a task if he or she could work uninterrupted and removed all waiting from the process. In addition to the time spent "touching" the work, process time includes the "talk time" for clarifying or obtaining additional information to perform the task, and the "think time" required to perform a task if analysis and/or review is involved. When interviewing workers, you may find it useful to ask them, "How long would it take you to do all of the activities in this step, from start to finish, if you were able to work on it uninterrupted?"

In office and service settings, process time is often expressed in minutes or hours and is typically obtained by interviewing the people who actually do the work rather than by conducting time/motion studies or other elaborate forms of operational research. That said, if true measurements (not desired standards) are relatively easy to obtain, accuracy beats approximation any day. But remember, you only need data that's "directionally correct" enough to draw accurate conclusions and make effective decisions. If scientifically obtained data wouldn't alter your conclusions or affect your decisions, there's no point taking the time to obtain it.

The facilitator will need to keep team members moving along and help them realize that if the lead time is four hours for a particular step (four hours from the work being made available until it's completed and passed on to the next person or department), it makes little difference if the process time for a task is five minutes or seven minutes. Either number will adequately illustrate the delay that exists and will provide a "good enough" baseline from which to measure improvement. Teams often get hung up on perfection. It's the facilitator's job to explain why debating over a few minutes that occur over the course of many hours isn't as important as is completing the map so the team can progress toward its key mission: implementation.

**Table 12-1.** Key Mapping Metrics

| KEY MAPPING METRICS | | |
|---|---|---|
| **Abbreviation** | **Metric Description** | **How Measured/Calculated** |
| **METRICS FOR EACH MBPM PROCESS STEP** | | |
| LT | Lead Time | Elapsed time, from the moment work is available to be worked on through completion of work and delivery to downstream customer. Includes all delays. Also referred to as "throughput time" or "turnaround time." |
| PT | Process Time | The "touch time" and "think time" it takes to perform the task if one could work uninterrupted. |
| %C&A | Percent Complete & Accurate | The percentage of occurrences of released work that doesn't require the downstream customer to "CAC" it:<br>1. **Correct** information<br>2. **Add** missing information that should have been supplied<br>3. **Clarify** information that should have been clear |
| **SUMMARY METRICS FOR THE ENTIRE MAP** | | |
| $\Sigma$CP LT | Critical Path Lead Time | The sum of the LTs for the process blocks/steps on the map's "critical path." When parallel activities exist, select the LT for the step belonging to the CP. |
| $\Sigma$CP PT | Critical Path Process Time | The sum of the PTs for the process blocks/steps on the map's "critical path." When parallel activities exist, select the PT for the step belonging to the CP. |
| AR | Activity Ratio | $(\Sigma \text{CP PT} \div \text{CP LT}) \times 100$ |
| RFPY | Rolled First Pass Yield | The product of the %C&As for all process blocks/steps on the map. (Convert percentages to decimals before multiplying). Multiply by 100 to express as a percentage. |
| PT | Total Process Time | The sum of the PTs for all process blocks/steps on the map. |
| # FTEs | Required Number of Full-Time Equivalents | The equivalent number of people, working full time (40 hrs per week), required to perform a task, based on the total PT and the volume of work. # FTEs = $(\Sigma \text{PT in hrs} \times \text{# occurrences}) \div 2{,}080$ hours worked per year. |
| # Steps | Number of Steps | Count the total number of Post-its®, including parallel activities. |
| %VA | Percent Value-Adding | Similar to AR, except you only use the value-adding critical path process times. % VA = $(\Sigma \text{VA CP PT} \div \Sigma \text{CP LT}) \times 100$ |
| **METRICS TO COMPARE CURRENT AND FUTURE STATE MAPS** | | |
| FC | Freed Capacity | (Pre $\Sigma$PT − Post $\Sigma$PT) $\times$ (# occurrences/year) = Annualized PT Saved. FC (in # of FTEs) = Annualized PT Saved (in hours) $\div$ 2,080 |
| Projected % Change | Projected Percent Change | {(Projected Future State Value − Current State Value) $\div$ Current State Value} $\times$ 100 |

**2. *Lead Time (LT)*** is the elapsed time from the moment work is made available to a particular worker or team, until it's been completed and made available to the next person or team in the process. Lead time includes the process time plus waiting and delays, and is often expressed in hours or days. Lead time is also usually obtained by interviewing the people who currently perform the work being analyzed. When interviewing workers, you may find it helpful to ask them, "What is your typical turnaround time for this activity, from the time the work is available to you until you've completed it and passed it on to your immediate downstream customer?"

Figure 12-3 illustrates the preferred convention for PT and LT placement on the Post-it®. Make sure you include the units of measure for each metric.

*Mapping tip #1*: When presenting the current state findings, it's helpful to express lead time in one unit of measure greater than the process time. So if your lead time is most easily understood in weeks, your process time might be expressed in days. If your lead time is in hours, your process time might be expressed in minutes. This technique makes the waste far more obvious (e.g., why does it take eight hours to complete only five minutes of work?), especially when the lead time is significantly longer than the process time. That said, the PT and LT eventually need to be converted into the same units of measure to calculate a few of the summary metrics. Some facilitators prefer to convert to like units of measure as the map is being created, whereas others prefer to convert PT and LT to similar units of measure just prior to calculating the summary metrics.

*Mapping tip #2*: With particularly complicated processes, it is sometimes helpful to determine lead time in "chunks," rather than include it for each and every step. (The same isn't true for process time, however). If a series of steps occur in any given department before a handoff to another department, you can obtain the typical lead time for the series of steps, rather than breaking it into individual components. Also for processes with very long total lead times (i.e., weeks or months), you can break the map into sections and assess lead time for that group of activities. For example, a three-week lead time may reside in one area for two business days, another for eight business days and a third for five business days. If you break the map into segments, place the segment lead time on the last Post-it® for that segment and leave the area below the line blank for all other steps (or place a "0").

*Mapping tip #3*: For teams new to lean terminology and these metrics, the facilitator will likely need to keep reminding them about the difference between process time and lead time. Teams often move more quickly through the metrics phase if they are asked first about the lead time, then the process time for a particular step. Because process time measures are somewhat new to office and service environments, it's usually easier for teams to determine their turnaround time from work being available to passing it on (lead time), than they are at how long it actually takes them to perform a task or series of tasks (process time).

*Mapping tip #4*: If the team is having difficulty determining the median that occurs 80 percent of the time for either the LT or PT, ask them for the longest time and how often that occurs. Then ask them for the shortest time and how often that occurs. The answers to these two questions often lead to a fairly accurate median that everyone can agree on.

**3. *Percent Complete and Accurate (%C&A)***, which reflects the quality of each process step's output, is obtained by interviewing downstream users of the upstream output and asking them what percentage of the time they can do their work without having to:

- **Correct** the information that was provided.

- **Add** missing information that should have been supplied.

- **Clarify** information that should have been clearer.

As shown in Figure 12-3, place the answer to this question on the lower left corner of the Post-it® for *the step that produced the output, not* the Post-it® of the downstream customer who you're interviewing. A C&A of 80 percent on a particular process step means that a downstream customer has to correct, add or clarify ("CAC") the upstream supplier's output about 20 percent of the time. For large maps, rather than determining the %C&A for each activity (which occupies significant time), you may want to ask the team to identify only those steps in which they receive output from upstream suppliers with a C&A of 80 percent or less. Answers to this question will reveal the greatest opportunities for error reduction.

Occasionally an internal customer several steps downstream from an internal supplier will assess the quality of the output from the upstream supplier to be lower than determined by the customer immediately downstream from the supplier. In this case, go back to the Post-it® for the step producing the output and reduce that step's %C&A further to reflect the further downstream customer's experience. This step is a most enlightening one, and can sometimes make team members uncomfortable to learn that their output hasn't been meeting their internal customers' needs, which can result in a little more "storming." But, with proper facilitation and a blame-free environment, these discoveries can provide the trigger for positive and productive dialogue between internal customers and suppliers regarding expectations and requirements.

## Critical Path Determination

Remember that *time* is the primary metric in the lean approach. As such, your map should accurately reflect the total elapsed time from the moment an order is placed or a request is made, until a product or service has been delivered. So, at this stage, you need to review your MBPM. Does it contain parallel steps (work that's being performed concurrently)? If so, you'll need to determine the *critical path* in preparation for the metrics summary phase. If the team has constructed the map properly, parallel activities will be depicted as two or more Post-its® aligned vertically (directly above or below one another), to illustrate that they are being performed concurrently.

To calculate the summary metrics, you need to determine the overall lead time (again, assuming that a ticking clock is running throughout the process). Concurrent activities must be reviewed to determine which *one* of the steps contributes most heavily to the ticking clock. In other words, which of the activities being performed in parallel form the "critical path?"

Typically, the steps that belong to the critical path are those with the longest lead times. But first you need to eliminate from consideration any of the non-value-adding parallel steps that lead to a "dead end" in the process, such as data entry, followed by filing. If the parallel activities take you down a path that never leads back to the customer (such as data entry, performed by filing the data input form), these parallel steps are not part of the critical path, no matter how long their lead times are. Once you've eliminated the "dead end" steps, review the remaining parallel steps, and select the one in the sequence with the longest total lead time.

Figure 12-4 represents a segment of an MBPM for a quoting process. Within this segment there are three parallel paths, or sequences, of activities. In determining the critical path, the top row is eliminated since it dead ends with the filing activity. Of the two remaining sequences of parallel activities, the steps performed by the finance department comprise the critical path since their collective lead time (seven days) is longer than the lead time for the activities being performed by the legal department (four days). In this example, the bold curved line indicates the critical path.

You can visually depict the critical path in a number of ways. Some facilitators place a brightly colored, smaller Post-it® on each critical path step, whereas others use a brightly colored marker and draw the critical path across the entire MBPM (such as shown in Figure 12-4). There are other options as well. The key is to make the critical path visually apparent. Mapping tip: Make sure your map is 100 percent complete before you determine the critical path.

*Mapping tip*: If the map's going to be rolled up and stored for any length of time, the team should secure all Post-its® with a small piece of tape to ensure they remain fixed in

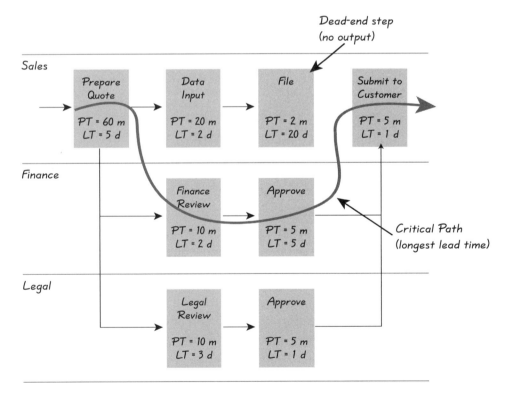

**Figure 12-4.** Critical Path Determination

their proper location. If the team wants to create an electronic version of the map for ease in sharing by e-mail and using as a standard work tool, the authors have created an Excel-based tool that is available through Productivity Press. Recognize that transforming manually created maps into electronic form is a form of waste and should only be performed if a high need exists for an electronic version.

## CURRENT STATE SUMMARY METRICS

Once the map is complete, the key metrics have been determined (PT, LT, and %C&A), and the critical path has been determined, it's time to calculate the summary metrics for the current state MBPM. If you look again at Table 12-1, you will see that it includes a complete listing of the metrics involved with mapping, including several discussed later in the book.

To begin, create the summary timeline by drawing a horizontal line across the bottom of your map. (*Note*: you may need to hang additional paper for this.) Label the line with "PT" and "LT" and the appropriate units of measure as shown in Figure 12-5. Place the process times for the corresponding critical path steps directly below the corresponding process steps and directly above the line you just drew (in the numerator position). Place

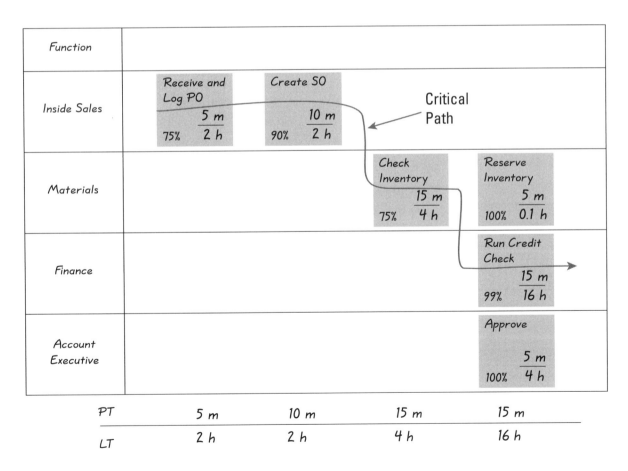

**Figure 12-5.** MBPM with Summary Timeline

the lead times for the corresponding critical path steps just below the line (in the denominator position).

The summary metrics are calculated as follows:

- *Critical Path (CP) Summation*—Add together the individual critical path PTs and LTs. Place the totals to the right of the time line as critical path summations (e.g. $\Sigma$CP LT and $\Sigma$CP PT). Validate the $\Sigma$CP LT with objective data, or a "gut check" if objective data is not available. Does the total CP LT match the team's experience of how much time generally elapses from the beginning to the end of the process? If it doesn't match objective data and/or the team's experience, review the LTs for the individual steps or process segments, and revise if necessary. Convert the CP PT and LT to the same unit of measure in preparation for the calculated metrics phase, described later in this section.

- *Rolled First Pass Yield (RFPY)*—This quality metric reflects the overall quality of the process. It tells you what percentage of the "things" pass through the process completely "clean;" that is, there's no need to correct, add, or clarify the work product or information at any point in the process. To calculate the RFPY, multiply together the decimal form for the %C&As for all of the steps (not just the critical path).

  The current state RFPY is typically (shockingly) low. For example, even if each person produces output with 95 percent quality, in a process with 30 steps, the RFPY reflects overall quality of only 21.5 percent. And if the %C&A at any process step is 0 percent (a surprisingly frequent finding), the RFPY for the entire process is naturally 0 percent.

  *Mapping tip*: If your map includes the %C&As for only those steps producing 80 percent quality or less, indicate that your baseline RFPY only includes the %C&A for a portion of your map. When comparing the projected or actual future state results with the current state, include the same process steps to assure your percent improvement results are accurate.

- *Activity Ratio (AR)*—This metric, which reflects the magnitude of the waiting and delays in the process, represents the ratio of the time "the thing" experiencing the process is being worked on versus the time it is idle, and is expressed as a percentage. To calculate the AR, convert your critical path PT (CP PT) and LT (CP LT) to the same units of measure. Then divide the sum of the critical path PTs by the sum of the critical path LTs and multiply by 100:

$$\frac{\Sigma\text{CP PT}}{\Sigma\text{CP LT}} \times 100 = \text{Activity Ratio (expressed as a percentage)}$$

  - **Two notes of caution:** In office environments, the current state activity ratio is often quite low—in the 5 to 15 percent range, which indicates ample opportunity for improvement. Naturally, you would like to get as close to 100 percent as possible—true flow. But this is extremely difficult to achieve in any environment, let alone office environments where multitasking is present to a large degree. So, for the first few rounds of improvement, focus on the degree of improvement rather than the actual numbers. If, for example, your current state activity ratio is 3 percent, designing a future state with a projected activity ratio of 6 percent is a 100 percent improvement (again, projected) that should be celebrated. But this number also indicates the tremendous need for ongoing improvement.

Second, be aware that those who are new to process measurement may not understand how improvements can impact ratio-type calculations, and may draw incorrect conclusions when interpreting the activity ratio. In the initial efforts to improve an office process, you may find that the Activity Ratio drops. But this isn't necessarily a bad thing. Remember, it's a *ratio*, expressed as a *percentage*. If you improve both the PT and the LT but the proportion shifts (e.g., the percent improvement for the PT is greater than the percent improvement for the LT), the ratio will drop. But reducing both the LT and the PT—your goal—is a success that should be celebrated. Enlighten team members and leadership to this fact so they understand that, although the AR has decreased, the team has made meaningful improvements.

- *Number of steps*—The number of process steps is an indicator of process complexity. Count the total number of Post-its® (include all of the parallel steps) to obtain this metric.

- *Total Process Time*—Total Process Time is used to calculate workforce requirements, described below. To obtain this metric, add together the PTs for all steps, not just the critical path.

  *Mapping Tip*: It's best to depict the total PT in the units of measure that are the easiest to comprehend. So even if you've captured each individual process step in minutes, you may want to express the total PT in hours or days. For example, 22.3 hours or 2.8 days is more easily understood than 1,338 minutes. And 1.5 days is easier to comprehend that 0.3 business weeks.

  Also, if you use days as a unit of measure, *make sure you specify whether it's calendar days or business days*. Two business days could equal four calendar days, if Friday and Monday are involved. And, in a Monday through Friday operation, 22 days equals 4.4 business weeks.

  If you are mapping a process in a 24/7 operation such as law enforcement or hospital services, use calendar days. For 8-to-5, Monday-through-Friday operations, the units of measure for days are usually expressed in "business days." For conversions from days to months, most offices are operational about 21 business days per month, though this is dependent upon the industry and how many holidays the organization typically recognizes. For example, the average number of business days worked per month tends to be lower in government and education and higher in healthcare organizations and small businesses with limited budgets.

- *Workforce Requirements*—If you want to calculate workforce requirements or measure the freed capacity created by the future state design, you need to convert the total PT (described above) to workforce requirements.

Full-time equivalent (FTE) is a measure of the number of staff required if they all worked full time, and generally assumes a 40-hour work week. For example: Two people, each working 20 hours per week, are equivalent to one full-time person or one FTE. It's helpful to measure the current state FTE requirements for two reasons: First, it can be used to compare current state staffing requirements according to the map versus actual staffing levels. (Note: This comparison is only valid when the staff responsibilities are limited to the work being mapped. If staff members have other responsibilities that you have not mapped, you may not know what percentage of their time focuses on performing the mapped process versus their other responsibilities.) Second, the FTE calculation provides a baseline from which you can measure freed capacity created from future state improvements that reduce process time.

To calculate FTE requirements, first add together the PTs for all of the process steps, not just the critical path steps. Convert the Total PT sum into hours if it isn't already. Multiply the PT sum by the number of occurrences per year (customer demand) and divide by 2,080 (the typical number of work hours per year):

$$\frac{(\text{Total PT in hours}) \times (\text{\# occurrences})}{2{,}080 \text{ work hours per year}} = \text{FTE Requirements}$$

- Other relevant metrics—Depending on the team's improvement focus, other metrics may be meaningful, such as:
  - *Productivity*—The number of "work units" processed per person per unit of time.
  - *Distance walked*—Distance walked measurements are often used in conjunction with a spaghetti diagram and are useful for illustrating:
    - The cost and productivity impact of unnecessary walking.
      - To convert distance to time, use 1 to 1.5 miles per hour as an average walking speed. This seemingly slow pace accounts for the number of times workers stop to talk with others or are stopped by others, or have to wait for equipment and/or people when they reach their destination.
      - To convert the distance walked into lost productivity from an FTE perspective, first convert the distance walked per occurrence into time (in hours). Multiply the resulting value by the number of times the process occurs per year. Divide the resulting product by 2,080 hours per year (the number of hours each FTE is typically scheduled to work).
      - To convert the distance walked metrics into dollars, for a conservative calculation, use the average hourly rate for the workers involved. To illustrate the truer cost of walking, you can include benefits and other workforce-related overhead expenses.
    - The benefits of co-locating people, equipment, or supplies (often used in creating the business case for purchasing additional equipment).
    - The benefits of eliminating hand-walking for approvals, input, or work expedition.

- *Morale, Turnover, Absenteeism*—These measurements are relevant when seeking to build a motivated workforce. Morale is best assessed by survey, whereas turnover and absenteeism data should be available from the human resources department.

- *Customer satisfaction*—Useful in any improvement effort, but especially relevant when seeking to retain customers and/or reduce customer complaints. The two key components of customer satisfaction are: 1) quality of the good or service received, and 2) on-time delivery percentage (based on customer expectation and need).

- *Overall Equipment Effectiveness (OEE)*—This metric is particularly useful when assessing how effectively capital-intensive and/or revenue-producing equipment is being utilized. OEE is also helpful in demonstrating the reliability for support equipment (which can impact productivity, safety, customer satisfaction, and departmental budgets), such as computers, law enforcement equipment, etc. Appendix A includes the formula for calculating OEE.

Now that the Kaizen Team members have documented the current state and obtained relevant metrics, they are prepared for the third and final pass of the MBPM—waste identification, the subject of the next chapter.

# CHAPTER 13

# IDENTIFYING WASTE AND PERFORMING ROOT CAUSE ANALYSIS

Once the Kaizen Team members have documented the current state, their next step is to identify the waste in the process—the *unnecessary non-value-adding* activities—that will become the team's target for elimination. The fastest way to accomplish this is to first identify the *value-adding* and *necessary non-value-adding* steps in the process. After this step, all remaining activities are considered waste that needs to be eliminated—or at least greatly reduced.

The final step in analyzing the current state is performing root cause analysis. Through root cause analysis, the team is able to identify the reason(s) for waste. They can then put countermeasures in place that address the root cause rather than implementing superficial improvements that only address the symptoms. This chapter addresses each of these final phases in understanding the current state.

## IDENTIFYING VALUE-ADDING AND NECESSARY NON-VALUE-ADDING ACTIVITIES

As discussed in Chapter 1, waste is defined as those activities that your external customer doesn't value and, therefore, isn't willing to pay for. But, before team members begin to identify the value-adding activities, a fundamental question needs to be answered: Through whose eyes will they make this determination? In other words, who is the customer? In many environments, it's clear that the customer is both the end user and the person who's paying directly for the products or services he or she receives. But in other environments, the end user isn't the paying customer—or at least not the immediate one. If the customer doesn't pay for—or only pays a small portion toward the services or products he or she receives (as found in government, healthcare, and social services)—the team needs to analyze each activity as though the customer were paying fully for the goods or services they receive. In still other situations, an intermediate party controls access to the product or service. Healthcare, distribution networks, and subcontracted services are examples of this. In these situations, because two or more external customers exist, the Kaizen Team needs to identify primary and secondary customers.

The *primary* customer is typically the end user of the product or service. The secondary customer is the person who's paying directly for the product or service and/or controlling access to the product or service. When primary and secondary external customers coexist, team members will differentiate between value-adding and non-value-adding activities by first viewing the process from the end user's perspective. After they've made that determination, they can view the process from the secondary customer's perspective. The reason why they shouldn't view the process only from the perspective of the secondary customer (who's typically closer to the process and, therefore, could be erroneously viewed as a better arbiter of value) is that improvement teams typically uncover more waste when they view a process from the end user's perspective. (*Note*: While considering internal customers' needs is a vital component of creating process flow, it's an organization's *external* customer's perspective that's considered when classifying process steps as value-adding or non-value-adding.)

After the team identifies the value-adding activities—which often comprise 10 percent or less of the current state activities—they will then classify the remaining non-value-adding activities as either necessary or unnecessary. (*Note*: Some lean practitioners prefer the terms *essential* and *nonessential*. It's your choice.) You may refer back to Chapter 1 for a review of how to determine whether a non-value-adding activity is necessary for the business to operate effectively or if it's unnecessary (waste). A word of caution: Be extremely judicious here, and challenge organizational paradigms. Teams often assume an activity is necessary simply because it's always been part of the process, or because someone who doesn't understand lean principles said so. The process for analyzing the current state will depend upon the documentation tool(s) used. For example, reviewing spaghetti diagrams and videotapes could reveal multiple back and forth trips, which could be indicators of unnecessary handoffs, excessive approvals, or poor quality requiring rework. These visual documentation tools could also reveal the need for co-location (people, supplies, or equipment) and other improvements to reduce motion or improve ergonomics. Survey and audit results may call for a Pareto analysis of the issues (discussed later in the chapter).

The Kaizen Team must analyze all current state documentation to identify waste, determine the root cause(s) for the waste, and design effective countermeasures, which are incorporated into the future state design. However, the process for analyzing the current state as depicted on a metrics-based process map is more involved.

## Analyzing the Current State MBPM

With the current state process documented in the form of an MBPM, it is time to analyze it. Here are the basic steps:

1. *Label all value-adding steps.* Write "VA" (representing value-adding) on several 2″ × 2″ or 3″ × 3″ Post-its® (pick a color you haven't used yet, so it'll stand out). Affix them on, below, or to the side of those process steps that the team feels the *primary* external customer (the end user of the product or service) values and would be willing to pay for if he or she paid directly for the services in question. Don't be shocked if the VA steps constitute 10 percent or fewer of the Post-its® on your map. This is a common finding and indicates ample opportunities for improvement. For processes in support areas such as human resources, finance, information technology, and maintenance, often *none* of the process steps are labeled "VA." (*Mapping Tip*: Post-its® don't stick well to other Post-its®, even the "super sticky" type. So you should either affix

the VA Post-its® directly to the mapping paper or tape them to the larger Post-its® to assure the VA labels remain affixed). If the process has multiple external customers, the team may wish to affix VA labels in different colors to differentiate the various customer perspectives.

2. *Label all necessary non-value-adding steps.* Write "N" (representing necessary) on several small Post-its® (it's best to use a different color than the VA labels), and affix these Post-its® to any process step that the customer is not likely to value and, therefore, would not be willing to pay for, but the step is absolutely necessary for the organization to successfully deliver its goods and/or services and remain in business.

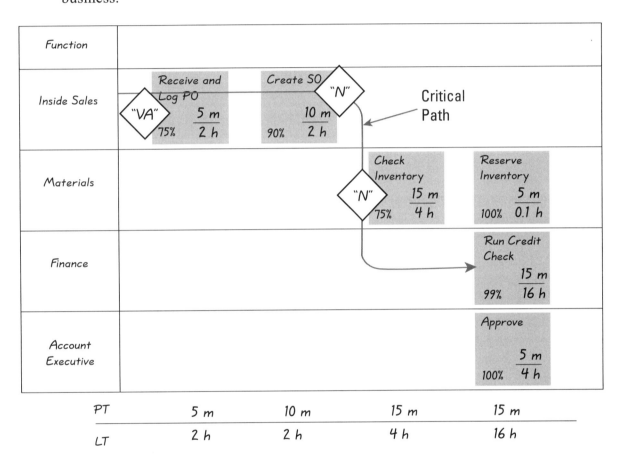

**Figure 13-1.** MBPM with VA & N Labels

The Kaizen Team needs to be extremely judicious when labeling process steps as N. They tend to "overdo" when labeling steps as "N." They need to differentiate activities that are *truly* necessary from those that *seem* necessary because that's the way they've always done it, or a well-meaning professional has said the activity is required. A skilled facilitator will challenge the team to classify as "N" only those steps that are truly essential. Analyzing activities put in place to meet a regulatory requirement can be especially tricky. A well-designed compliance process should include the *minimally necessary steps to ensure 100 percent compliance, 100 percent of the time*—and no more. But well-meaning attorneys and compliance officers who have not been exposed to lean thinking often "require" activities that are not truly necessary to meet a requirement 100 percent of the time. The same situation exists when "required" overprocessing is present, such as inspection steps put in place to "catch" poor quality rather than eliminating the root cause for repetitive errors. As the Kaizen Event progresses, the Kaizen Team may need to educate leadership about the operational costs of overprocessing waste, including direct and indirect expenses associated with workforce frustration and reduced productivity. If the Kaizen Team meets resistance from leadership, the facilitator often gets involved to assure leadership that processes can be designed that meet the key tenet of effective process design—*minimum effort and expense to achieve optimal outcomes*—without exposing the organization to increased risk. Note: At this stage of the mapping process, less than 50 percent of the Post-its® typically carry the "VA" or "N" labels (and often far less than 50 percent).

3. *Confirm that all unlabeled steps represent unnecessary non-value-adding activities.* Scan the map one more time to assure that all remaining (unlabeled) steps represent waste and are, therefore, targets for elimination. *Note*: Some lean practitioners prefer to have their teams classify and label every single step. Labeling only those that are value-adding and necessary non-value-adding likely creates a stronger visual statement about the degree to which waste exists in the process and prevents the map from becoming cluttered with labels.

   - *Calculate additional summary metrics.* Now that the team has identified which activities are value-adding, two additional metrics can be used to provide further understanding about the current state and set the stage for innovative future state design: *Percent Value-adding (%VA)*—the percentage of critical path lead time during which value-adding work is being performed. To calculate %VA, add together the process times for the critical path steps that are labeled VA (do not include the "N" steps). Divide by the total lead time for the critical path:

$$\%VA = \frac{\text{Sum of PT for all Critical Path VA Steps}}{\text{Total Critical Path LT}} \times 100$$

   Since some of your process time is typically consumed by non-value-adding activities, the %VA is usually lower—often *significantly* lower—than the Activity Ratio described in Chapter 12. And if you're analyzing a support process in which no value is being provided (from your external customer's perspective), the %VA is 0.

   Some lean practitioners prefer not to use this metric for support processes that are necessary to operate the business but do not deliver direct value to the customer. They fear it will demotivate a team that's been charged with improving a process. But, when discussed in a constructive manner, a 0%VA finding can drive Kaizen Teams to be even more innovative in their efforts to reduce waste than if they ignored the fact that *none of the activities in the process are value-adding when viewed from the external customer's perspective*. If the team ignores a 0%VA finding, it also risks perpetuating the disconnect that often exists between internal support departments and external customers. To become lean enterprises, internal support departments need to think as much about the organization's external customers as those who provide direct value. This is another reason why Kaizen Events are so powerful when used in office and technical environments.

- Percent Value-Adding Steps (%VA Steps): the percentage of process steps in which value-adding work is being performed. To calculate %VA Steps, count the number of VA steps and divide by the total number of steps in the process (including all parallel activities):

$$\%VA\ Steps = \frac{\#\ VA\ steps}{Total\ \#\ Steps} \times 100$$

In most cases, neither of these metrics are used for ongoing measurement, but they're often helpful for illustrating the amount of waste and, therefore, opportunity present in the current state. In addition to the shock value provided by a 0–10% VA finding, it can be a powerful stimulant for change for a team to learn that only 7 out of 46 steps add value in the eyes of the external customer. Remember, if an activity is non-value-adding, it merely adds organizational expense.

4. *Highlight the process steps that contain the greatest waste.* The facilitator should review the Event objectives once more with the team and then have them highlight those steps that contain some of the most obvious and largest wastes. Examples include steps (or process segments) with exceptionally long lead times, poor quality (low %C&A), and other barriers to flow such as batching. Extended process times are also relevant, because reducing process time reduces lead time. If freeing capacity is an event objective (so the organization can absorb additional work without increasing staffing by its usual proportions), reducing work effort (process time) is a legitimate improvement objective.

The team can visually highlight the most significant opportunities for waste reduction in several ways: by placing a specific color Post-it® above the relevant process step, by circling the step or the metric targeted for improvement with a brightly colored marker, or by turning the Post-it® on its side. The key is creating a clear visual to guide the team as it begins prioritizing improvements.

At this point in the Kaizen Event, the team members are typically clear about where the waste lies in the process. But they may not know why it exists. So, before they begin designing the future state, they need to dig a little deeper and uncover the root cause(s) for the waste they've identified. The root causes that team members uncover will prove the true target for elimination rather than the waste itself, which is merely a symptom of an underlying problem.

# ROOT CAUSE ANALYSIS (RCA) TOOLS

As discussed in Chapter 1, and noted in the last column of Table 1-3, waste is a symptom of an underlying root cause. This means that the team's primary target for elimination isn't the waste itself—it's the root cause of that waste. Root cause is defined as the *fundamental reason for the breakdown or failure of a process* which, when properly resolved, prevents a recurrence of the problem. If the Kaizen Team doesn't peel back the layers of the onion to reveal the true root cause of waste, it risks creating two undesirable outcomes: 1) designing suboptimal solutions that treat only the symptoms or only partially resolve the problem; and 2) designing solutions that resolve the problem short term, but allow waste to creep back into the process because the root cause hasn't been fully eliminated. Without proper root cause analysis, the team risks jumping to conclusions and/or creating "Band-aid®" fixes.

Those familiar with Total Quality Management (TQM) or Six Sigma methodologies will find some familiar friends here. The fundamental tools for root cause analysis include:

- The Five Whys
- Cause-and-Effect Diagrams
- Check Sheets
- Pareto Charts

## Five Whys

The *five whys* is a simple tool that reveals the root cause of a problem. It's accomplished by asking "why?" several times until you have determined the ultimate reason for the problem. When investigating an issue, turning to the five whys keeps teams from talking only about symptoms, and from automatically accepting the initial response they receive about what the problem is. The five whys encourage team members to uncover the deeper issues that are causing problems.

Here's an example of the five whys at work: During a Kaizen Event, one of the team members, Jim, revealed that he was having difficulty keeping up with the value-adding work for which he was responsible and shared that he was spending 25 minutes per day generating an error report for his supervisor. The team embarked on the five whys and reached a surprisingly common conclusion:

a. Why #1 – They asked Jim *why* he compiled this daily error report. He told the group that he didn't know what the report was used for but that his supervisor required it.

b. Why #2 – The team called the supervisor and asked her *why* she required Jim to run the report. She said it was among the daily reports her predecessor had listed on a daily reports log and admitted that she hadn't found time to figure out what she should be doing with the data.

c. Why #3 – So the team called the predecessor (who still worked for the company) and asked *why* he had required the report. He said he had created the report two years earlier when the data entry clerk had been making a lot of errors. The report highlighted these errors so a review team could fix them before they were passed on to the customer.

d. Why #4 – The next question—*why* was the data entry clerk making errors?—also included a current state analysis component—are the errors still occurring today? To the team's surprise, they learned that the data entry errors hadn't occurred for quite some time. They further learned that, at the time the report was originally created, the company was receiving orders by fax and the quality of the output for this particular fax machine was poor. So the order entry people had difficulty reading the orders. They raised the issue but the supervisor couldn't get approval to buy a new fax machine.

In this case, the team members discovered the root cause in only four whys. And they discovered that this organization did what a lot of companies do: They added an inspection step rather than correcting the problem through root cause analysis and mistake proofing. It was likely far more expensive to add the inspection step than it would have been to purchase a new fax machine. But here's the real kicker: A new fax machine *was* finally purchased and, at the time of the Kaizen Event, had been in place for 10 months. That's why the data entry errors were no longer occurring. But no one had revised the process to reflect the improved state. So the reason for the admittedly inappropriate fix was long gone, but the old process remained because no one had taken the time to stop and look at it. This is the value of the focused attention that Kaizen Events allow. It creates an environment that enables a team to understand the true nature of a defined problem and design the most effective improvement. In this case, a simple five-minute activity revealed that the report could be discontinued immediately, with no consequences to the organization or downstream customers to the process, freeing 25 minutes of Joe's time per day, during which he could perform value-adding work or participate in continuous improvement activities. An added benefit of performing this root cause analysis step was that the team discussed the possibility of automating order submission to eliminate the need for data entry altogether. This idea was placed on the Improvement Ideas List (Tab 7 on the Kaizen Event tools) for consideration as a follow-on improvement activity.

The five whys tool doesn't always reveal waste's root cause but, because of its simplicity, you should always attempt it. If the process issues are too varied or complicated for the simplicity of the five whys, you can graduate to the cause-and-effect diagram.

## Cause-and-Effect Diagram

As shown in Figure 13-2, the *cause-and-effect diagram*, also referred to as a *fishbone* or *Ishikawa diagram* (after its developer), is a visual tool that aids in brainstorming and documenting potential causes and subcauses for an undesired effect or outcome. The cause-and-effect diagram provides structure to the team's brainstorming efforts to reduce the risk of overlooking a valid reason for a particular outcome. Six categories of reasons are considered, referred to as the "6 Ms" as an easy way to remember the categories. Some improvement professionals have replaced two of the original "Ms" with labels they feel are more

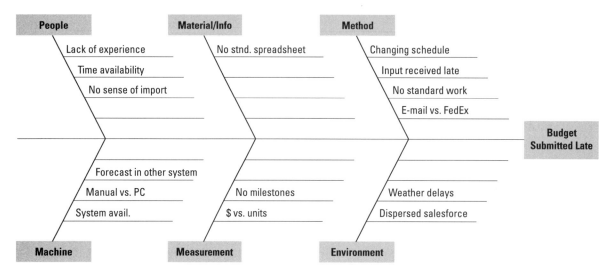

**Figure 13-2.** Cause-and-Effect Diagram for Late Budget Submissions

appropriate for today's work environments. Table 13-1 lists both types, as well as their meanings. It's your choice which set of labels you want to use. Some problems call for different labels all together. Pick the ones that best fit the problem you're trying to solve.

**Table 13-1.** Cause-and-Effect Diagram Label Definitions

| CAUSE-AND-EFFECT DIAGRAM LABELS | | |
|---|---|---|
| **Original Labels** | **Modified Labels** | **Explanation—Could the issue be related to:** |
| Man | People | The people performing the task. Do they possess the necessary skills? Have they been properly trained? Do they understand the purpose of their role? Do they care? |
| Material | Material/Information | The material or information being used. Is material of poor quality? Is information 100% complete and accurate? Are materials available? |
| Machine | Equipment | The equipment being used. Does it function properly? Is it available when needed? Is it up-to-date technology? Is it properly maintained? Does it produce high-quality output? Is it reliable? Are proper tools/supplies available? |
| Method | Process | The procedure/process in place. Does a defined process/standard work exist? Is it up-to-date and correct? Is it easy to follow? Does it contain visuals? Is it being adhered to? Is there a process for revising procedures as improvement opportunities are identified? |
| Measurement | Measurement | The measurement itself. Do metrics exist? Are they easy to understand? Does the report say what you think it's saying? Do the numbers mean what we think they mean? Are they accurate? Is the right thing being measured? |
| Mother Nature | Work Environment | The physical work environment, whether inside or outside. Is it too hot or cold? Is there adequate space? Is lighting adequate? Are there distractions such as noise, odors and interruptions? Are ergonomic issues present? Do good visuals exist? Is outdoor weather a factor? |

The cause-and-effect diagram does not provide solutions. It enables the Kaizen Team to consider the full spectrum of possible reasons for a defined outcome or problem. A finance department created the cause-and-effect diagram in Figure 13-2 in response to its ongoing problem of budgets being submitted late, which created a crunch in the department.

The next step after creating a cause-and-effect diagram is to narrow down the list of possible causes to the most likely contributors. The team members can winnow their choices based on process knowledge, objective data (if available), or through informal polling. From the narrowed list, the team can begin identifying the most likely contributors, which may require the use of a check sheet to tally the frequency of occurrences.

## Check Sheets

A *check sheet* is a simple analytical tool that is used to collect and record process data in an organized way, for a short period of time. The results enable Kaizen Teams to focus their attention on higher-incidence root causes rather than lower-incidence ones. Table 13-2 shows a check sheet for late product deliveries. Check sheets also provide factual data that helps the team transition from relying on subjective information (I think . . ." or "it seems that . . .") to drive improvement decisions to using objective data, which reduces the risk of invalid conclusions.

**Table 13-2.** Sample Check Sheet

| Reason | Occurrences | | | | | | |
|---|---|---|---|---|---|---|---|
| Material shortage | III | | | | | | |
| Quality issue requiring rework | IIII | | | | | | |
| Staffing/absenteeism | I | | | | | | |
| Order entry error | IIIII | IIIII | I | | | | |
| Changing customer requirements w/ no adjustment to promised delivery date | IIIII | IIIII | IIIII | IIII | | | |
| Equipment failure | I | | | | | | |

Maintaining a check sheet should not be a cumbersome, long-standing process. You can have your staff tally occurrences on check sheets for a limited period time. The Kaizen Team needs just enough reliable data to make sound decisions. If a particular process problem is clear enough before the Kaizen Event and/or a cause-and-effect diagram has already been created, check sheet tallies are often done as homework prior to the event. Except for high-volume processes, it can be tough to get data quickly enough during an event to impact the team's decisions. Once a check sheet is complete, the data is then often used to create a Pareto chart, a visual prioritization tool.

## Pareto Charts

Pareto charts, named after their developer, Vilfredo Pareto, are visual aids for defining and prioritizing issues. Based on the notion that most of the outcomes in a situation can be traced back to a small number of contributors, the chart helps improvement teams focus on the "vital few" reasons for an issue rather than the "trivial many."

As shown in Figure 13-3, Pareto charts rank occurrences in the order of frequency, from the most to the least frequent. Constructed from check sheet tallies, survey results, and the like, Pareto charts help Kaizen Teams leverage their time and energy by focusing on resolving 20 percent of the contributors that account for 80 percent of the occurrences. They concentrate their efforts on eliminating the root cause(s) for the few categories that account for the majority of the issues.

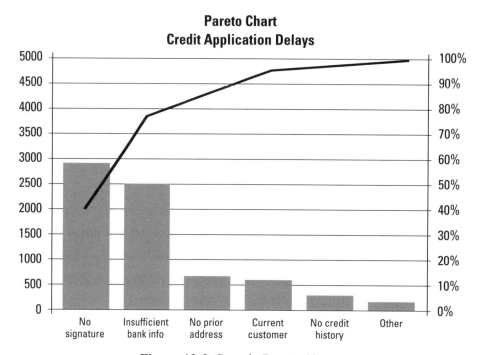

**Figure 13-3.** Sample Pareto Chart

The results of check sheet tallies, presented mathematically, reach the same conclusions as a Pareto chart. However, Kaizen Teams often benefit by seeing the results visually displayed. While a quick glance at a list of issues and their frequencies will tell the team which issues are the most frequent, a Pareto chart provides an obvious way to see which combination of issues occupy the top 80 percent and should be the team's highest priority. If cause-and-effect diagrams and check sheet tallies have been created (or other data compiled) prior to the Kaizen Event, creating the Pareto chart can be one of the team's first prioritization exercises. So now that the team has identified the root causes behind the wastes, how exactly should it go about resolving the issues? Which wastes should the team members eliminate first? What tools do they need to apply? What should the MBPM look like when they've eliminated waste and resolved the process problems that impede flow? These questions are answered in the next chapter, Brainstorming and Prioritizing Improvement Options.

# CHAPTER 14

# BRAINSTORMING AND PRIORITIZING IMPROVEMENT OPTIONS

Now that the Kaizen Team members have identified the root causes for the waste that they discovered in the target process, it's time for them to begin designing the future state. But without a structured approach, teams often fall short of their innovative capabilities, or they focus their attention on lower priority improvements instead of the most critical process needs. Structure also helps teams pass through the "storming" and "norming" team development stages, and move into the "performing" phase, during which the team generates the desired results.

This chapter focuses on a five-step process that provides the structure to help teams generate aggressive outcomes:

1. Review the current state map with "future state eyes."
2. Stimulate innovative thinking, and reduce resistance to new ideas.
3. Provide improvement tools training (or refresher).
4. Conduct a brainstorming session to generate improvement ideas.
5. Evaluate and prioritize improvement ideas.

## REVIEW THE CURRENT STATE MAP

First, the facilitator should have the team members review the Event objectives once again, and their current state findings (MBPM, photos, data, spaghetti diagrams, etc.), now that they are fully focused on creating an improved state. As they study the MBPM (if created), they should pay particular attention to the areas they highlighted earlier that offer the greatest opportunities for improvement, and consider the following questions:

1. How could the team design the process so that the "thing" passing through the process moves from one value-adding ("VA") or necessary ("N") step to the next, *bypassing all unnecessary, non-value-adding steps*?

2. How could the team create flow in the process so that the product (service or good) being delivered *never stops* and never has to be reworked?

3. Does the process include batching, buildup of queues/work-in-process (WIP), motion, unbalanced work, excessive multitasking, excessive handoffs and/or approvals that the team could eliminate or reduce?

4. Which steps have low *%C&A*? How can the team standardize and mistake proof the work to reduce variation and errors?

5. Which process steps have *long process times* that, if reduced, would also reduce the lead time?

## STIMULATE INNOVATION

Next, to stimulate creativity and innovative thinking, and reduce the natural resistance to change, the facilitator should discuss the change process and share techniques for stimulating innovation. During discussions about the key elements for successful change and the role of paradigms in resisting change, it is useful to show Joel Barker's DVD, *The New Business of Paradigms*,[1] to help team members stretch their thinking and become more receptive to innovative ideas.

## PROVIDE IMPROVEMENT TOOLS TRAINING

Once the team has been primed to accept new ideas, the facilitator should provide a brief training session to introduce (or review) the most relevant tools that could be used to improve the particular target process. A skilled facilitator will know which tools prove the most relevant, given the event objectives, current state findings, the type of process being improved, and how many improvement efforts the process has gone through. In the early stages of improvement, office and service environment Kaizen Teams typically focus on removing the "noise" in the process—the gross obstacles to flow—and standardizing the process. Once a standard exists, Kaizen Teams in subsequent events to further improve the process can more effectively balance the work, create pull systems, and level load demand. A third phase of improvement may be needed to achieve more refined process control. Table 14-1 lists some of the more common tactical-level improvement tools that Kaizen Teams often turn to. As mentioned in the Preface, it's beyond the scope of this book to offer detailed explanations about each improvement tool available. Consult the many resources available to deepen your understanding of how to apply these tools.

## BRAINSTORM TO GENERATE IMPROVEMENT IDEAS

The key to an innovative future state lies in the quality and volume of ideas the Kaizen Team produces and the subsequent prioritization of those ideas. To discover improvements that will yield the greatest results, facilitators often rely on classic brainstorming, an idea-generating team activity for identifying and solving problems. It is based on the concept that teams generate more creative ideas in an interactive group environment than do individuals working independently. The typical steps for this phase of improvement are:

1. Define the problem
2. Generate ideas via brainstorming
3. Review and evaluate ideas
4. Evaluate, prioritize, and select ideas

---

1. Joel Barker Productions, 2001.

**Table 14-1.** Lean Improvement Tools

| IMPROVEMENT TOOLS | |
|---|---|
| **Standard Work/Quality at the Source** <ul><li>Visual work instructions</li><li>Checklists</li><li>"Cheat sheets"</li><li>Flowcharts</li><li>Data entry rules</li><li>Mistake proofing</li><li>Metrics-based process maps</li><li>Interdepartmental service agreements</li><li>Other job aids</li><li>Samples of good and bad products</li></ul><br>**Co-location/Cells** | **Visuals Management / 5Ss** <ul><li>Metrics boards</li><li>Signage</li><li>Labeling</li><li>Color coding</li><li>Workplace organization</li></ul>**Pull Systems** <ul><li>One-piece flow</li><li>FIFO lanes</li><li>Kanban</li></ul>**Work Balancing and Level Loading** <ul><li>Multifunctional workers</li><li>Takt time</li><li>Heijunka systems</li></ul> |

Since brainstorming is the critical transition point as the team moves from documenting the current state to creating an improved process, the following section looks at this process more closely.

## Define the Problem

First, to prevent the Kaizen Team from straying from its path, the facilitator restates the problem(s) for which the team is seeking solutions. The specific issue the team is looking to solve may be one of the items included within the Event Drivers/Current State Issues or Event Objectives sections of the Kaizen Event Charter. Alternatively, the problem for which the team is looking for solutions may be a subset of the aforementioned issues and objectives (e.g., the team may have identified lead-time reduction within one specific step as the specific issue to be brainstormed). The facilitator should remind the team about its goal several times during the brainstorming session to reduce the risk of team members personalizing process solutions, and to ensure the team stays on track.

## Generate Ideas via Brainstorming

Before the idea generation phase begins, the facilitator should encourage the group to relax (instilling a playful environment helps), and review the three primary rules for brainstorming:

- *There are no bad ideas*—no matter how outlandish, silly, seemingly impossible, or even illegal they may be. At this point, quality isn't a goal—quantity is. Successful brainstorming requires idea generation without analysis, judgment, or logic. *All* ideas are acceptable and encouraged—even those that violate company policy, or break an industry standard. This no-holds-barred thinking often generates more practical and appropriate solutions as participants build on each others' ideas.

- *It's okay to build on the ideas of others.* For the previously stated reasons, team members should be encouraged to contribute new variations of ideas already mentioned.

- *Avoid judgment* until all ideas are on the table. Successful brainstorming requires that people suspend their natural tendency to evaluate, criticize, and be quick to judge. Since it's common for people to begin evaluating ideas as they're being suggested, it's the facilitator's job to intercede immediately by reminding the team of this classic brainstorming rule. Don't let the team move out of the creativity mode.

While there are many ways to structure brainstorming sessions, the two methods described below typically generate good results:

- *Round robin.* In this approach, the facilitator asks each team member, one-by-one (usually in seating order), for an idea. If a person doesn't have an idea to offer during a particular round, he or she says "pass," and the facilitator moves on to the next person. The facilitator repeats this process until the ideas stop flowing or time runs out (see timing considerations later in this chapter).

- *Free-for-all.* This approach often works best for teams that include shy or inexperienced team members, because it reduces the anxiety that sometimes occurs when it's "your turn" in round robin sessions. In the free-for-all approach, team members offer their ideas at any time, in no particular order. Since they aren't required to give a response in this approach, and since it is the facilitator's job to stimulate the team to generate as many ideas as possible, the facilitator must draw out quiet team members to distinguish between shyness and a lack of ideas.

An essential element of successful brainstorming involves the speed and timing for generating ideas. Obtaining ideas rapidly reduces the risk of doubt entering in, which causes team members to censor or filter their ideas. The adage introduced in Chapter 2 that rings especially true during brainstorming sessions is "think long, think wrong."

Another essential element for successful brainstorming is establishing a session endpoint up front, so the team knows what the boundaries are. Here, the facilitator may either: 1) set a time limit; or 2) set a goal for a specific number of ideas. The best bet may be a combination of the two: Set a time limit and an idea goal, based on the complexity of the problem and anticipated volume of ideas (for example: 20 minutes or 40 ideas). With this approach, the facilitator ends the session when the designated time runs out or the idea limit is reached, whichever comes first. When setting a quantity goal, set the bar high to reduce the risk that the team quits before it has generated all possible ideas. Some additional tips for running a productive brainstorming session are:

- Keep the mood light, interjecting humor whenever possible.

- Give frequent positive feedback—say, "Good!" and "Excellent idea!" and "Thank you!"

- Move quickly! A quick pace generates a greater number of ideas. Say, "Next" while you're still writing the previous idea on the board.

- Continuously remind the team not to censor themselves, nor evaluate any ideas.

- Remind the team that it's okay to build on each other's ideas.

During the session, the facilitator should record and number the ideas on a flip chart or white board so the team can see the ideas that have been suggested, which prevents excessive duplication and stimulates variations on the ideas presented. As the team studies the suggested ideas, it will often stimulate other ideas. (*Note to facilitators*: You'll have to write fast. Ask the team to help you keep track of the ideas in case you fall behind in writing. You can also have a second person record every other suggestion.)

To keep the ideas flowing, try these techniques:

- Gently prod the team using the pressure of time: "Five more minutes!" Encourage a quick pace by saying, "Next." "Next." "Next."

- The facilitator is authorized to contribute ideas.

- If team members laugh at a "ridiculous idea," remind them that they're judging, record the idea, and challenge the team by asking, "If that won't work, what will?"

- When the flow of ideas begins to slow, prod the team to produce ten more ideas. When they slow further, ask them: "What if we brought in the CEO? What might he or she suggest?" "What might the VP of sales & marketing suggest?" "How would you solve this problem if you owned the company?" Keep doing this (with smaller and smaller quantity targets as the pace slows) until no more ideas are generated—or until many of the ideas being suggested are becoming impractical and/or unreasonable because the team has exhausted the pool of viable ideas.

When the idea generation phase ends, congratulate the team members, and encourage them to give themselves a round of applause. A five- or ten-minute break at this point will help the team shift from brainstorming, a right-brain activity that requires creativity, to the evaluation stage, which is analytical and relies more heavily on the left portion of the brain.

## EVALUATE, PRIORITIZE, AND SELECT IDEAS

Next, the team must begin the process of eliminating ideas that aren't practical, wouldn't solve the defined problem, or are outside of the event scope. After evaluating their ideas, team members select which improvements they will implement during the remainder of the event.

### Evaluate Ideas.

Evaluating ideas for their appropriateness for improving process performance involves four steps.

1. *Eliminate duplicate ideas*. When generating ideas quickly and without evaluation, duplicates sometimes occur. In addition, two team members may suggest the same improvement, expressed in two different ways.

2. *Combine similar ideas*. Look for ideas that, while different, are similar in how they would be implemented. For example, perhaps quality could be improved in several different areas by implementing a single standard work checklist.

3. *Eliminate ideas that don't conform to law, ethics, safety criteria, industry standards, and, in some cases, organizational policy.* Organizational policy is fair game to be challenged when improving processes and a common step in streamlining office-based work processes. However, all ideas that violate law, established standards, etc.—or would place the organization at risk—should be eliminated.

4. *Eliminate ideas that are beyond the scope of the Kaizen Event or are not relevant for accomplishing the Event objectives.* Maintaining focus is a key success factor in Kaizen Events. The team should eliminate all ideas that will not directly help achieve the event objectives, as well as those that go beyond the team's boundaries of empowerment.

At this point, the facilitator should number the feasible ideas. As he/she is doing so, the Kaizen Team may discover that they've generated more ideas than can be implemented within the remaining time allotted for the event. As shown in Figure 14-1, the Idea List (Tab 7 on the Kaizen Event Tools file) can be used to record all of the improvement ideas generated during the brainstorming session (*Note*: The Idea List can also house those ideas generated by the workforce prior to the Event, and additional ideas that are suggested during the Event. The "now" column is checked next to those ideas that will be fully implemented during the Kaizen Event.)

| Kaizen Event Improvement Ideas | | | | | |
|---|---|---|---|---|---|
| Executive Sponsor | | | Event Name | | |
| Value Stream Champion | | | Event Dates | | |
| Facilitator | | | | | |
| Team Lead | | | | | |
| | Improvement | | Now | Later | Owner / Work Group |
| 1 | | | ☐ | ☐ | |
| 2 | | | ☐ | ☐ | |
| 3 | | | ☐ | ☐ | |
| 4 | | | ☐ | ☐ | |
| 5 | | | ☐ | ☐ | |
| 6 | | | ☐ | ☐ | |
| 7 | | | ☐ | ☐ | |
| 8 | | | ☐ | ☐ | |
| 9 | | | ☐ | ☐ | |
| 10 | | | ☐ | ☐ | |

**Figure 14-1.** Improvement Ideas (partial view)

Next, the team needs to prioritize the ideas and decide which ones they will fully implement during the event versus those that need to be implemented at some later point.

## Prioritize Ideas

To ensure the team spends its time wisely and avoids trying to take on too much, the facilitator leads the team in prioritizing the improvement ideas they generated. The PACE chart (Figure 14-2), is a simple and effective prioritization tool that provides a systematic way to rank ideas. Similar to other prioritization tools, the PACE chart consists of four quadrants in which the Kaizen Team places its ranking for each improvement idea, based on two criteria:

how easy the team believes the improvement would be to implement, and to what degree they feel the improvement would benefit the organization. PACE is an acronym for **P**riority – **A**ction – **C**onsider – **E**liminate, which reflects the order in which improvements should be implemented and/or eliminated from consideration. Without this degree of structure, teams often wrestle with prioritization and enter into extended debates, robbing them of the time they need to actually implement the improvements.

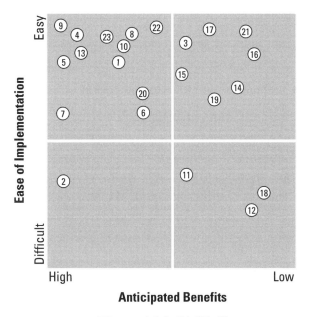

**Figure 14-2.** PACE Chart

Figure 14-2 shows a completed sample PACE Chart. Here a Kaizen Team generated 23 improvement ideas, then ranked them in terms of implementation ease and anticipated benefit to the organization. *Ease* (*y* axis) includes issues, such as: cost, degree of leadership support, complexity, time requirements, competing priorities, anticipated workforce acceptance or resistance to the improvement, customer perception, technical difficulty, and other issues unique to the process and organizational culture.

The team also evaluated each improvement's likely *benefit* (*x* axis) to the organization, in relationship to the Kaizen Event objectives and the five primary aspects of organizational performance: quality, cost, delivery, safety, and morale. To what degree would the improvement impact organizational performance in this/these area(s) and achieve event objectives?

The facilitator leads the team in evaluating one idea at a time and ranking it, one axis at a time. In other words, determine first where the idea should be placed on the *y*-axis from difficult to easy, then determine where it should be placed in terms of benefit. The ranking process moves along more quickly if the facilitator places his or her hand at the bottom left corner of the grid, and begins moving it slowly from bottom to top, instructing the team to tell him or her to stop when the facilitator's hand has reached the *y* axis location that best approximates how easy it would be to implement the improvement. From the spot, the facilitator begins moving his or her hand slowly to the right. The team tells him or her to stop when his or her hand reaches the position that approximates the degree to which the improvement would benefit (as defined by the team) the process and the organization. The facilitator writes the idea's number in that location. And so on. Keep in mind that the objective is to evaluate the ideas relative to each other, so don't let the team overanalyze and spend excessive time debating the exact placement of each idea's number.

## Select Ideas

After the improvement idea numbers have been placed on the PACE chart, in the location that best represents how easy and beneficial each improvement would be, the facilitator draws prioritization "bands" that group the improvements into four prioritization categories.

As shown in Figure 14-3, you'll notice that the bands are not evenly spaced across the prioritization grid. Rather, they are placed with a slight bias toward the easier-to-implement, "quick hit" improvements. The ideas that fall into the "P" (*priority*) section are typically implemented first because they have been classified as the easiest to adopt and have the highest anticipated benefit. The next round of improvements (possibly during a follow-on Kaizen Event) would include those ideas in the "A" (*action*) section since, although they have a lower anticipated benefit they, too, are easy to implement. Ideas that fall into the "C" (*consider*) section should be evaluated more closely, to determine if implementation is really as difficult as the Kaizen Team ranked it on the matrix, and, if so, whether the outcome is worth the effort. Improvements in the "C" section are often strong candidates for return on investment (ROI) analyses before proceeding with implementation.

Because the ideas that fall into the "E" section would be difficult to implement and yield low benefits, and because you likely have higher priorities waiting for space on your

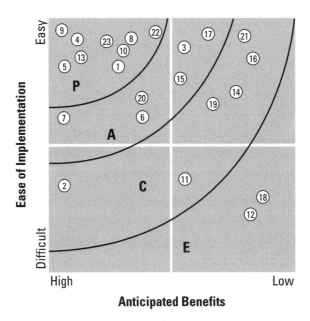

**Figure 14-3.** PACE Chart with Prioritization Bands

improvement schedule, you *eliminate* these "E" ideas. Another common development in organizations that are aggressively implementing improvements is that once they have implemented the "P" and "A" ideas, the process will have shifted enough that it requires a fresh brainstorming and prioritization activity. So, in many cases the ideas in the "C" and "E" sections are never implemented. In other cases, as the organization gains experience and expertise in continuous improvement, ideas that teams initially perceived as being difficult to implement become easier and more feasible to put into place.

At this stage of the Kaizen Event, the team now knows what specific improvements they will be implementing. With the tools training the team members received prior to brainstorming, the facilitator can now lead them into the most exciting aspect of the Kaizen Event—designing and testing the actual improvements.

# CHAPTER 15

# DESIGNING AND TESTING IMPROVEMENTS

As a result of brainstorming and prioritizing improvement ideas, the Kaizen Team members now know what they are going to implement, and they are usually eager to dive in and produce results. But to ensure they make the best use of the time available and avoid going off in too many directions at once, a work plan is essential. This chapter will cover the structure under which teams typically produce the greatest results. As mentioned in the Preface, it's beyond the scope of this book to delve into specific applications for the variety of lean tools available for making process improvements. Many resources are available that address how to create cells, implement 5S, develop pull systems, create standard work, etc. Rather, this book focuses on the *process* for making change.

The work plan, whether formal or informal, specifies how the team will implement the improvements—the "do" and "check" stages of the micro PDCA cycle.

## CREATING A WORK PLAN

With the facilitator's guidance, the Kaizen Team should review the improvements selected for implementation within the Event and decide which team members are most appropriate for designing each improvement. Simple improvements may only require the involvement of one or two team members, whereas more extensive improvements may require the entire Kaizen Team's engagement.

To maximize the team's output, it's often helpful to break the full Kaizen Team into smaller work groups of two to four team members, each tasked with specific improvements. For example, while one work group creates a job aid for performing a particular task, another one could establish new service standards and creating a visual tracking tool to monitor process performance. At the same time, a third work group could focus on calculating takt time and balancing the work for a particular portion of the process. When the first work group completes the job aid (and has tested it, as described in the next section), they may move on to another improvement, such as working with on-call IT staff to mistake proof data entry or 5Sing a shared drive that's a vital part of the process being improved. And so on. If a particular improvement requires the entire Kaizen Team's attention, or a work group wants the full team's input on an issue, the facilitator calls the work groups back together, and then splits them apart again as needed.

The Owner/Work Group column on the Improvement Ideas list (discussed in Chapter 14) can be used to keep track of work group assignments. (*Note*: The "later" column is included so you can also use this tool to archive ideas that are either outside the scope of the Kaizen Event or will require more time than is available during the Event.)

If the Kaizen Team divides into smaller work groups, the facilitator should hold status report sessions with the entire team at least twice a day. These 20- to 30-minute sessions enable the facilitator to monitor progress, and create cross-pollination among the work groups to ensure that the improvements are synchronized and consistent with each other and with event objectives. Throughout the day, the facilitator should remain actively engaged with each of the work groups to identify and remove obstacles to success, stimulate creativity, and teach improvement tools, as needed.

Before releasing the Kaizen Team to begin designing improvements (moving from the "planning" stage in the micro PDCA cycle to the "do" stage), the facilitator should set the time for the first status report session (when everyone needs to return to Kaizen Central) and remind the team of the following:

- The goal is to implement measurable, incremental improvements, so focus on what you can *fully* implement within the event itself. Remind team members that they aren't trying to solve world hunger in one Kaizen Event.

- All improvements should make work *easier*, not more difficult, and no improvement should produce a negative overall impact. The work groups must think through the improvement carefully to avoid creating unintended negative consequences.

- They are not implementing permanent, perfect improvements that can never be altered. Continuously improving how work is done is the fifth lean principle—seek perfection. The Kaizen Team should focus on designing an improvement that will generate positive measurable results and avoid the paralysis that can occur if team members become overly concerned with creating perfection. They should view their initial designs as well thought out experiments rather than changes that are set in stone. This spirit of experimentation also helps reduce resistance among the workforce that will be impacted by the improvement.

- Piloting works well for larger scale improvements. If, for example, the team wants to change a process that affects the entire organization, it might consider rolling out the change in one department, one regional office, or with one customer group first, and work out the bugs before rolling it out across the entire organization. Pilot rollouts should be determined and clearly defined while initially scoping the event and drafting the Kaizen Event charter.

- Only leave Kaizen Central if the team needs to get input from people who are not on the team, physically observe the process or the area being improved, or test the improvement (described below).

This last bullet point is a critical step in a Kaizen Event and one that teams often fail to perform. While the Kaizen Team includes representation from a broad cross section of the workforce, specific departments may only have one or two representatives on the team. So, to create the best improvements and obtain broad-scale buy-in that sets the stage for sustainability, the Kaizen Team members should consult with peers outside the team as they are designing and testing the improvements. The greater the number of users affected by the change, the more important this level of involvement becomes. There is nothing more frustrating to a workforce or more damaging to your Kaizen Events than having a team sequestered four days only to have an improvement fail because it was designed with only one person's perspective and/or wasn't thoroughly tested. Testing improvements is a necessary step in minimizing the risk of failure.

## TESTING IMPROVEMENTS

The primary purpose of testing—the "C" (check) in the micro PDCA—is to work out the kinks in the improvement prior to full implementation to ensure the Kaizen Team has considered all options and has created as fail-proof a way of operating as possible. Testing also reduces the risk that an upstream improvement creates negative, unintended consequences downstream. Most importantly, testing helps determine training requirements (discussed in Chapter 16) and the "teeth" the team needs to put into place to sustain the improvement (discussed in Chapter 17).

In the design phase, the Kaizen Team creates drafts, prototypes, samples, and so forth of the planned improvement—*which may be hand drawn at this point*. In office and service Kaizen Events, testing ranges from reviewing the draft for a job aid to ensure it's as complete and accurate as possible, to conducting a test run for a new order-entry process, to placing cardboard models in a work area to test a new layout before furniture is physically moved.

As the Kaizen Team creates the drafts or prototypes for the improvements, it will need to decide how to test the improvements. Will it test the improvement in the "real world" or will it need to simulate the change first? While improvements generate greater results and are far more sustainable when tested in the *real situation* in which they will occur, simulation is advisable when making high-risk improvements, changing a low-volume or infrequent process, or implementing improvements in a customer-facing environment. In all cases, Kaizen Teams need to test their improvements in the area(s) directly impacted by the change(s) before rolling out the improvement. When testing improvements affecting the workforce in locations physically removed from Kaizen Central, the team can use e-mail and conference calls to solicit feedback.

This brings up an important point. Because it is difficult to predict up front the specific improvements the team will focus on, scheduling testing can be logistically challenging. The earlier in the process the team can predict 1) what needs to be tested, 2) when the testing will likely occur, 3) how long it will last, and 4) who needs to be involved, the smoother the testing phase. If testers don't have sufficient time to plan for the test, and have multiple priorities competing for their attention, they may rush through the test, and, as a result, provide poor feedback. Without adequate review and feedback, the improvement may need major adjustments immediately following the Kaizen Event, which places the improvement at higher risk for failure.

Once the testing requirements have been determined, the team will need to decide how many reviewers/testers they should involve and who specifically would be a reliable reviewer/tester. Engage as many people who will be impacted by the improvement as possible. If the improvement involves a small department, the team should try to engage the majority of the staff in the review and test phase. If the department is large, the team should solicit input from an appropriate representative sample.

The event facilitator should encourage the team to be strategic when selecting workers to test improvements. Teams should be including a sample of the workers who will be using the improvement or doing work a new way, as well as some downstream customers who will receive altered input (the improved output from the upstream supplier). When possible, they should select at least one person from the following categories of users:

- Someone relatively new to the company or to the job.

- Experienced workers.

- At least one influence leader (someone whom the workers respect and tend to follow).

- A chronic complainer (when complainers are part of the improvement process, they often become the greatest advocates for change).

If the Kaizen Team integrates feedback from these four types of workers, it is far more likely to implement an effective improvement with staying power.

Another testing requirement is that the Kaizen Team needs to receive rapid response from the testing process. Be aware that nonteam member colleagues who are not on the Kaizen Team may not understand the team's time constraints and may be slow in providing feedback. It's best that the Kaizen Team prep any colleagues he or she approaches about what is meant by *rapid* improvement, as well as the team member's role in the Kaizen process. Communicating the need for a rapid response early on (such as while conducting pre-event communication and training) is helpful. As the organization becomes more seasoned with Kaizen Events, the workforce will become more familiar with the rapid response that is needed during an event.

For process steps that are not particularly lengthy, testing may take as little as 30 minutes to complete. Before commencing with the test, make sure the testers know exactly what they should be doing and how long they have to accomplish it. If the team is able to test improvement in real situations, have the tester try the new process with the next few occurrences of whatever work they're doing. If standard work is being created, the testers should review a draft of new or revised job aids, checklists, "cheat sheets," process flowcharts, and the like for complete and accurate information displayed in as user-friendly a manner as possible. To maximize improvement quality, the team should encourage the testers to be critical and detailed with their feedback.

At least one of the Kaizen Team members responsible for the improvement should be present during testing to *observe*, *measure*, *record*, and *inquire*. Since experimentation is a key component of designing an improvement, it's best if the "scientist" directly *observes* the results of his or her experiment. In addition, team members themselves should measure and record results. If one of the objectives is to reduce the process time for a particular activity from 15 minutes to 5 minutes, one of the team members needs to *measure* the improved process (taking into account that learning curves will create slower process times initially) and *record* the results to share with the rest of the Kaizen Team. One of the most important elements of testing is *inquiring* how the worker performing the improved process feels about it and whether or not he or she sees opportunities for additional improvements.

The Kaizen Team members should record the testers' suggestions and, if they are sound, take one of three actions:

- If sufficient time remains in the event, incorporate the suggestion into the process.
- If the suggestion would benefit the process, but insufficient time remains in the event to incorporate it into the improved process, add the enhancement to the 30-Day List (discussed in Chapter 17).
- If the suggestion is beyond the scope of the event, it should be added to the Idea List ("later" categories) or Parking Lot Issues (discussed in Chapter 17) and discussed with leadership.

If testing is merely reviewing documentation for a new process, the testers can read it on their own, mark up the document, and then meet with the responsible kaizen work group to review their findings. But if the test is a trial run for a new process that involves physically performing a task, the responsible Kaizen Event work group should be present to observe the process in action. Likewise, if the test involves physically moving office equipment or furniture, the Kaizen Team members responsible for that improvement should direct the move. Team member presence during the test enables the "adjustment" process. If problems arise, Kaizen Team members have the authority to adjust the process immediately and retest. The challenge for the Kaizen Team is to make any necessary adjustments as quickly as possible, so they can prepare for the training that needs to occur before the Kaizen Event concludes.

Once testing is complete, the team has incorporated the testers' feedback and has finalized the improvement, it's time to implement. In most office, service, and technical environments, the bulk of implementation is accomplished through training the effected workforce. Only with effective training and communication will the Kaizen Team achieve the ultimate goal that marks a successful Kaizen Event: The work must be performed differently *immediately following the Kaizen Event*. Chapter 16 addresses the step-by-step approach for this key success factor.

# CHAPTER 16

# IMPLEMENTING IMPROVEMENTS

Implementation is the stage during which the workforce transitions to the improved process. The implementation process goes more smoothly when the launch—the "go live" date—is definitive. One day the work is performed the old way, and the next day it is performed the new way. When shifts are present, the transition occurs between the two shifts closest to the end of the Kaizen Event. In each case, training is required to teach the workforce how to perform work the new way. What are the new steps? Who passes work to whom? If 5S has been part of the Kaizen Event, workers need to know where everything is located and what the new standards are for maintaining the environment. So the Kaizen Team's final step in implementing an improvement is providing workforce training. Here, in the "performing" stage of team development, the team moves into the "act" stage of the micro PDCA cycle.

The key question that the Kaizen Team must answer when considering its implementation strategy is, *"What preparation does the workforce need so the improvement is fully effective the next business day (or the next shift)?"* The same question applies to your customers, suppliers, and other external stakeholders if the improvement changes how they will interact with your organization. Even if the improvement doesn't affect outsiders' experience with your organization, you may want to communicate the improvement to demonstrate the organization's commitment to continuous improvement. Your goal is a smooth implementation that minimizes disruption and maximizes the ease of operating in the "new world order" that the Kaizen Team has created. The workers involved should have no doubt about what to do, and the downstream customers of upstream improvements should have no surprises.

Continuous improvement is about changing behavior—how we do things—to achieve improved performance. Proper training is essential to instill worker *confidence* in the new process, which leads to *competence* and, by extension, performance excellence. Effective training builds both knowledge (understanding "why") and skills (demonstrating "how"). It must be relevant, thorough, timely, and include the proper mix of training materials and methods to accommodate the range of learning styles any given workforce has: written/visual aids, verbal instruction, and demonstration (if relevant). If possible, the Kaizen Team should create a "test environment" that allows trainees to perform the improved process in a safe environment, where errors won't matter. This learn-do interactive training model results in faster learning than nonparticipatory methods.

While effective training doesn't *guarantee* improvement sustainability, it's unlikely that a process will have staying power without a properly trained workforce. When workers understand why an improvement was made, and are given proper instruction to develop competency, the improved process has a far greater likelihood of being sustained. If either or both of these elements are missing—or if the workers encounter problems with the new process and don't know whom to go to with their concerns—they will likely revert to their old familiar ways of getting work done. *Lack of appropriate training is a common reason why organizations fail to sustain improvements.*

So how do you train workers on a new process during a Kaizen Event? Quickly and effectively. This requires training in new and highly innovative ways that can quickly and effectively sell the change and prepare the workforce to perform differently. The primary lean tenet applies to training as well: Expend the minimal training effort required to achieve optimal worker performance. *Optimal performance* is the key. While workers typically experience a learning curve, by the end of the training, the affected workers need to have received all the necessary instruction and tools to ensure they can perform the new process effectively and with confidence. They should feel 100 percent prepared to operate in the new way.

## PLANNING FOR TRAINING

Training on the new process typically occurs on the last day of the event, although some teams are able to begin training workers the day before. But, before training can occur, the training approach must be developed, including the creation of training materials and the development of the training approach. In many cases, the team will only have access to the workers for a limited amount of time. How can teams achieve these seemingly incongruent realities and still offer effective training? They accomplish this through effective training materials, and the application of innovative "just-in-time, just-the-facts" approaches. When designing the training effort, key considerations include:

- How many people need to be trained?
- Where are the trainees physically located? In one building? Scattered across the country—or the world?
- What are the educational levels and learning styles for the targeted workers? (e.g., highly visual, more cerebral, etc.)
- Can you use a train-the-trainer approach to maximize the speed at which large groups of workers are trained?
- How much time will be required?
- What training mediums will be employed (e.g., in person, by phone, via e-mail with attachments, webinar-based, etc)?

Face-to-face training is by far the most desirable method for teaching a new process. The training is best if done in person and includes demonstration and trial runs. If geography is an issue, you can employ train-the-trainer methods, webinars, and other electronic means. The only hard and fast rule to abide by is to *never* rely solely on independent learning—it is typically ineffective. While you may use e-mail with attachments, computer-based training, or create learning modules that reside on a shared drive, the workforce affected by the improvement must have real-time access to a knowledgeable trainer, either in person or by phone.

Here's an example of an innovative and effective approach a Kaizen Team used when implementing a new process across a large cross section of their organization: The Kaizen Team had only four hours to train 500 engineers in six locations across the country on the new process for ordering materials. They had improved a process that had previously taken ten business days to complete, and projected the process could now be completed in two days (80 percent improvement). This team's training model required significant planning and excellent communication, but the success of this Kaizen Team proves that it's possible. The training, which the team began planning for on the second day of the five-day event, included global voice mails, e-mails with visual standard work attachments, written acknowledgement from the engineers that they understood the new process, and designated mentors that were available to assist the engineers for the first 30 days of the process. Because the training was complete, concise, relevant, and timely, the implementation went smoothly, and the new process has been sustained.

## TRAINING FORMATS

Depending on the number of people you need to train, their physical locations, the available technology, the nature of the improvement, and the learning preferences of the group to be trained, the Kaizen Team can choose from the following training methods and options. Often, a combination of methods provides the most effective training:

- *Work site training.* Training is often most effective if it's conducted in the physical location in which the improvement is being implemented (especially if 5S was employed). This approach is especially helpful with phone-based staffs that have difficulty leaving their area for more than a few minutes. In this case, the Kaizen Team creates and delivers a "roving training program," during which they teach the new process to the affected workforce one-on-one or in small groups.

- *Conference room training.* If the improvement involves a large group, and if a practice session conducted directly in the work area is not necessary, it may prove most efficient to conduct training sessions in conference/meeting/computer rooms. To provide maximum flexibility and to accommodate workers' schedules, teams often hold multiple training sessions throughout a two- to six-hour window. In this case, it's best if the workers commit to a session, so the Kaizen Team can plan accordingly. You might want to use a first-come-first-served approach and set a maximum number of attendees for each session.

- *Lunch 'n learn.* For simple improvements, the team could conduct training during a lunch 'n learn session. When the organization provides food, attendance is usually higher.

- *Global voice mail (accompanied by an e-mail with attachments).* You should only employ this training approach when no other viable option exists, but it can be extremely effective if well-executed. Here's how it works: Most voice mail systems allow at least a two- to three-minute message, permitting a fair amount of concise, well-organized information to be relayed. In this model, the Kaizen Team creates a carefully worded script, and has several people review it for clarity and accuracy before recording the message. At least one point of contact is included in the message so the recipients can ask questions. (*Note*: The team should consider the number of recipients and possible volume of questions when determining how many points of contacts to include.) When combined with e-mail, this option can produce strong results.

- *E-mail with attachments.* E-mail by itself is a woefully ineffective training device, but when combined with a descriptive voice mail, in-person training and/or assigned points of contact or mentors, it can be an effective component of a well-designed training program. It's best that the e-mail require a response to the sender confirming that the recipient received it, read it and understands the new process fully. The attachments could include new standard work tools, photos (with compressed file sizes), and PowerPoint presentations explaining the improvement, etc. It's best to follow-up the e-mail with in-person training, but e-mail accompanied by voice mail and with designated point of contacts may be the only way to roll out a new process across an entire organization with multiple locations.

- *Mentor(s)/Points of contact.* Assigning mentors to help the workforce get up to speed on a new process is a wise move. The mentors reinforce training, provide assistance when workers get stuck, and receive ongoing feedback from workers, which fuels future improvements. This model works best when Kaizen Team members serve as the mentors.

- *Train the Trainer.* When you need to train large groups of people, it's often helpful to have multiple trainers. Remember that the only failed Kaizen Event is one in which implementation doesn't occur. So, if you're using this method for training, the Kaizen Team must train the trainers and have the trainers train the affected workers *before the event ends*.

- *Webinars.* Webinars present a newer option for training large numbers of people simultaneously. However, there are disadvantages such as the risk that participants respond to e-mails or perform other work during the session, and the trainer is unable to read trainees' body language to gauge his or her understanding and acceptance. However, webinars do present a viable option when the trainees are geographically dispersed and/or travel extensively. Here, mentors should also be designated to provide follow-up support to workers.

A number of other training options exist. The key is selecting the most interactive, hands-on option that also accomplishes the primary goal of the Kaizen Event—full implementation of improvements, which includes workforce training, by the end of the event.

## GATHERING FEEDBACK

No matter which training method(s) the Kaizen Team chooses, it must identify and communicate one *single* point of contact for users and affected stakeholders to send feedback to regarding the improvement—and communicate this person's contact information during the training component. The point of contact (designated feedback gatherer), evaluates the feedback and suggestions for additional improvements to determine whether the issue is one that requires immediate process modification or is simply an enhancement. For the latter category of suggestions, it's best to wait until the process has been in place for a designated period of time, and then include these enhancements with other modifications that have surfaced along the way.

## ATTENDANCE

Since training the majority of the workforce affected by the improvement must occur within the Kaizen Event itself, *attendance at workforce training must be mandatory*. The only reason a worker wouldn't receive training within the event is if he or she is sick, on vacation, on jury duty, or has scheduled personal time off. If training on the improved process isn't a top priority, the workers won't know how to properly perform the new process, jeopardizing the chances that the improvements will be sustained.

The team should use a sign-in sheet to keep track of who's been trained and who needs to receive make-up training within the first few days following the Kaizen Event. If 100 percent of the affected workforce is not available to receive training during the Kaizen Event, the first task on the 30-Day List should be to provide makeup training to the affected workforce. Timing is critical, however; training must be held the moment people become available. Otherwise, a portion of the workforce will operate in the improved way, and a portion will operate the old way, creating process chaos at best and complete failure at worst. If training is held via conference call, one of the Kaizen Team members should document who attends the training. If e-mail is one component of your training, a designated person should keep a record of who confirms understanding the new process.

## TRAINING CONTENT

Determining training content is another strategic decision the team needs to make. The staff that they are training is the internal customer for that effort and, as such, they should feel the experience was of high value. In terms of training content, this is the Kaizen Team's opportunity to not only build worker confidence and competence in the new process, which ensures the process performance, but it's also an opportunity to sell the what's-in-it-for-me benefits of lean thinking and Kaizen Events to a broader section of the workforce. Additionally, it's an opportunity to demonstrate how the results from Kaizen Events impact the organization's overall business strategy. You may find the content format in Table 16-1 helpful to use as a foundation for providing context, and one that you can adjust as necessary. In the spirit of providing efficient, high-value training, you should cover all of these topics quickly and effectively. Remember that this training focuses on learning how to perform a new process, not teaching everyone about lean. However, it's important that any training include the minimal context. Naturally, hard or soft copies of the new standard work, including job aids and process flows should be available to each training participant. Kaizen Teams need to allow for copying time when they're planning for the training component.

**Table 16-1.** Training Content and Time Frames

| Content | Time Frame |
| --- | --- |
| Lean Principles Review | 1 minute |
| Why the Kaizen Event Was Held | 1 minute |
| Current State Findings (high-level summary) | 2 minutes |
| Future State Design (including options considered as discarded) | 2 minutes |
| Anticipated Benefits (both direct and indirect) | 2 minutes |
| New Process/Work Tools Overview (review detailed work procedures) | 10–20 minutes |
| Ongoing Monitoring (metrics, audits, key contact) | 2 minutes |

This format will work for most improvements. However, you may run across an improvement that will take longer than 20 minutes to train the workforce on, especially if workers are given an opportunity to try the new process. But make sure the training is greatly streamlined, so that the team demonstrates lean principles by delivering high quality training in the shortest amount of time necessary.

Another key consideration is how much of the Sustainability Plan (discussed in Chapter 17) will be shared with the trainees. Ideally, the Kaizen Team has already decided:

- How the process will be monitored (who will do it and which metrics will be used).

- When the 30-day audit will occur and who will lead the audit.

- Who's responsible for gathering user input and modifying the process as needed.

- What rewards or consequences will be put into place to ensure compliance.

- How new hires will be trained to reduce variation in process performance.

If available, you should share these details with the affected workforce. If the team has finalized all of the sustainability details by the time training occurs, the trainers should let the participants know that they'll receive follow-up information within a week. Someone from the team should also make sure that this communication activity is placed on the 30-Day List.

Once the content is determined, it becomes easier to identify which team member(s) should conduct the training. If the Kaizen Team is providing face-to-face training, it should select someone who understands the new process extremely well, is comfortable in front of a group, and is a strong communicator. Teams sometimes choose several instructors, each leading a specific component of the content. In some cases, others on the Kaizen Team are present at the training to help answer questions or help during demonstrations, even if they aren't serving as primary trainers.

While training is occurring, the rest of the Kaizen Team should begin preparing for the wrap-up, which includes:

- Creating a metrics-based process map that represents the improved state (if relevant and not yet created).

- Finalizing the metrics that will be reported.

- Drafting the Sustainability Plan (discussed in Chapter 17).

- Drafting the Event Report (discussed in Chapter 17).

- Preparing for the team presentation (discussed in Chapter 17).

- Identifying documentation that may need to be updated to reflect the altered process, such as ISO documentation or detailed standard operating procedures.

- Finalizing the 30-Day List of improvement-related tasks that will not be completed by the close of the Kaizen Event (discussed in Chapter 17).

- Finalizing the Parking Lot Issues (discussed in Chapter 17).

With the workforce trained and the new process either up and running, or scheduled for rollout the next business day or shift, it is time to wrap up the event. In Chapter 17, you will learn how the team should document and communicate its accomplishments during the final presentation and how it prepares for disbanding as a team, the adjourning phase in Tuckman's team development cycle.

# CHAPTER 17

# EVENT WRAP-UP

While one portion of the Kaizen Team is delivering new process training to the workforce impacted by the improvements, the remaining team members focus on activities that will formally conclude the event. The activity that culminates the Kaizen Event is the team presentation, discussed later in the chapter. The Kaizen Event Tools file on the CD contains a number of tools to help the Kaizen Team communicate its results and set the stage for sustainability, several of which are shared during the final presentation:

- Kaizen Event Report (Tab 8)
- Sustainability Plan (Tab 9)
- 30-Day List (Tab 10)
- Parking Lot Issues (Tab 11)
- Team Presentation Agenda (Tab 12)

This chapter describes each of these tools and provides tips for a successful conclusion to the Kaizen Event.

## KAIZEN EVENT REPORT

The Kaizen Event Report (Figure 17-1) summarizes the actions the team took to achieve the event objectives, and the results the improvements are projected to generate. At this stage of the improvement process, the results are *projected* because the affected workforce typically experiences a learning curve and becomes progressively proficient in the new way of operating. Process performance measurements taken immediately following the Kaizen Event often fall short of the team's improvement projections; however, with practice (and, on occasion, additional process adjustments and/or workforce training) the workers become more comfortable with the new process and produce results that approach—and, in some cases, exceed—the Kaizen Team's initial projections. Remember that projected improvement results are based on the team's knowledge of the process and its estimate of how the improvements will impact performance. And because the process owner may receive post-implementation feedback that requires the Kaizen Team to adjust the process further during the first 30 days after the event, the 30-day audit (described in Chapter 18) is typically the first time the team reports "actual" results and compares them against its projections.

Anyone from the Kaizen Team may take the lead on completing the Event Report, but it's often the team lead. If the team is busy with other activities, the facilitator sometimes steps in as well. The report is completed as follows:

## Kaizen Event Report

| Executive Sponsor | | Event Name | |
| Value Stream Champion | | Event Dates | |
| Facilitator | | | |
| Team Lead | | | |

| Event Objectives | Key Improvements Implemented | Before Photos, Graphs and/or Data |
|---|---|---|
| 1 | | |
| 2 | | |
| 3 | | |
| 4 | | |
| 5 | | |

| Measurable Results | | | | | Collateral Benefits | After Photos, Graphs and/or Data |
|---|---|---|---|---|---|---|
| | Metric | Unit of Measure | Before Measurement | Projected After Measurement | Projected Change | | |
| 1 | Lead Time | | | | | | |
| 2 | Process Time | | | | | | |
| 3 | Rolled First Pass Yield | % | | | | | |
| 4 | | | | | | | |
| 5 | | | | | | Team Members | |
| 6 | | | | | | | |
| 7 | | | | | | | |
| 8 | | | | | | | |
| 9 | | | | | | | |
| 10 | | | | | | | |

**Figure 17-1.** Kaizen Event Report

- *Header.* The header, which lists key event leadership, the event name, and the event dates auto-populates when data is entered into the corresponding cells on the Event Charter.

- *Event Objectives.* This section houses up to five key event objectives. Rather than auto-populating from the Event Charter information, these cells are designed for manual data entry, in the event the objectives are modified during the Event. Occasionally, as the team members perform their current state analysis, their objectives become clearer and are modified from the original objectives set forth in the charter. Or the charter may initially list general goals that the team converts to measurable objectives as they obtain baseline current state metrics early in the event.

- *Key Improvements Implemented.* Here, the team lists the most significant improvements they implemented that will impact each objective. The facilitator should encourage team members completing the Event Report to use action-based language (verb/noun), such as: merged two roles, created standard work, eliminated handoffs, created data-entry quick guide, rearranged department, revised drawing standards, cross-trained work teams A and B, implemented monitoring system for interdepartmental service agreements, etc. While some improvements may impact more than one objective, each improvement should only be listed once on the report.

- *Before Photos, Graphs and/or Data.* This section houses relevant visual information that demonstrates the current state as it existed prior to the Kaizen Event. Photos are useful for physical improvements, whereas graphs, charts, and other forms of visual data work well when quantifiable improvements exist. Root cause analysis tools such as cause-and-effect diagrams and Pareto charts can be included in this section. A button located in the upper right corner of the Event Report enables the team to easily insert separate files containing visual data, which auto-size to fit the space provided.

- *Measurable Results.* For the vast majority of Kaizen Events, the team will report the projected outcomes for three key metrics: *total lead time* for the process being improved (critical path only), *total process time* (critical path only), and *rolled first pass yield* (the product of the %C&As for each process step). If these three metrics are not relevant for the improvement implemented (this is rare), the team should leave the corresponding cells blank. This section includes seven additional rows to house additional measurements that are relevant. Additional metrics may include:
    - On-time delivery (customer perspective)
    - Activity ratio
    - % value-adding activity
    - Space occupied (square footage or number of storage areas)
    - Productivity
    - Customer-received quality (internal or external customer)
    - Number of "items" in queue
    - Longest time in queue
    - Number of steps in the process
    - Number of handoffs and/or approvals
    - Percent complete and accurate for the output of a particular process step
    - Process time at bottleneck
    - Distance traveled
    - Paid overtime
    - Shipping expenses (or other direct expenses)
    - Number of rework loops
    - Staff motion (distance walked)
    - Overall process cost
    - Freed capacity/number of full time equivalent staff (FTEs) required
    - Overall Equipment Effectiveness
    - Customer satisfaction scores/Number of customer complaints
    - Customer retention
    - Workforce satisfaction scores/turnover/absenteeism
    - Inventory (volume/dollars/turns)
    - Revenue per employee or work team

    And there are many more. The current state issues that drove the need for the event and the particular improvements implemented will dictate the metrics that are most relevant for measuring event success and ongoing improvement progress.

**171**

Each metric listed should include the *Unit of Measure* (minutes, hours, feet, miles, percentage, etc.); the *Before Measurement*, based on the performance level prior to the Kaizen Event; and the *Projected After Measurement*, based on the team's projections about the degree to which improvements implemented during the event will impact the "before" performance levels. The *Projected Change* column auto-calculates based on the before and projected after metrics. The cells in this section will auto-populate the corresponding cells on the 30- and 60-Day Audit Reports (Tabs 14 & 15, discussed in Chapter 18).

A word about 5S-specific events: Teams often overlook the relevance in tracking lead time, process time reductions, and quality gains that occur through 5S activities. For events that include 5S, consider including these three key metrics when conducting your current state analysis and reporting projected results.

- *Collateral Benefits.* Collateral benefits are improvement outcomes for which the team has not yet obtained measurement, or those results that have been traditionally referred to as "intangible," "indirect," or "soft" benefits (e.g., improved morale, better communication, reduced stress, etc.) "Collateral" is the preferred term because most *"soft benefits" can indeed be quantified and tied to financial performance.* Ideally, the Kaizen Team creates the means to measure all relevant performance issues—including collateral benefits—during the event.

- *Team Members.* This section is auto-populated from the Event Charter and serves as a record of who was involved in a particular improvement activity.

- *After Photos, Graphs, and/or Data.* This section houses visual information (photos, graphs, charts, diagrams) that illustrates the actual or projected improvements implemented during the event.

The Kaizen Event Report serves many purposes: 1) a summary document that the team reviews during the team presentation; 2) a tool for communicating and archiving the team's success; and 3) a tracking tool that provides structure for ongoing monitoring activities (discussed in Chapter 18). The Event Report should be distributed broadly, posted in prominent places, and housed in a designated location on a shared drive. Event leadership should also consider sharing the report with board members, key customers and suppliers, and other external stakeholders to highlight the effectiveness of the Kaizen Event approach for making improvements.

## SUSTAINABILITY PLAN

As shown in Figure 17-2, the Sustainability Plan (Tab 9 in the Kaizen Event Tools file) offers a standard work approach for the Kaizen Team to identify and track the critical success factors for sustaining improvements. Ideally, the Sustainability Plan is 100 percent complete by the end of the event, and the facilitator should push for this. However, it's often added to the 30-Day List and finalized during the team's first weekly post-event meeting. The plan should be complete enough for the team members to share key elements during the workforce training on the last day of the Kaizen Event. In any case, the Sustainability Plan

## Kaizen Event Sustainability Plan

| | | | |
|---|---|---|---|
| **Executive Sponsor** | | **Event Name** | |
| **Value Stream Champion** | | **Event Dates** | |
| **Facilitator** | | **"Go Live" Date** | |
| **Team Lead** | | **"Go Live" Location** | |
| **30-Day Audit Date** | | **60-Day Audit Date** | |

| Communication / Training | |
|---|---|
| **Requirement** | **Plan** |
| Provide training for those who missed initial training. | *Who will deliver it and when?* |
| Integrate new process into ongoing department training. | *Who leads identification of training that need to be updated (ongoing and for new employees), when will training be in place?* |
| Update Value Stream Map. | *Which value stream map(s) need to be updated, who will do it and when?* |
| Update training records to reflect who has been trained. | *Who maintains training records?* |
| Communication to affected parties who were not advised during event. | *Who communicates? How? To whom?* |
| Post Event Report, 30-Day List, Sustainability Plan. | *Who is accountable? Where posted?* |
| Update SOPs and other ISO or regulatory documents impacted by changes. | *Who identifies relevant documentation? Who updates it? By when?* |
| Communicate and post 30-day and 60-day audit results. | *Who communicates? How? To whom? Where posted?* |
| Communicate audit results to stakeholders and leadership team. | *Who communicates? Via what medium?* |
| Communicate process performance levels. | *How is process performance going to be communicated to workers? Are additional visuals needed? Who owns this activity?* |
| | |
| | |
| | |
| | |

**Figure 17-2.** Sustainability Plan—Page One

must be 100 percent complete by the end of the first week following the Kaizen Event. Once finalized and approved, the Sustainability Plan should accompany the Event Report when it's distributed and posted.

Because organizational culture plays such a strong role in sustaining improvements, the Sustainability Plan is a flexible shaping tool, which allows each team to determine the specific elements that will ensure that the gains they achieved are sustained, and continue to improve with further process refinement. The header includes cells that auto-populate from the Event Charter, as well as four cells that relate to the post-event process audits and "go live" location and date as determined by the Kaizen Team. The "go live" date is typically the next business day or shift after the event concludes. The team should establish the 30- and 60-day audit dates before the event concludes, and share its post-event follow-up plans with leadership during the team presentation.

The plan is a two-page document, organized into two sections that represent the two primary elements required for sustainability: 1) excellence in *communication and training*, and 2) ongoing and relevant *monitoring and measurement*. The Requirements column includes common elements found in sustainable improvement efforts. While these cells are locked to prevent alteration, additional cells are available under each section for user-defined activities that are specific to the improved process and organizational culture. The Plan column includes italicized questions to guide the team in creating an effective Sustainability Plan. As they develop a strategy, they should overwrite the italicized suggestions with their own specific plan elements.

The final step in creating the Sustainability Plan is obtaining approval from the two parties who are ultimately accountable for the Event results—the value stream champion and process owner. You may opt for a less formalized approach, but workers usually follow plans more closely when leadership in their own area signs them.

The event leaders and Kaizen Team should review the plan each week during its four-week follow-up period (discussed in Chapter 18) to ensure that the "teeth" for sustainability are firmly in place. The value stream champion is typically accountable for the Sustainability Plan, though the person overseeing its direct execution is the identified process owner—the person closest to the work that is responsible for process performance and design, which includes monitoring to ensure sustainability and identify future improvement opportunities. If, prior to the Kaizen Event, a process owner wasn't designated, the Kaizen Team will need to work with leadership (possibly during an interim briefing) to identify the person who will monitor process performance and have the authority to refine the improved process on an ongoing basis.

The Sustainability Plan is perhaps the most important document in the Kaizen Event Tools file and requires careful consideration. Creating this plan is not easy because it forces the organization to confront cultural issues that may need to be addressed to achieve an environment that will sustain improvements. However, through the process of assigning accountability and conducting consistent follow-up, you can slowly shift your culture into one that supports ongoing process improvement.

## 30-DAY LIST

The 30-Day List (Figure 17-3) helps the Kaizen Team and event leaders track open action items that must be completed after the formal event concludes for the team to declare the improvement 100 percent implemented. Action items may include receiving and installing visuals that had to be ordered, conducting make-up training for those workers who missed the new process training held during the event, or updating ISO documentation to reflect the new process. Some teams include post-event follow-up activities such as the weekly status meetings and the 30-day audit on their 30-Day List as well.

The most important goal in compiling this 30-Day List is to *keep it as short as possible!* There are two reasons why the facilitator should encourage the team to get as close as possible to 100 percent implementation during the event and to limit the number of items on the 30-Day List. First, the improvements need to be implemented fully enough by the end of the event that the work can be performed the new way on the next business day or shift following the event conclusion. Secondly, once the Kaizen Team disbands, the focus, sense of urgency, and teamwork members established during the event wanes, making it more difficult to accomplish necessary follow-up tasks.

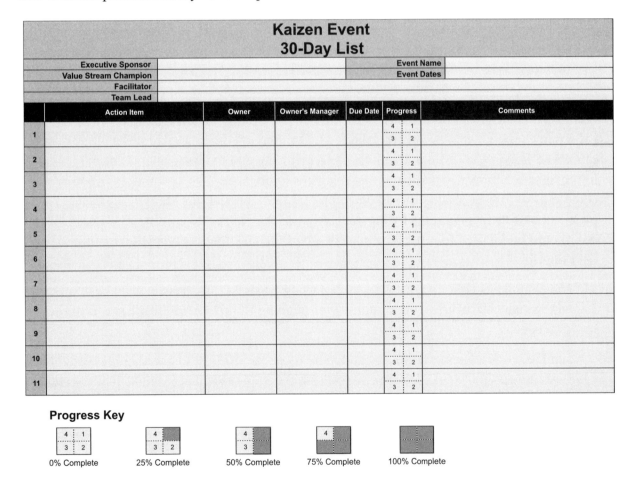

**Figure 17-3.** 30-Day List (partial view)

Following the Kaizen Event, the team should review the 30-Day List on a weekly basis to monitor progress (discussed in Chapter 18). Each action item should have an owner assigned to it (a Kaizen Team member) along with a due date to create clear accountability and time frames for completing the assigned task. The list also includes a column for each task owner's manager. The list should be distributed to the task owner's direct supervisor or manager, so he or she is aware of the additional responsibilities his or her staff member agreed to.

The progress column provides a visual method for quickly assessing the status for post-event action items. Whoever is leading the weekly post-event status meetings (typically the team lead, value stream champion, or facilitator; discussed further in Chapter 18) is responsible for updating the status column, as well as posting and distributing the updated 30-Day List. As an open action item moves toward completion, the 30-Day List is progressively color-coded green to communicate progress as follows:

| Action Item Progress | Color-Coding Progression |
| --- | --- |
| 0 percent complete | No shading |
| 25 percent complete | Upper right (#1) quadrant is color-coded green |
| 50 percent complete | Bottom right (#2) quadrant is also color-coded |
| 75 percent complete | Bottom left (#3) quadrant is also color-coded |
| 100 percent complete | The entire status square is color-coded green |

The quadrant turns green when the 30-Day List owner deletes the number in the quadrant that represents the percentage of the task that is complete. For example, when the task is 25 percent complete, list owner deletes #1 from the upper right quadrant and the quadrant turns green. When the task is 50 percent complete and the list owner deletes 2 from the lower right quadrant, it will also turn green. And so on. When the action item is 100 percent complete, all four quadrants should be green. It is possible that the team will partially complete some of the action items by the conclusion of the Kaizen Event. In this case, the status box should be updated to reflect the percentage of the task that is completed by the end of the event.

The Comments column houses notes regarding progress, any obstacles the task owner encounters, new discoveries, opportunities for ongoing improvement, feedback from the workforce, etc.

The Kaizen Team reviews the key action items on the 30-Day List during the team presentation (discussed in the next section), so leadership understands that, once an improvement is implemented and the event formally concludes, the work isn't always 100 percent complete.

The 30-Day List is also a tool for communicating how the task owner is delivering on his or her commitments. The list should be posted in the relevant work areas and/or on continuous-improvement communication boards to demonstrate that leadership is supporting the improvement process beyond the structured Kaizen Event, and that the team is making ongoing progress. You can store the 30-Day List electronically, but be sure it is also physically posted in a prominent location.

## PARKING LOT ISSUES

During Kaizen Events, it's common for issues and discoveries to arise that are beyond the scope of the event. A "Parking Lot" list provides the structure for capturing and making recommendations for further action on these issues (see Figure 17-4). It also provides a psychological tool for team members to air ideas, get them in writing, and quickly redirect their attention back to those issues that are within the event scope and boundaries.

| Kaizen Event Parking Lot Issues | | | | |
|---|---|---|---|---|
| Executive Sponsor | | | Event Name | |
| Value Stream Champion | | | Event Dates | |
| Facilitator | | | | |
| Team Lead | | | | |
| | Issue / Discovery | Team Recommendation | | Owner |
| 1 | | | | |
| 2 | | | | |
| 3 | | | | |
| 4 | | | | |
| 5 | | | | |
| 6 | | | | |

**Figure 17-4.** Parking Lot Issues (partial view)

During the team presentation, the team shares these Parking Lot issues and accompanying recommendations for action with leadership who, in turn, take responsibility for prioritizing the recommendations and assigning ownership, as appropriate. The team presentation is not an appropriate forum for debating the issues, but rather to obtain leadership's commitment regarding follow-up. The Kaizen Team members do not typically assign ownership for these items, nor do they review the Parking Lot list in their post-event follow-up meetings. Leadership should consider the Parking Lot list when planning future improvement activities. As with all of the Kaizen tools, the header on this sheet populates automatically when you draft the Charter.

## TEAM PRESENTATION

The team presentation is the concluding activity in the Kaizen Event, during which the team presents its accomplishments to leadership and, if preferred, a cross-section of the workforce experiencing the improvements. The presentation generally lasts one hour, but can run anywhere from 30 to 90 minutes. The newer the organization is to Kaizen Events and the larger the audience, the longer the presentation will typically be. In early Kaizen Events, the team presentations provide a learning environment for leaders to begin "letting go" and grow comfortable with worker-defined solutions. In making that transition, they often have many questions about the process, how the team selected particular implementation strategies, and follow-up commitments. In contrast, narrowly scoped events in seasoned organizations often only need a 30-minute window for the final presentation.

The team presentation serves many purposes. In addition to formally concluding the Kaizen Event, it:

- Provides a forum for the team members to share their success and gain public recognition for their effort.

- Serves as a sales tool to the rest of the organization about the effectiveness of Kaizen Events—especially when each team member is given the opportunity to express what he or she experienced during the event.

- Assists the organization in learning more about Kaizen Event benefits and challenges, which helps in planning future events.

- Enables the organization to leverage the momentum created by Kaizen Events and the team's enthusiasm across the organization.

- Communicates the change that will take effect the next business day or shift.

For the first few Kaizen Events, a broad cross section of the organization's leadership team should be encouraged to attend as the team presentation provides deeper understanding about the elements surrounding rapid improvement and cultural issues that may need to be addressed to pave the way for becoming a lean enterprise. As the organization matures with Kaizen Events, it may be preferable for the team to present only to relevant leadership who oversee the specific areas impacted by the improvements made. As mentioned in Chapter 8, the event leaders may want to segment the invitations to the team presentation into two categories: required attendance and invitation. The importance of this concluding activity cannot be overstated: leadership attendance (by phone, if necessary) at the team presentation demonstrates commitment to the process and is a key success factor in ongoing rapid improvement efforts and in the sustainability of the particular improvements implemented. *If relevant leadership places other responsibilities in a higher priority than demonstrating their support to a team who has expended significant effort in improving organizational performance, it sends a disheartening message to the team.* The level of leadership engagement reflects organizational culture, and is a strong indicator for the likely success of future rapid improvement efforts.

The team presentation is not meant to be an excessively formal activity with PowerPoint-heavy presentations. Preparation typically takes 30 to 60 minutes; in no case should it require more than 90 minutes of the team's time. To reduce the team's prep time and give them more time to complete critical implementation tasks, the facilitator often plays a strong role in helping the team organize the material they will present. Often, while a portion of the team is training workers on the new process, the remaining team members begin pulling together material for the team presentation.

The venue for the presentation is identified during pre-event planning. Ideally, you hold the presentation in Kaizen Central because the team can easily reference flip charts, maps, and other visuals that are typically hanging on the wall. If the presentation is held in another location, the team will need time to set up the room, robbing them of vital work time.

While actual presentation agendas may vary slightly, the Team Presentation Agenda, shown in Figure 17-5 and located on Tab 12 of the Kaizen Event Tools, provides a sample

| Kaizen Event Team Presentation Agenda | | |
|---|---|---|
| **Value Stream Champion** | **Event Name** | |
| **Facilitator** | **Event Dates** | |
| | **Agenda Item** | **Presenter(s)** |
| 1 | **Opening Comments**<br>• Team introductions<br>• Agenda<br>• "Rules" for attendees | |
| 2 | **Scope and Objectives**<br>• Process being addressed<br>• First & last steps<br>• Specific conditions<br>• Event drivers/current state issues<br>• Objectives<br>• Boundaries & limitations | |
| 3 | **"Before" Condition**<br>• VSM and/or MBPM review<br>• Relevant metrics<br>• Photos (if relevant) | |
| 4 | **Key Improvements Implemented**<br>• Key improvements and accomplishments implemented during the event<br>• Tools used | |
| 5 | **"After" Condition**<br>• New process description<br>• Projected results (direct and collateral) | |
| 6 | **Key Open Action Items**<br>• 30-Day List | |
| 7 | **Sustainability Plan**<br>• Potential obstacles that could prevent attaining projected performance levels | |
| 8 | **Parking Lot Issues**<br>• Define what a "parking lot" item is | |
| 9 | **Lessons Learned**<br>• Greatest success; greatest challenge<br>• Team feedback (each individual) | |
| 10 | **Facilitator Feedback** | |
| 11 | **Question and Answer**<br>• Leadership feedback to team | |
| 12 | **Team Recognition** | |
| 13 | **Wrap-up** | |

**Figure 17-5.** Team Presentation Agenda

agenda that the team can refer to in preparing for the presentation. Several of the agenda items contain subpoints that should be covered while addressing each item. The tool also includes a column to house the names of the team members who will be presenting each topic. The facilitator typically asks for volunteers to cover one or more of the agenda items, but *strongly encourages* all team members to present at least a small portion of the agenda. This approach provides team members with the professional development opportunity to further develop their presentation and leadership skills, and aids in driving workforce-level ownership into the improvement process. Since there are thirteen agenda items, and the team is limited to ten people, some team members will cover more than one item. The team and facilitator should assign time frames for each agenda item so the presentation stays on schedule.

The facilitator plays a minor role during the final presentation. He/she can kick off and conclude the presentation if the team doesn't feel comfortable in that role, but the team should present all other content. The facilitator can add comments throughout to highlight issues and clarify what's being said, but the team members should deliver the bulk of the presentation. This can make shy or junior team members nervous but, as mentioned above, worker-level recognition and development is an important element of an organization's journey to becoming a lean enterprise. You can pair reluctant team members with someone more seasoned and perhaps cover only one of the subpoints.

For those team members who are intensely uncomfortable with the thought of presenting to leadership (and potentially their peer group), the facilitator can allay their concerns with the following strategies and encouragement:

- Give them time to practice their section of the presentation. Remind them that they will be talking for five minutes or less, and can script their portion in advance if they'd feel more comfortable.

- Remind them that they've worked hard and have achieved significant results in a short period of time, and deserve recognition for their effort. Presenting is a way to achieve recognition.

- Highlight that the team presentation is an excellent career development opportunity in a safe environment, and that the facilitator and fellow team members will support the nervous presenter.

- Point out that the facilitator will open the session with a reminder to leadership that some of the team members haven't presented much before and, therefore, may be nervous. After a statement like this, leadership typically becomes even more supportive of team success. Verbalizing team members' apprehensions often helps reduce their own anxiety as well.

- Remind the audience the presentation is casual by design. The facilitator and fellow team members should chime in and help other team members if they struggle with details, calculations, terminology, etc.

- Allow nervous team members to pair up for the presentation.

- As a last resort, allow them to present from their seats.

If, after all that, a team member still refuses to participate, the facilitator should let it go, but encourage him or her to study fellow team members' presentation techniques so he/she can see that it's easier to present than one may think upfront. One last note: Sometimes pushing team members beyond their comfort zone prods them to present, and they may even thank you for pushing them. This is a judgment call the facilitator needs to make.

One more tip in encouraging team-wide involvement in the final presentation: It's some-time best to delay mentioning the participatory requirements for team members until the morning of the team presentation to avoid creating anxiety in shy team members and shifting their focus from achieving results to their concern about the presentation. This approach may seem unfair, but the facilitator needs to do whatever he/she can to keep the team focused on designing and implementing improvements.

To keep the presentation from becoming overly formalized, and unnerving shy team members further, flip charts are the medium of choice for communicating content rather than sophisticated PowerPoint presentations that require excessive time to prepare. Here again the lean tenet applies: Minimum effort to achieve optimal outcomes. Organizations with a more formal culture may initially balk at this "back to basics" approach. However, lean is about eliminating non-value-adding activities, and converting information that has already been recorded on flip charts is redundant work and robs the team of the valuable time needed to design and implement improvements. If the organization wants to share the results in formal settings, such as board meetings and customer gatherings, PowerPoint presentations can be prepared after the Kaizen Event has concluded. That said, using PowerPoint to show before and after photos and to project other improvement-related visuals is acceptable.

Finally, the facilitator should ask the group gathered for the team presentation to follow fundamental meeting management rules:

- Cell phones and other devices are silenced

- The presentation begins and ends on time

- One conversation at a time; no sidebar discussions

- Express concerns freely (don't leave in silent disagreement)

In addition, the group should be reminded that the improvement(s) are not likely to be "perfect," nor are they set in stone and cannot be adjusted as discoveries for further improvement are made. Finally, the facilitator should mention the fundamental Kaizen Event rule that no one has veto power outside of the team (unless a policy is being challenged, which should have revealed itself and been resolved—with leadership's input—during the event). Finally, the facilitator should monitor the time frames for each agenda item and move the group along if they begin to go off schedule. Follow-up sessions can be scheduled if specific leaders want more information than time allows.

## TEAM RECOGNITION AND CELEBRATION

As discussed in Chapter 7, it's important to formally recognize the team's achievements. In a matter of days, team members have designed and implemented improvements that have traditionally required weeks or months to accomplish, and they have made sacrifices to do so. Most team members are acutely aware that work is piling up in their absence, and they often receive additional pressure from colleagues during the event. While it's typically fulfilling to serve as a Kaizen Team member, it's not easy.

Organizations vary widely regarding how they approach recognition. At the very least, during the team presentation, team members should receive a heartfelt thank you from leadership and a recognition certificate such as the one shown in Figure 17-6. This certificate template is also included on the CD and, if desired, can be customized with your company logo and/or printed onto formal certificate paper (after removing the template borders).

# Certificate of Achievement

*Presented by*
*<Company Name>*


*Recognizing*
## *<Participant Name>*

*For serving on the <name of event> Kaizen Team and contributing to*
*organizational performance improvement*


*<Month, Date, Year>*

| _____ | _____ |
| --- | --- |
| <Name of senior leader or executive sponsor> | <Name of value stream champion or facilitator> |
| <Title> | <Title> |

**Figure 17-6.** Recognition Certificate

Chapter 7 lists a wide range of additional recognition options (typically arranged for by the Event Coordinator), including gift cards, T-shirts, or polo shirts with the company logo, baseball hats, movie tickets, coffee mugs, etc. Many organizations treat the Kaizen Team and those who helped during the event planning and execution phases to a lunch, dinner, pizza party, or some other group activity. Celebrations like these are a small gesture, given the effort the team has put forth, and degree to which the results they generated will benefit the organization.

## DISBANDING THE TEAM

Before disbanding, the team should complete two final activities. First, they need to finalize the Idea List generated during the Event (discussed in Chapter 14) and turning it over to whoever oversees continuous improvement in the organization. The continuous-improvement champion can then work with leadership to prioritize these ideas into the organization's ongoing improvement plans. Secondly, the team should assign due dates and owners for at least the most immediate tasks listed on the Post-Event Activities sheet (Tab 13 on the Kaizen Event Tools file and discussed further in Chapter 18).

At this point in a Kaizen Event, the team is typically both exhausted and exhilarated. They have accomplished a tremendous amount in a very short period of time. They also have bonded as a team. As the event concludes, the team begins experiencing the fifth stage of team development as defined by Tuckman—adjourning, also referred to as mourning. The facilitator should aid them in transitioning back to their regular work by reminding them that they will continue to work together for the next four weeks as they conduct the post-event activities and transition improvement responsibility to the area supervisors and managers, described in Chapter 18. The team is also welcome to plan social outings, similar to what juries sometimes do after being sequestered together. This helps teams cope with the "adjourning/mourning" aspects of team development.

This concludes Part III of the book and the "Act" phase of the micro PDCA cycle that occurs during the execution phase of Kaizen Events. It also concludes the end of the "Do" phase of the macro PDCA cycle. The next chapters address follow-up activities that are essential for assuring sustainability and ongoing improvement—the "Check" and "Act" stages of the macro PDCA cycle.

# PART IV

# Beyond the Kaizen Event: Sustaining and Expanding

# CHAPTER 18

# FOLLOW-UP ACTIVITIES

The improvement cycle is not over when the Kaizen Event concludes. In many ways, the toughest work is just beginning: measuring and monitoring, assuring sustainability, and continuously improving the process—the "C" and "A" in the macro PDCA cycle. The Post-Event Activities checklist (Tab 13 on the Kaizen Event Tools file) lists a number of key tasks that the team needs to complete following the Event (see Figure 18-1), including sending thank-you notes, communicating event results, monitoring the process, completing the 30-Day List, and conducting formal audits.

| Kaizen Event Post-Event Activities | | | | | |
|---|---|---|---|---|---|
| **Executive Sponsor** | | | **Event Name** | | |
| **Value Stream Champion** | | | **Event Dates** | | |
| **Facilitator** | | | | | |
| **Coordinator** | | | | | |
| | ✓ | Task | Due Date | Owner | Comments |
| **1 Week After** | | | | | |
| 1 | ☐ | Observe the new process the first day or shift following the event. Make real-time adjustments, if needed. | | | |
| 2 | ☐ | Hold first of four weekly post-Event meetings with Kaizen Team to assess progress on 30-Day List, monitor process performance, identify and resolve new problems, and conduct lessons learned sessions. | | | |
| 3 | ☐ | Send thank you's to all team members, on-call support, and others who helped. | | | |
| 4 | ☐ | Broadcast results organization-wide (via e-mail, newsletter, etc.) | | | |
| 5 | ☐ | Post-Event Report and Sustainability Plan on improvement communication board(s) and shared drives. | | | |
| 6 | ☐ | Assess if new process is being followed. | | | |
| 7 | ☐ | Take corrective action if process is not being followed. | | | |
| 8 | ☐ | If controlled procedures/processes were changed, update relevant documentation as necessary. | | | |
| 9 | ☐ | Plan future improvement activities, if needed. | | | |
| 10 | ☐ | Share "later" ideas on Ideas List with relevant leadership and continuous improvement staff. | | | |
| 11 | ☐ | Modifiy process further if it needs additional improvement. | | | |
| 12 | ☐ | | | | |
| 13 | ☐ | | | | |
| **2 Weeks After** | | | | | |
| 14 | ☐ | Meet with team to assess progress on 30-Day List. | | | |
| 15 | ☐ | Measure process to validate projected future state metrics. | | | |
| 16 | ☐ | Adjust process, if needed. | | | |
| 17 | ☐ | Interview process workers and those affected by the improvements to assess success and need for future improvements. | | | |
| 18 | ☐ | | | | |

**Figure 18-1.** Post-Event Activities Checklist (partial view)

As with all of the Kaizen Event tools, the header auto-populates with information from the corresponding cells on the event charter. In addition to the typical post-event activities that are listed, the checklist includes additional cells to house activities that are unique to your organization or the particular Kaizen Event. Ideally, the team has reviewed the checklist prior to the official conclusion of the event and has assigned due dates and ownership for some of the most immediate follow-up activities, such as scheduling follow-up meetings, observing the process the next day or shift, and making adjustments, if necessary. The checklist should be reviewed during the weekly post-event follow-up meetings, described below.

## WEEKLY FOLLOW-UP MEETINGS

Holding weekly post-event follow-up meetings is arguably the most important activity in the Kaizen Event process for stabilizing the new process, assuring sustainability, and demonstrating the effectiveness of rapid improvement. Without a formal structure to monitor progress, track results, and conduct valuable lessons-learned activities, Kaizen Event improvements often slip and diminish over time. Consistent focus on the process will ensure that old work habits are broken and replaced with new ways of operating. These follow-up meetings should be scheduled before the Kaizen Team disbands at the end of the event

The *entire* Kaizen Team should be present for these 30 to 60-minute follow-up meetings. Members who traveled to the event can attend the meetings by phone; however, to achieve the greatest effectiveness, all other team members should be required to attend in person. Supervisors and/or managers in the areas impacted by the improvement should also attend the meetings to begin transferring authority for process design and implementation from the Kaizen Team to frontline management, who may or may not have been on the Kaizen Team. Additional participants could also include a representative from a centralized continuous-improvement department, if one exists.

Ideally, the meetings are held at gemba (where the work is actually performed) or include a visit to gemba, so the team can talk with the workers, see the process in action (if possible), and hear firsthand what's going well and what, if anything, is problematic. Through this real-time analysis, process adjustments can be made or additional training provided to continue driving toward optimal process performance. If an internal event facilitator led the Kaizen Event, he or she should lead the follow-up meetings. If an external facilitator was brought in and he/she will not be present for the follow-up meetings, the team leader or value stream champion should lead the meetings.

The weekly meeting agenda should include items such as:

- *Process performance and stabilization*—analyze measurements; review new problems that may have arisen; adjust the process; retrain as needed.
- *Workforce feedback*—does the workforce see value in the new process?
- *30-Day List progress*—are tasks being completed as assigned?
- *Sustainability Plan*—finalize and execute the plan.
- *Prepare for the 30-day audit*—review the audit tool and decide who will facilitate the various aspects of the audit.

- *Lessons learned*—what went well with the Kaizen Event? What would you do differently the next time?

Whoever leads the post-event meetings should communicate progress to leadership and physically post the updated 30-Day List, Sustainability Plan, and Post-Event Checklist in the affected areas and/or continuous-improvement communication board.

## PROCESS STABILIZATION

A critical element in process stabilization is providing feedback to the staff regarding process performance in the form of real-time visual metrics. Selecting the *relevant few* process performance metrics (in lieu of the common mistake of including the *trivial many*) is instrumental in driving the desired behaviors. Process performance results also indicate the further improvement activities that are required.

Teams often ask how much they should adjust the process during the first few days or weeks post-implementation. If the process has an obvious problem that is unrelated to the learning curve associated with new processes, the team needs to make immediate change, demonstrating the true spirit of kaizen. Engaging in rapid intervention when problems arise sends a strong message throughout the organization that incremental improvements are both necessary and expected, and are a key component in the organization's mission to seek perfection. However, you also want to allow adequate time for the process to stabilize between each round of improvements, to avoid workforce burnout and confusion from constantly relearning how to perform the work. If you make too many minor changes too quickly, you risk perpetuating the chaos that you seek to eliminate through well-executed process simplification.

Recall that the Sustainability Plan calls for naming a single process owner who is responsible for the overall performance of the process. Process ownership should be established before the Kaizen Event concludes and communicated to the workforce during the training session on the last day, so workers know whom they should contact if they encounter issues or roadblocks with the new process, or discover opportunities for continued improvement.

If further process modifications occur in the days immediately following the event, the team should reconvene to modify associated standard work documents, job aids and controlled processes (e.g., FDA, ISO, Joint Commission, etc.) to reflect the change. Remember, all process modifications require communication and workforce training.

## POST-EVENT PROCESS AUDITS

Thirty and 60 days after the improvements have been implemented, the Kaizen Team conducts audits to measure process performance and drive ongoing improvement. Again, it's best if all Kaizen Team members participate in the audits, so they can experience firsthand the fruits of their labor, continue their learning cycle, and strengthen their role as ombudsmen for rapid improvement.

In advance of the audit, you need to select a lead auditor. This is often the event facilitator, but if the facilitator was external and/or is unavailable for the audit, someone will need to lead the activity. Ideally, the lead auditor is someone who is respected within the organization, is 100 percent objective, and has no stake in the process. If one of the Kaizen Team members volunteers for the role, he or she needs to be aware that objectivity is vital for accurate audit results and an effective post-audit process.

The audit results are reported on the two-page 30-Day Audit Report (Tab 14 of the Kaizen Event Tools file on the CD). As shown in Figure 18-2, the header contains several cells that auto-populate from the event charter, as well as two cells that the lead auditor will manually complete: lead auditor and the audit date.

## 30-Day Audit Report

| | Criteria | Yes | No | Corrective Action Needed | Owner |
|---|---|---|---|---|---|
| | Executive Sponsor | | Event Name | | |
| | Value Stream Champion | | Event Dates | | |
| | Lead Auditor | | Audit Date | | |
| 1 | Are workers following the process as designed in the event (or authorized modifications made since the event)? | ☐ | ☐ | | |
| 2 | Is there evidence that all workers, including those new to the area, have been trained on the new process? | ☐ | ☐ | | |
| 3 | Is process performance being measured and reported as set forth in the Sustainability Plan? | ☐ | ☐ | | |
| 4 | Is the area manager monitoring and supporting compliance to the new process? | ☐ | ☐ | | |
| 5 | Are consequences for not following the new process design in place? | ☐ | ☐ | | |
| 6 | Have any unintended consequences (positive or negative) arisen? Check with downstream customers. | ☐ | ☐ | | |
| 7 | Is anyone resisting the new process? | ☐ | ☐ | | |
| 8 | Are all aspects of the Sustainability Plan being followed? | ☐ | ☐ | | |
| 9 | Are workers pleased with the improvements? Do they feel their work has been simplified? | ☐ | ☐ | | |
| 10 | | ☐ | ☐ | | |
| 11 | | ☐ | ☐ | | |
| **30-Day List Status** | Number of action items due by audit date | | | | |
| | Number of action items completed | | | | |
| | % of action items completed | | | | |

**Figure 18-2.** 30-Day Audit Report (Page One)

Page one of the 30-Day Audit Report focuses heavily on obtaining anecdotal data—a key element in monitoring the change process—and includes the suggested assessment criteria for the audit team to ask the workers performing and the managers overseeing the improved process. The Corrective Action Needed column houses notes regarding corrective actions that the audit team feels should be taken. The Owner column indicates who is responsible for following through on the suggested corrective action.

The 30-Day List Status section in the bottom left corner of the audit report (page 1) aids in monitoring the Kaizen Team's progress on the 30-Day List. The bottom cell, "*% of action items completed,*" auto-calculates once the numbers of action items are entered into the two cells above. Ideally, everything on the 30-Day List is completed by the 30-day audit, yielding 100 percent in the bottom cell. If it is less than 100 percent, leadership notification and/or intervention may be needed to provide team members with the necessary resources to complete their action items. Sharing positive findings with leadership signals them to recognize team members for their diligence in completing their action items.

The second page of the audit tool (Figure 18-3) reports the key metrics relevant to the process. The first five columns in the Performance Metrics section auto-populate from the corresponding cells on the Event Report. The audit team should measure the new process (interview is acceptable if actual measurement is difficult to obtain), and enter the data received into the *Actual After Measurement* cells.

## 30-Day Audit Report

| Executive Sponsor | | Event Name | |
|---|---|---|---|
| Value Stream Champion | | Event Dates | |
| Lead Auditor | | Audit Date | |

### Performance Metrics

| Metric/Activity Being Measured | Unit of Measure | Before Measurement | Projected After Measurement | Projected Change | Actual After Measurement | Actual Change (from Before Measurement) | Comments |
|---|---|---|---|---|---|---|---|
| Lead Time | | | | | | | |
| Process Time | | | | | | | |
| Rolled First Pass Yield | % | | | | | | |
| | | | | | | | |
| | | | | | | | |
| | | | | | | | |
| | | | | | | | |
| | | | | | | | |
| | | | | | | | |
| | | | | | | | |

### Additional Comments

**Figure 18-3.** 30-Day Audit Report (Page Two)

Cells in the next column, *Actual Change (from Before Measurement)*, auto-calculate and represent the true change (expressed as a percentage), rather than the projected change the team made during the Kaizen Event. *Note*: The percent change will carry a negative sign if the new value is less than the value of the before measurement. In some cases, a successful improvement will be reflected by a negative percentage (e.g., lead time). In other cases a positive percent change is desired (e.g., rolled first pass yield). You will need to evaluate whether obtaining a negative number in the percent change cells is a desirable or undesirable outcome, based on the particular attribute being measured.

The comments column next to each metric houses information that further explains the results. An additional comments section is provided at the bottom of the audit report to note key observations, lessons learned, ongoing issues, or suggestions for further improvements.

After the team has completed the audit, analyzed the results, and assigned any necessary corrective action activities, a designated person (lead auditor, value stream champion, continuous improvement leader, etc.) should distribute the report to the Kaizen Team, value stream champion, executive sponsor for the Kaizen Event, and relevant leadership across the organization. Organizations holding their first few Kaizen Events may wish to hold formal briefings to present the audit findings to the event leaders, senior leadership, and perhaps the entire leadership team, to provide additional learning opportunities about leadership's role in supporting the rapid improvement process.

The audit report should also be posted in the areas affected by the improvement, in common areas where continuous-improvement communication boards are maintained, and on designated shared drives. Through diligence in ongoing measurement and heightened awareness about process performance, the team's improvements will be sustained and organizational performance will improve.

If the audit reveals a need for corrective action, a small work group consisting of key Kaizen Team members and the supervisors/managers for the affected areas should meet on a regular basis for a few weeks following the audit to assess progress. While the entire Kaizen Team need not be present for these follow-up meetings, it's helpful to share the outcomes of these meetings with team members, so they continue to see the impact their work is having on the organization.

The purpose of the audits is to ensure that the improvements implemented by the Kaizen Team have taken hold, the new process is being followed, and the improvements are having the intended effect. By the time the 60-day audit is complete, the process should be stabilized, and an ongoing monitoring program should be firmly in place with key performance indicators clearly defined, which drive ongoing improvement efforts and identify the need for additional staff education and training. Many organizations ultimately fail in sustaining their improvements because they don't continue to aggressively measure and analyze their processes. This type of monitoring should occur on a daily basis so that real-time corrective actions can take place, if necessary. It does no good to ignore process performance for six or twelve months and then measure it, only to learn it hasn't been performing well for the past six or twelve months. This is the true role of supervisors and managers: to monitor processes real time and identify the need for further improvements when necessary.

So now that the organization has completed a cycle of improvement, how does it keep the momentum going? How do you drive change throughout the organization? That's the subject of our next chapter, Creating a Kaizen Culture.

# CHAPTER 19

# CREATING A KAIZEN CULTURE

Creating a kaizen culture is a multifaceted journey that requires proper execution of change, leadership commitment, and an infrastructure that provides ongoing support for improvement efforts. All too often, one of the three elements is missing, resulting in slow progress at best, and organizational damage at worst. You've probably seen it: An organization embraces a new way of thinking and experiences a few early successes. Leadership and workforce enthusiasm mounts. Momentum is created. And then the organization's well-intended efforts begin to fizzle. Results wane, resistance builds, and—through the eyes of an understandably cynical workforce—the new approach becomes yet another failed improvement initiative.

This scenario doesn't have to happen. Through recognizing the aspects of human nature that cause people to either embrace or reject change, and including in your plans the necessary elements for effective change, you can stimulate the culture shift that's necessary to embed continuous improvement into an organization's DNA. When this happens, organizational performance begins to soar. Your goal is to minimize the reasons people resist change so you can create a kaizen culture, which is a fundamental building block on the journey to becoming a high-performing organization.

## UNDERSTANDING THE CHANGE PROCESS

If you study the institutions around you—schools, government, suppliers of the goods and services you purchase, and your own organization—you begin to notice common elements that, if present, create effective change and, if absent, lead the individuals within the organization to resist new ideas and ways of operating. Think about it: When was the last time you experienced a change that you were happy with? What made it a more positive experience than usual? Now think about the opposite reactions you've had. What was missing in the way the change was executed? Why did you resist the change? Think about the elements that need to be in place for you to personally embrace change. Your workforce needs these same elements.

While change management theories abound, Table 19-1 presents a model created by the authors of this book, which views the change process from strategic and tactical perspectives. This model defines the roles of the individuals involved in the change process, the elements that must be present for effective change, and the range of potential results if any of the elements are absent.

The required elements are relevant at both macro and micro levels. At a macro level, leadership must create the environment for sustainable improvement. Without leadership

**Table 19-1.** Creating Effective Change

| Stage | Role | Required Elements | Potential Results if Required Elements are Absent |
|---|---|---|---|
| **Strategic** | **Senior Leadership** | **Purpose**<br>• Communicate the compelling business case, burning platform, *why is change necessary?*<br><br>**Plan**<br>• Provides vision, direction and key milestones<br><br>**Objectives**<br>• Must be measurable | **Ineffective Action**<br>• Shotgun change/ band aids<br>• Suboptimization/disconnected<br>• False starts/reverting to old ways<br>• Renegade behavior/lashing out/anarchy<br><br>**Inaction**<br>• Confusion/stagnation/frustration<br>• Apathy<br>• Resistance |
| **Tactical** | **Middle Management & Supervisors**<br>(Resources & Support) | **Motivation**<br>• Incentives, WIIFM (what's in it for me?), rewards & consequences<br>• Inclusion/involvement<br>• Respect & recognition<br>• Results<br><br>**Guidance**<br>• Facilitation<br>• Executable action plan<br>• Measurement/metrics<br>• Continuous monitoring | |
| | **Workforce**<br>(Execution) | **Skills**<br>• Improvement tools<br>• Change management tools<br><br>**Time**<br>• Provides focus | |

commitment and support, the best laid plans will fail. Middle management may be able to drive change for a period of time, but it will be limited in scope, and managers will encounter too many obstacles for the change to be sustained over the long haul. While these managers may be able to successfully implement small improvements, without senior leadership support, these limited improvements will not likely impact organizational performance across the entire value stream.

At a macro level, leadership must communicate the reason for change. This seemingly logical element is often absent from improvement efforts. People need to understand the compelling need—the burning platform—for a particular improvement. To make significant progress, a sense of urgency must be instilled. All too often, people aren't told *why* something must occur, so they operate in a vacuum, which invites resistance. Leadership must also provide a clear plan that communicates its vision and provides direction to those who will implement the change. And finally, leaders must establish measurable objectives to define the degree to which their vision has been successfully implemented.

At a micro level, properly executed Kaizen Events provide the structure to ensure that the tactical elements for effective change are in place, which trigger progressive shifts in culture. These internal shifts, in turn, produce high-performing organizations, which customers, workers, and investors are all eager to engage with. Kaizen Events fulfill these vital tactical requirements in the following ways.

## Motivation

Most human beings have a natural inclination to seek pleasure and avoid pain, a principle that provides insight into what motivates people's behavior. Human nature also operates heavily from a "what's in it for me?" perspective, especially in organizations where interpersonal connections are based, in large part, on impersonal goals and objectives. To implement effective change, clear incentives must be provided for people to embrace the change. You need to engage with workers at an emotional level, even though they are expected to operate in a somewhat unemotional manner.

People often think of incentives in financial terms, but human nature is often more significantly shaped by the *intrinsic* rewards received. In Kaizen Events, the intrinsic incentives of inclusion (cross-functional teamwork) and control (authority to improve one's work environment) drive teams to achieve unparalleled performance. When Kaizen Teams begin to see the results of their efforts—and receive visible recognition—energy is generated that propels them to excel even further. When teams face the possibility of reduced intrinsic rewards because the clock is ticking, and the end of the event is nearing, they often step it up yet another notch, and they are able to accomplish even greater amounts of work in ever shorter time periods. In properly executed Kaizen Events, the incentives are embedded into the team's psyche by providing continuous and visible recognition for their efforts.

## Guidance

Organizations often try to make improvements without providing adequate guidance and resources, which results in frustration, improvements that aren't lasting, or change that doesn't qualify as an improvement. Kaizen Events provide the skilled facilitation and executable action plans (the Event Charter) that are necessary for a team to generate results that align with leadership's vision.

Without a clearly defined action plan, leadership's attempt to realize their vision is a long shot at best. Most organizations are far more proficient at analyzing and planning than they are in tactical-level execution. After all, action seems riskier than thinking. But is it? *Is the risk of action higher than the risk of inaction?* An executable action plan creates a safety net of sorts—structure, expectations, time frames, and clear accountability. Without it, organizations experience false starts, misdirection, and "treadmill behavior."

From the moment the charter is being developed, Kaizen Events provide a series of action plans that drive the improvement effort itself, sustainability of the improvement, and ongoing improvements. Daily action plans are established by the facilitator to keep the Kaizen Team focused and on track. At the conclusion of the event, the Sustainability Plan, 30-Day List, and Parking Lot serve as action plans for sustainability and provide the foundation for ongoing improvement efforts. In addition, the heavy emphasis on data-driven decisions and ongoing measurement—all part of the action plans put in place during the event—provides the necessary direction for creating informed and sustainable change.

## Skills

The "learn by doing" environment that defines Kaizen Events provides the setting for effective and lasting skills development. Throughout the event, skilled facilitators teach, monitor, and provide feedback. And team members learn in the most effective way: *by doing*. By the end of the Kaizen Event, six to ten people have developed a valuable new set of skills that they can continue to apply and share with others long after the event has concluded. Even seasoned team members report that the degree of learning that takes place during a Kaizen Event continues to exceed their expectations. This newly acquired knowledge and skill set creates a more valuable and motivated workforce.

## Time

We live in a world in which multitasking is encouraged and expected. But, without focus, work quality diminishes, frustration rises, and the pace of change slows. Kaizen Events provide the necessary focus to hone in on one problem at a time (one-piece flow) and eliminate interruptions that invite poor quality and long mental setup times. As a result, solutions are better thought out and implemented more quickly. And the compressed time frame also reduces the risk of analysis paralysis or allowing doubt to alter what are otherwise good decisions.

While some people seem hard-wired from birth to embrace change, others are extremely uncomfortable with the prospect. If every change effort includes the previously mentioned elements—*and they are effectively communicated*—you will progressively shift natural resisters toward the comfort end of their acceptance spectrum. You will, in effect, hard-wire your workforce to embrace change. But you won't accomplish this vital step in creating a kaizen culture by telling people what to do. *They need to be actively engaged in the process.* The key to success is threefold: 1) clear communication of the vision; 2) extensive workforce involvement in executing that vision at a tactical level; and 3) strong leadership commitment and support along the way. So what does leadership commitment look and feel like? Read on.

# DEMONSTRATING LEADERSHIP COMMITMENT

Your workforce consists of perceptive individuals. No matter how inexperienced or seasoned they are, they observe carefully and listen closely. They study leadership for clues about what's going on behind closed doors and cues for how to behave. If they sense an incongruity between a leader's words and action, they will view the action as the more reliable indicator. So leaders must remember that, from workers' perspectives, it doesn't matter what leaders *think*, and it doesn't matter what leaders *say*. It matters what they *do—especially in terms of rapid improvement*.

The following nine actions are necessary to demonstrate leadership's commitment to continuous improvement, and lead the transformation into a kaizen culture. To the extent that any of these nine behaviors are missing, the leader risks dashing not only any hope of realizing the culture shift he or she seeks, but possibly creating an intransigent, apathetic workforce in the process.

1. *Be engaged in the planning stage.* Especially in early Kaizen Events, leadership must ensure that the event supports organizational and value stream objectives. To minimize downstream conflict, leaders must agree upon the scope, timing, and goals of the improvement effort. Any gains realized by Kaizen teams are put at risk if leadership isn't fully committed and/or hasn't bought into the change process from the get-go.

2. *Authorize workers to make changes.* Lean thinking requires leaders to focus on what their role is meant to be: developing strategy. As discussed, the tactical decisions about how to implement improvements belong to the people performing the work. You should remind company leaders that their actions, not their words, are the primary indicators of their willingness to "let go" of tactical decision making. No matter what company leaders say, if they don't authorize frontline workers to make tactical decisions—with boundaries, of course—they will stifle the organization's efforts to improve performance.

3. *Avoid becoming an "anchor dragger."* While it may take time for leadership to fully understand lean principles, leaders who refuse to embrace the approach eventually become an impediment to organizational progress. Their traditional command and control mindset can sabotage the organization's efforts to become lean. Leaders who refuse to adopt new ways of thinking and behaving should be encouraged to find work in a more traditionally minded organization.

4. *Allow for dedicated Kaizen Team members.* Leadership must be willing to relieve workers of their daily duties to participate on Kaizen Teams. This is especially true when high-performing workers (whose managers are often reluctant to give up for two to five days) are needed for a team. This requirement is an especially painful one for organizations that are only "one deep" in particular work areas. But pain indicates the need for root cause analyses and resolution. In this case, organizational healing begins with having backup for every position to provide coverage in times of sickness, vacations, family leave, jury duty, and continuous improvement activities—or if a worker suddenly leaves the organization.

5. *Attend interim briefings.* As described in Chapter 10, the Kaizen Event includes interim briefings, during which the team shares their progress and seeks leadership guidance regarding key issues. When a leader doesn't show up, it sends a strong message to the team about the leader's priorities.

6. *Attend the team presentation.* For the same reasons stated above, leaders need to attend the team's presentation that concludes the Kaizen Event. In addition to serving as an educational and communication tool, the presentation is sometimes the only time team members receive verbal and in-person recognition for their efforts. And the dialogue that typically occurs during the presentation is often the most powerful tool the organization has for promoting lean thinking and Kaizen Events.

7. *Become comfortable with—and endorse—rapid decision making.* A key success factor for Kaizen Events centers around the organization's ability to make decisions quickly in real time. Leaders must participate in this process when, for example, the team needs authorization to modify a policy or challenge a long-standing paradigm within the organization. Leaders sometimes say, "I'm not comfortable making a decision this quickly. I need more information." But when teams probe to determine what relevant data would help the leader make a decision, they sometimes find that adequate data has nothing to do with it. So leaders need to understand up front that rapid decision making is an expectation—assuming adequate data is available. No one will force a leader to make a decision if he or she truly doesn't have enough data to make an informed decision. But the expectation needs to be firmly established up front that lean thinking requires as much a shift in the speed at which decisions are made as the speed at which goods and services are delivered to your customers.

8. *Become comfortable with "it doesn't have to be perfect" thinking.* Assure leaders that you would never advocate making a change unless it carried with it a high likelihood of improving organizational performance. Remind them that the fifth lean principle is "seeking perfection" through calculated experimentation and incremental change, rather than waiting for perfection to begin making improvements. Remind leaders that the goal is to remove non-value-adding waste, not about implementing a perfect process. And, finally, remind leaders, as you do with team members, that nothing is set in stone. Further improvements can, *and will*, be made down the road.

9. *Monitor the new process and its results.* Supervisors and managers are ultimately responsible for mentoring the processes they oversee. While the Kaizen Team plays a large role in measuring process performance during and immediately following an event, the responsibility quickly shifts to those who are closest to the work on a daily basis. But if measurement falls apart after the event—if management fails to fully embrace its role in the process and perform accordingly—the improvement will be difficult to sustain.

While leaders can and should display many other behaviors to demonstrate their commitment to continuous improvement, if they follow these nine previously mentioned behaviors, they will clearly see the wheels of productive change start to spin.

## DEVELOPING A CONTINUOUS-IMPROVEMENT INFRASTRUCTURE

An important goal of holding Kaizen Events is to help the organization learn how to apply the lean philosophy and relevant improvement tools, and create a support system that encourages "kaizen behavior" every minute of every day. While your specific continuous-improvement approach is important in the beginning, your longer term journey requires the "cellular uptake" of lean thinking into your organization's genetic code. You want to create a continuous-improvement infrastructure that enables you to view every process through a lean lens, and approach every problem with the same speed, diligence, and inclusiveness that is offered by Kaizen Events. What you need is a permanent shift in culture, and that's not going to happen by holding a Kaizen Event every month or two, nor by relying on external consultants for an extended period of time. It will take at least one person or, in larger organizations, a core team of skilled individuals to strategically direct and coordinate improvement activities. This means building a dedicated staff to:

- Provide ongoing lean training to leadership and the workforce.
- Oversee improvement identification and prioritization.
- Schedule, plan and facilitate improvement activities, such as value stream mapping, Kaizen Events, and longer term projects.
- Manage process monitoring efforts to aid in assuring sustainability.
- Assist leadership in identifying and resolving obstacles to cultural transformation.

How many full time equivalents (FTEs) does it take to make significant progress on the lean journey? First, it is important to understand that it's not the number of people that matters—it's how many hours they have available to focus on improvement activities. On the high end, a number of 400-employee organizations have three full-time lean specialists who are overwhelmed with improvement-related work. Several 800-employee organizations have two full-time specialists. One 1,500-person organization has three full-time employees dedicated to continuous improvement and a team of 25 trained facilitators who have split roles—75 percent operational responsibility (with staffs, in some cases) and 25 percent lean work. The shared role resources spend a little less than one day a week focused on continuous-improvement activities. Progress is significantly slower when improvement efforts are led by resources with shared operational responsibilities.

The authors of this book recommend a 1:100 ratio—one full-time employee, skilled in and dedicated to continuous improvement, for every 100 employees. While aggressive, it's a ratio that can generate significant results and measurable payback.

Another relevant issue in establishing an infrastructure to support ongoing Kaizen Events is determining how often to hold events. Given a four- to six-week planning cycle, two to five days for the event itself, and a formal 30- to 60-day follow-up period, the organization risks burnout if it attempts too many formal Kaizen Events in a given time period. With adequate support, most organizations can handle about *four events per 100 employees per year*.

When you begin holding more than one or two events per month, you should publish a calendar as far in advance as possible listing when the events will be held, and the specific area of focus (if known). Larger organizations may want to plan six months in advance. But, while advance planning is critical, it's important not to fill every available Kaizen Event slot with predetermined improvements. Companies that hold frequent events find it best to hold every third or fourth slot open to accommodate higher priority needs that may arise, and follow-up Kaizen Events to further improve processes. If the schedule is filled with predetermined Kaizen Events, you'll spend unnecessary time reprioritizing and rescheduling.

When scheduling Kaizen Events in advance, another consideration is whether to "go deep" or "go broad." You may want to continue making improvements to your target value stream. Or you may want to move on to a completely different value stream. A third option exists if you've used the pilot approach to implement an improvement: You may want take the improvement organization-wide.

It is often wise to "go deep" and continue making improvements to the same value stream, leveraging the momentum created during the improvement process. However, three circumstances substantiate moving on to a new value stream:

- *Burnout.* After two or three Kaizen Events, even if the events are scheduled four to six weeks apart, the workforce in the target area can experience burnout. Event planning, execution, and follow-up require significant energy. Sometimes it's best to let an area live with its improvements for awhile, and allow team members to recharge their batteries before planning another Kaizen Event. In the meantime, to keep the spirit of kaizen alive, they can make smaller continuous improvements—just-do-its—that don't require Kaizen Events.

- *Extenuating competing priorities.* Sometimes an organization reaches a point in which more aggressive continuous-improvement approaches, such as holding Kaizen Events, needs to take a back seat to competing priorities that are consuming significant energy across the organization. During these periods, the organization should emphasize the need for ongoing, incremental improvement but step away from formal Kaizen Events for a few months. Situations that may benefit from this strategy include physical moves, significant mergers and acquisitions, implementation of new IT systems, entering a heavy sales cycle, or key leadership turnover, to name a few.

  Continuous improvement should be ongoing no matter what stressors the organization faces, but formal Kaizen Events can wait until an excessively challenging period has passed, or they can be held in areas less impacted by the temporary situation. On the other hand, you have to guard against resistance to Kaizen Events due to routine, competing organizational priorities. Organizations will always need to juggle competing priorities, and if you use this thinking, there will never be a "good" time to make significant improvements.

- *Significant improvement has been achieved.* While you should continuously seek perfection, there is an appropriate time for moving away from an area that has undergone significant improvement and begin making equally impressive improvements in another area. Once a process is consistently performing well and resources are in place to quickly resolve performance slippage should it occur, it's time to move on to another area that can benefit from Kaizen Events, and to spread learning across the organization.

The most important thing in assessing next steps is to keep your finger on the pulse of the organization to identify: Where's the pain? Who needs help? Who's open to change? How can we spread organizational learning and share best practices? Answers to these questions shape your Kaizen Event schedule.

## CONCLUSION

An organization with a kaizen culture carries a passion for improvement and displays "patient persistence" as it relentlessly removes barriers to flow and enhances organizational performance. As noted in Matthew May's *The Elegant Solution*,[1] Toyota implements one million ideas each year—that's 3,000 ideas per day. Some of those ideas are single hits, some are home runs. The key to Toyota's success is their mission to provide value to the customer, and their kaizen work ethic. Through daily kaizen and strategically employed Kaizen Events, you too, can deliver superior customer value, defined as faster goods and services, at lower cost, and with higher quality.

As depicted on Figure 19-1 (which you were introduced to in Chapter 1) a motivated workforce with proper leadership direction and a well-developed skill set will drive improvements that produce flow, customer loyalty, and ultimately, optimal organization performance. *Your workforce is the key to your success.* Treat your workers with respect. Teach them how to apply lean principles and tools. And, most importantly, give them the authority to make the improvements. Give them "freedom with boundaries" and your organization will soar. You will be on your way to building a lean enterprise that can thrive during strong economic times and survive the inevitable downturns. You will properly serve your customer and provide value to your shareholders. Further, you will provide the work environment to attract and retain the talented workforce you need to provide ongoing value to your customers and shareholders.

*The Kaizen Event Planner* provides the principles and key tools to guide you as you hold your first Kaizen Event, or provide additional structure to the planning and execution approach you've been using. As you progress on the lean journey and incorporate properly executed Kaizen Events into your implementation strategy, remember that, if you relentlessly seek out and eliminate waste and create an environment that results in a fulfilled workforce, improvements to your bottom line and market share will follow. Remember, too, that incremental improvements add up. You don't have to hit a home run every time. Consistent base hits, doubles, and triples will drive up your score more quickly than the occasional grand slam.

---

1. Matthew May, *The Elegant Solution*. New York: Free Press, Oct 2006, p. xi.

**Figure 19-1.** Building a Lean Enterprise

Now it's time for you to take action: Define your product families, select a value stream for improvement, create current and future state value stream maps, select improvements that are best implemented through the Kaizen Event structure, and begin planning! *Best wishes for successful Kaizen Events and continuous forward progress on the journey to becoming a lean enterprise.*

# Appendices

# APPENDIX A

# LEAN TERMINOLOGY

**Activity Ratio (AR).** An indicator of process efficiency, equal to the sum of the critical path **Process Times** for all the individual steps divided by the sum of the critical path **Lead Time**.

**Andon.** A visual control device used to show the current status of the process and/or system. The visual control usually takes the form of a lighted overhead display or series of lights that can signal normal and abnormal conditions in the process.

**AR.** See **Activity Ratio**.

**Autonomation.** A machine or process that immediately stops whenever a defect or abnormal condition occurs. This technique is an essential element in introducing one-piece flow to a process. Also referred to as **Jidoka**. Compare with **Mistake Proofing**.

**Barriers to Flow.** Any barrier, physical or not, that prevents the passing of one unit of work directly to the next process without the work stopping.

**Batch and Queue.** A processing method where multiple pieces of work (often referred to as a "batch" or "lot") are processed and/or passed together from one operation to the next. Upon arrival at the next process, some or all of these pieces of work may wait in a "queue" to be worked on. Contrast with **One-Piece Flow**.

**Cause-and-Effect Diagram.** A visual root cause analysis tool used to brainstorm and document potential causes and subcauses for an undesired effect. The primary causes often used are referred to as the "6Ms," standing for: man, machine, materials, methods, measurement, and Mother Nature (*Note*: More recently, "people" and "environment" are being used in lieu of man and Mother Nature.) Also referred to as an **Ishikawa Diagram** (after its developer) or **Fishbone Diagram** (due to its shape).

**Cells.** See **Layout for Flow**.

**Changeover.** The activity of converting a process from performing one type of work to another. Changeover time is the elapsed time from when the last good unit of the run is completed until the first good unit of the following run is completed. Changeovers can be physical (changing a fixture) or mental (orienting one's self with the next "job"). Long changeovers often result in batch processing, inhibiting the ability to achieve one-piece-flow. This term is also commonly called **Setup**.

**Checklist.** A form used as a reference to ensure all of the key steps in a process have been completed. Checklists are often integrated into the standard work for an operation.

**Checksheet.** A simple form used to tabulate information regarding the type and frequency of an occurrence. Checksheets are often used to quantify data and provide direction for corrective actions or continuous improvement activities. Results from checksheets often provide the input data for creating Pareto charts.

**Co-location.** See **Layout for Flow**.

**Complete and Accurate (%C&A).** See **Percent Complete and Accurate**.

**Continuous Flow.** A work process management system wherein workers only work on one unit at a time, and only one unit of work moves from process to process. Implementation of continuous flow can have significant impact on reducing throughput time, minimizing waste, and improving value-adding activity. This concept is also referred to as **Single-Piece Flow** or **One-Piece Flow**. Contrast with **Batch and Queue**.

**Continuous Improvement.** A philosophy of frequently reviewing processes, identifying opportunities for improvement, and implementing changes to get closer to perfection. See **Kaizen** and **Kaikaku**.

**Countermeasure.** A change to a process, designed to reduce or eliminate the root cause of an undesired symptom.

**Critical Path.** When parallel activities occur in a process, the critical path is the sequence of activities along the path with the longest lead time through the process from request to delivery.

**Cross-Functional Team.** A team composed of individuals representing different functions or departments within a given process. The team may be formed for a specific activity (e.g., a Kaizen Event), or the team may be more permanent in nature (a cross-functional team, co-located and cross-trained; put in place to support a specific product or customer).

**Cross-Training.** Training individuals to perform a variety of tasks and skills. In a lean environment, the focus of cross-training should be to increase competence along the value stream in order to optimize performance of that value stream.

**CS.** See **Current State**.

**CT.** See **Cycle Time**.

**Current State (CS).** All of the steps that are performed to complete the work as it is operating in today's environment (this is often quite different from how a written procedure states it should be done) as well as the issues and performance (metrics) of the process.

**Cycle Time (CT).** The frequency, or interval, of work being completed. Compare to **Process Time**; contrast with **Lead Time**.

**Downstream.** As viewed from a reference point, downstream processes are activities that take place after the reference point (e.g., transmitting a quote to the customer is a downstream process from writing the quote). Contrast with **Upstream**.

**Effective.** Measure of quality. How well is it done? All processes must be both efficient and effective. Contrast with **Efficient**.

**Efficient.** Measure of speed. How fast is it done? All processes must be both efficient and effective. Contrast with **Effective**.

**Eighty (80%) Percent Rule.** See **Pareto Principle**.

**FC.** See **Freed Capacity**.

**FIFO.** See **First In First Out** and **FIFO Lanes**.

**FIFO Lanes.** A type of **Pull Production** that is often used in administrative and nonstandard product environments. A FIFO lane is a coupling mechanism, which defines the maximum work-in-process (WIP) level between two processes. FIFO lanes are typically physical in nature, which provides supplying process workers with a clear visual indicator when they have authorization to produce and when they should stop (e.g., five color-coded folders between the design and estimating steps indicate design activities should stop if all five folders are full with work for the estimating process). Compare to **Kanban**.

**First In First Out (FIFO).** An order sequencing and control approach, which ensures that the first order entering the system is the first order to be worked on.

**First Pass Yield (FPY).** A quality metric that indicates process performance. First pass yield is expressed as a percentage and is calculated by dividing the number of "right the first time" units of work by the quantity of work entering the process. Similar to **%C&A**.

**Fishbone Diagram.** See **Cause-and-Effect Diagram**.

**Five Ss (5Ss).** An approach utilizing workplace organization and visual controls to improve performance. It is derived from the Japanese words *seiri*, *seiton*, *seiso*, *seiketsu*, and *shitsuke*. The English equivalents are sort, set-in-order, shine, standardize, and sustain. Safety is often referred to as the sixth "S," but in traditional 5S programs, safety is assumed to be predominant throughout.

**Five Whys.** A root cause analysis tool used to identify the true root cause of a problem. The question "why" is asked a sufficient number of times to find the fundamental reason for the problem. Once that cause is identified, an appropriate countermeasure can be designed and implemented to eliminate recurrence.

**Flow.** The smooth, uninterrupted movement of a product or service through a series of process steps. In true flow, the work product (information, paperwork, material, etc.) passing through the series of steps never stops.

**Flowchart.** A schematic representation of a process, from start to finish, including inputs, outputs, paths, steps, and decision points. Traditional process maps are often depicted in flowchart form. Also referred to as a **Process Flowchart**. Contrast with **Metrics-Based Process Map**.

**Flow Stopper.** See **Barriers to Flow**.

**FPY.** See **First Pass Yield**.

**Freed Capacity (FC).** The amount of capacity created as a result of process improvements, typically expressed in number of full time equivalents (FTEs). It is calculated by subtracting the post-improvement sum of process times (in hours) from the pre-improvement sum of process times (in hours), and multiplying that value by the number of occurrences per year. To determine the freed capacity (the new number of FTEs required), divide the resulting product by 2,080 (number of scheduled work hours per year).

**FS.** See **Future State**.

**FTE.** See **Full-Time Equivalent**.

**Full-Time Equivalent (FTE).** Number of resources (usually people) required to run a process or series of processes if they were employed full time on that activity. For people, the number is usually based on 2,080 hours per year (i.e., 2,080 hours of work = one FTE) or 40 hours per week. Example: Four people working 20 hours per week each on the same activity, equals two FTEs.

**Functional Arrangement.** The grouping and management of resources based on similar activities or operations, as opposed to physically arranging and managing a work team based on the sequence of process steps. An example would be where all the design engineers sit together, separate from the drafting staff. Contrast with **Layout for Flow**.

**Future State (FS).** A plan for how a process is planned to be running at a defined point in time in the future. Serves as the primary input for the development of an implementation plan. Future state value stream maps are usually developed looking three to twelve months into the future.

**Gemba.** A Japanese word for the "real place" or the place where the work actual occurs. To understand the real issues that affect a process, it is critical to go to gemba and see what is actually happening.

**Genchi Genbutsu.** A Japanese term that refers to seeing for yourself. Genchi genbutsu is the act of going to gemba.

**Heijunka.** See **Level Loading**.

**Ishikawa Diagram.** See **Cause-and-Effect Diagram**.

**Jidoka.** See **Autonomation**.

**JIT.** See **Just-in-Time**.

**Just-in-Time (JIT).** A process management system utilizing the concept of flow to produce goods and provide services only when needed and only in the quantity needed.

**Kaikaku.** Radical process improvement over a short period of time—innovation. Changes of theses type are often implemented during the course of a **Kaizen Event**.

**Kaizen.** An improvement philosophy in which continuous incremental improvement occurs over a sustained period of time, creating more value and less waste, resulting in increased speed, lower costs, and improved quality. When applied to a business enterprise, it refers to ongoing improvement involving the entire workforce including senior leadership, middle management, and frontline workers. Kaizen is also a philosophy that assumes that our way of life (working, social, or personal) deserves to be constantly improved.

**Kaizen Event.** A structured, team-based, problem-solving activity of short duration used to improve processes throughout an organization. Activities typically include: 1) team training, 2) current state analysis, 3) future state design, 4) prioritization of improvements, 5) train on new process, and 6) implementing the selected improvements. Duration is typically one to five days. The event team is focused on the process 100 percent of time during the event and is cross-functional in composition. Also referred to as Kaizen Blitz and Rapid Improvement Event (RIE).

**Kanban.** A type of **Pull Production** system whereby the downstream process signals the upstream process to replenish what has been consumed. Kanbans typically pull by part number. Kanban means signboard in Japanese. Compare to **FIFO Lanes**.

**Layout for Flow.** The co-location of processes and/or equipment in sequence to permit one-piece flow and the flexible deployment of workers to operate multiple processes (resources). The resources found in cells are often cross-functional in nature. Also referred to as **Cells**, or **Cellular Arrangement**. Contrast with **Functional Arrangement**.

**Lead Time (LT).** The amount of time it takes for a product (or service) to go through the system, from the first operation to the final operation, including processing, delays, movement, queues, etc. At a process level, the process lead time begins when the work is received and ends when the work is delivered to the next downstream customer. Lead Time = Process Time plus Wait Time (or delays). Also referred to as **Throughput Time** or **Turnaround Time**.

**Lean.** The philosophy of aggressive, continuous improvement executed through defining value from the customer's perspective; mapping the value streams; creating flow; working at the pull of the customer; and pursuit of perfection.

**Level Loading.** The leveling of quantities and types (mix) of products/services produced for the customer. Also referred to as **Heijunka** or **Production Smoothing**.

**Line Balancing.** See **Work Balancing**.

**LT.** See **Lead Time**.

**MBPM.** See **Metrics-Based Process Mapping**.

**Metrics-Based Process Mapping (MBPM).** A visual, micro-level process mapping technique that separates tasks into separate rows based on who the person or functional area is that is performing the tasks. These rows are sometimes referred to as swim lanes. The tasks are depicted in a sequential format such that a timeline can be created, which depicts total lead time. MBPM process blocks contain at a minimum the: process time, lead time, and %C&A for that step. Contrast with traditional **Flowcharts**.

**Mistake Proofing.** A device or procedure designed to prevent the generation of defects. The English translations for this Japanese phrase are: poka, which means "error" and yoke, which means "to avoid." Also referred to as **Poka-Yoke**.

**Muda.** A Japanese word for waste. See **Non-Value-Adding** and **Waste**.

**Multifunctional Workers.** Individuals trained and qualified to perform a variety of tasks. In a lean operation, workers are typically cross-trained on operations upstream and downstream of their primary work, so they can support the value stream should problems occur.

**Necessary Non-Value-Adding.** Activities that add no value from the customer's perspective but are required in order to operate the business. This could include legal and regulatory requirements, as well as certain internal business processes, which would put the business at risk if eliminated in today's environment. Necessary non-value-adding is often referred to as Type I Muda. Contrast with **Unnecessary Non-Value-Adding**.

**Non-Value-Adding (NVA).** A task that the customer does not care about and would be unwilling to pay for if he/she knew the incremental cost of that task. The attribute of a task or activities that can be eliminated from a process without deterioration of the function, performance, or quality of a product or service as viewed by the customer. Two types of non-value-adding activity exist: **Necessary NVA** and **Unnecessary NVA**.

**NVA.** See **Non-value-adding**.

**OEE.** See **Overall Equipment Effectiveness**.

**One-Piece Flow.** See **Continuous Flow**.

**Operation.** An activity performed on a product or service. An operation is a component of **Process**. Also referred to as **Task**.

**Overall Equipment Effectiveness (OEE).** A measure of how effectively equipment is utilized during scheduled operating time. OEE = (% time available) $\times$ (% of designed output rate) $\times$ (% First Pass Yield). OEE is particularly useful when assessing how well critical equipment is utilized. Examples include medical equipment in healthcare, duplication equipment in the publishing industry, computers in many industries, vehicles and equipment in law enforcement, etc. Factors such as cost and available capacity are key determinants in evaluating OEE.

**PACE Chart.** A graphic used to help quickly prioritize a list of improvement ideas based on ease of implementation and anticipated benefit.

**Pareto Chart.** A graph or chart, based on the Pareto Principle, that ranks occurrences from the most frequent to the least frequent. Pareto charts are often used to prioritize improvement activities. **Checksheets** are a common input to creating a **Pareto Chart**.

**Pareto Principle.** The concept that most of the effects in a situation can be traced back to a small number of contributors. In the early 1900s Wilfred Pareto observed that 80 percent of the property in Italy was held by only 20 percent of the population. Joseph Juran later observed that this 80/20 relationship is, in fact, quite common and coined this phenomenon as "The Pareto Principal."

**PDCA.** See **Plan–Do–Check–Act**.

**Percent Complete and Accurate (%C&A).** A quality metric used to measure the degree to which work from an upstream supplier is determined by the downstream customer to be complete and accurate (or error free). In other words, to what degree does the downstream customer need to: 1) correct information that is incorrect; 2) add missing information that should have been supplied by an upstream supplier; and/or 3) clarify information provided. Out of 100 "things" passing to the downstream customer, what percentage is complete and accurate and do not require one of the three above actions before completing the task? The number is obtained by asking the immediate, or successive, downstream customer(s) what percentage of the time they receive work that is 100 percent complete and accurate.

**Percent Value-Adding.** See **Activity Ratio**.

**Plan–Do–Check–Act (PDCA).** The basic steps to be followed in making continuous incremental improvements (kaizen), adapted by W. Edwards Deming from Walter Shewart's PDSA Cycle (S = Study).

**Poka-Yoke.** See **Mistake Proofing**.

**Process.** An operation or group of operations that receives inputs, performs an activity, and then provides outputs to an internal or external customer.

**Process Flowchart.** See **Flowchart**.

**Process Time (PT).** The amount of time is takes to perform a task (or series of tasks) if the worker could work uninterrupted. For example, if one enters data for 2 minutes, places a call to obtain additional information, waits for 10 minutes for the call to be returned, talks with the information supplier for 3 minutes, and finishes data entering in 1 minute, the process time is six minutes (2 + 3 + 1). Process time plus wait time (or delays) = lead time. This time is related to **Takt Time** such that if every operation in a complete process has a process Time equal to or less than the takt time, then the product or service can be made in **One-piece Flow**. Also referred to as **Touch Time** or **Cycle Time**.

**Product Family.** A group of products or services that pass through similar process steps. In the service sector, product families are often referred to as **Service Families**.

**Production Smoothing.** See **Level Loading**.

**PT.** See **Process Time**.

**Pull Production.** A **work-in-process (WIP)** management approach whereby the downstream process authorizes upstream production through the consumption of work. Common pull systems include **One-Piece Flow, Kanban** and **FIFO Lanes**.

**Push Production.** A system where an upstream process produces as much as it can without regard to the actual requirements of the next process and sends them to the next process whether they have capacity to begin work or not. Push Production typically results in queues of work building up, which result in delays.

**Queue Time.** The amount of time that product, people, information, or material waits to be worked on. Also referred to as "wait time."

**RCA.** See **Root-Cause Analysis**.

**Reliability.** The ability of a process to produce the same results (product or service) over repeated cycles.

**RFPY.** See **Rolled First Pass Yield**.

**Rolled First Pass Yield (RFPY).** A quality metric for determining the percentage of work going through a series of process steps that is error free. RFPY is the product of the percent yield (or **%C&A**) of all of the process steps. For example, in a three-step process, if the %C&A is 80 percent at the first step, 75 percent at the second step, and 90 percent at the third step, the rolled first pass yield = 80% $\times$ 75% $\times$ 90% = 54%. In this example the 54 percent RFPY means that only 54 percent of the things going through the process pass through the process "completely and accurately."

**Root Cause Analysis (RCA).** A problem-solving approach whereby the underlying cause of a problem is first identified and only then is the corrective action or solution designed. The intent of RCA is to reduce or eliminate recurrence of the same problem. RCA tools include **Five Whys, Cause-and-Effect Diagrams, Check Lists** and **Pareto Charts**.

**Sensei.** A Japanese word for teacher or master. In lean circles, sensei typically refers to an individual who has been led numerous lean transformations.

**Service Family.** See **Product Family**.

**Setup.** See **Changeover**.

**Single-Piece Flow.** See **Continuous Flow**.

**Spaghetti Diagram.** A diagram representing the physical path taken by a product (or service) as it travels through all the steps required to transform a requirement into a deliverable. This can also be used to draw the path walked by those involved in completing the required activities to deliver the product (or service). The diagram derives its name from the way it commonly looks after mapping a process because the diagram looks much like a plate of spaghetti.

**Stakeholder.** Anyone who has an interest in a process, typically the suppliers, customers, and people who actually perform the work.

**Standard Work.** Documentation of the best known method for completing a task or activity. This becomes the way for everyone working on that process to perform the work. This also becomes the baseline for future work. In the words of Taichii Ohno, "Where there is no standard, there can be no kaizen (improvement)."

**Takt Time (TT).** The pace at which work must be completed in order to meet customer demand. To calculate, divide the available work time by the customer demand for that period. For example, if a call center receives 900 calls per shift, and there are 27,000 seconds of available work time, the takt time is 30 seconds per call. Therefore, one call must be completed every 30 seconds to meet customer demand. Takt, a German word, meaning pace, is the heartbeat of any lean system. **Process Time** divided by **Takt Time** yields the number of workers required to support a specific product.

**Task.** See **Operation**.

**Throughput Time.** See **Lead Time**.

**Total Quality Management (TQM).** A management approach which evolved out of the work of quality pioneers including Deming, Juran, Ishikawa and Shewart. TQM focuses on the delivery of quality product and quality services to achieve customer satisfaction, concepts that provided the foundation for the Toyota Production System.

**Touch Time.** See **Process Time**.

**TQM.** See **Total Quality Management**.

**TT.** See **Takt Time**.

**Turnaround Time.** See **Lead Time**.

**Upstream.** As viewed from a reference point, upstream processes are activities that take place prior to the reference point (e.g., receiving a request for a quote from the customer is upstream to writing the quote). Contrast with **Downstream**.

**Unnecessary Non-Value-Adding.** Activities that add no value from the customer's perspective nor are they necessary to properly run the business. These activities are often legacy in nature ("we've always done it that way"). Unnecessary non-value-adding activities are often referred to as Type II Muda.

**VA.** See **Value Adding**.

**Value.** A customer-defined desired feature or attribute provided at the right time and at an appropriate price.

**Value Adding (VA).** Any activity which, from the ultimate customer's perspective is of value, such that the customer is willing to pay for that activity, or that that activity is a condition of doing business with that customer.

**Value Stream.** The specific activities required to design, order, and provide a specific product or service from the point of product (or service) concept, through launch, ordering raw materials, production, and placing the product (or service) in the hands of the customer. From a shareholder's perspective the value stream could also include the steps and time required until the receipt of revenue.

**Value Steam Map (VSM).** A high-level, visual representation of all of the process steps (both VA and NVA) required to transform a customer requirement into a delivered good or service. A VSM shows the connection between information flow and product flow, as well as the major process blocks and barriers to flow. Value stream maps are used to document current-state conditions as well as design a future state. One of the key objectives of value stream mapping is to identify non-value-adding activities for elimination. Value stream maps, along with the Value Stream Implementation Plan are strategic tools used to help identify, prioritize, and communicate continuous improvement activities.

**Visual Management.** An approach to managing products, people, and processes using low-cost, easy-to-understand visual devices. These devices, when properly utilized, will quickly and effectively communicate objectives, performance, operating conditions, and problems.

**VSM.** See **Value Stream Map**.

**Waste.** Any activity that consumes resources, but does not provide value as defined by the customer. Also referred to as **muda** or **non-value-adding activities**. The eight common types of waste are:

- Overproduction
- Overprocessing
- Waiting
- Inventory
- Defects
- Motion (by people)
- Transportation (of product/material)
- Underutilization of people

**WIP.** See **Work-in-Process**.

**Work Balancing.** Designing processes so that the Process Time for each person is equal or slightly less than the Takt Time that is required to meet customer demand. Also referred to as **Line Balancing**.

**Work-in-Process (WIP).** Work that has been made available to be worked on, has been initiated, or has been completed but has not yet been released to the downstream customer.

# APPENDIX B

# ADDITIONAL RESOURCES

## BOOKS

### Toyota Production System, Lean Enterprise Principles, and Kaizen

Imai, Masaaki, *KAIZEN: The Key to Japan's Competitive Success.* New York: McGraw-Hill, 1986.

Imai, Masaaki, *Gemba Kaizen: A Commonsense, Low-Cost Approach to Management.* New York: McGraw-Hill, 1997.

Laraia, Anthony C., Patricia E. Moody, and Robert W. Hall, *The Kaizen Blitz: Accelerating Breakthroughs in Productivity and Performance.* New York: John Wiley & Sons, 1999.

Liker, Jeffrey, *The Toyota Way.* New York: McGraw-Hill, 2003.

Liker, Jeffrey and David Meier, *The Toyota Way Fieldbook.* New York: McGraw-Hill, 2005.

May, Matthew E., *The Elegant Solution: Toyota's Formula for Mastering Innovation.* New York: Free Press, 2006.

Mika, Geoffrey, *Kaizen Implementation Manual* 5th Edition. Dearborn: Society of Manufacturing Engineers, 2006.

Ohno, Taiichi, *The Toyota Production System.* New York: Productivity Press, 1988.

Womack, James P. and Daniel T. Jones, *Lean Thinking.* New York: Free Press, 2003.

Womack, James P., Daniel T. Jones, and Daniel Roos, *The Machine that Changed the World.* New York: Harper Perennial, 1991.

### Value Stream Mapping

Keyte, Beau and Drew Locher, *The Complete Lean Enterprise.* New York: Productivity Press, 2004

Rother, Mike and John Shook, *Learning to See.* Brookline, MA: LEI, 1998.

Tapping, Don and Tom Shuker, *Value Stream Management for the Lean Office.* New York: Productivity Press, 2003.

### Miscellaneous Lean Tools

Fabrizio, Tom and Don Tapping, *5S for the Office.* New York: Productivity Press, 2006

Hadfield, Debra and Shelagh Holmes, *The Lean Healthcare Pocket Guide.* Chelsea, MI: MCS Media, 2006.

MCS Media, *The Lean Office Pocket Guide.* Chelsea, MI: MCS Media, 2005.

Productivity Press, *The Lean Office: Collected Practices and Cases.* New York: Productivity Press, 2005.

## ARTICLES

Shapiro, Benson et. al, "Staple Yourself to an Order," *Harvard Business Review*, July–August 1992.

Spear, Steven, "Learning to Lead at Toyota," *Harvard Business Review*, May 2004.

Spear, Steven, "Decoding the DNA of the Toyota Production System," *Harvard Business Review*, September-October 1999.

## DVDS

*Time: The Next Dimension of Quality*

*Joel Barker's The New Business of Paradigms*

*Race Without a Finish Line*

## PROFESSIONAL ASSOCIATIONS, TRADE ORGANIZATION, WEBSITES

The following organizations and web sites offer a wide variety of resources, including conferences, print material, electronic newsletters, job boards, user groups, mapping supplies, etc.

American Society for Quality, www.asq.org

Association for Manufacturing Excellence, www.ame.org

Institute of Industrial Engineers, www.iienet.org

Lean Podcasts, http://www.leanblog.org/2006/07/leanblog-podcast-main-page.html

Lean Enterprise Institute, www.lean.org

Society for Health Systems, www.shsweb.org

Society for Manufacturing Engineering, www.sme.org

www.changethis.com

www.nwlean.net

www.superfactory.org

# INDEX

# ABOUT THE AUTHORS

**Karen Martin,** Principal Consultant for Karen Martin & Associates, specializes in applying Lean principles and tools in office, service, and technical environments.

She has provided performance improvement support to organizations in a broad range of industries, including: construction, distribution, education, engineering services, financial services, government/military, healthcare, information technology, insurance, manufacturing, oil and gas production, and publishing.

Karen's quality and process orientation evolved from her early career as a scientist (B.S. Microbiology, Pennsylvania State University) and was further developed while serving as the Director of Quality for a healthcare organization that managed healthcare for 22 million Americans. She also served as the Director of the Institute for Quality and Productivity at San Diego State University, where she oversaw the university's Lean Enterprise and Quality Business Practices programs. Her passion for workforce development and implementing change led her to a graduate program in adult learning (M.A. Education, California State University, Bakersfield).

Karen is known for her keen diagnostic skills and ability to lead teams in generating aggressive results. Her broad understanding of operations design, customer value, regulatory issues, and business management stems from her experience building the infrastructure for several start-up operations with triple-digit annual growth. She is an instructor for the University of California, San Diego's Lean Enterprise program and San Diego State University's Advanced Lean program. Karen also serves as an Industry Advisor for the University of San Diego's Industrial Engineering program and is licensed as a Clinical Laboratory Scientist. She can be contacted through www.ksmartin.com.

**Mike Osterling** is the President of Osterling Consulting, Inc., a firm that leads organizations on their Lean journey. Mike has played a pivotal role in leading Lean transformations across a broad range of industries including aerospace, automotive, consumer goods, medical products, oil production, pharmaceuticals and construction.

With more than 15 years of management experience abroad, Mike has led and supported Lean implementations in the U.S., Mexico, Australia and Europe. A dynamic leader with proven team-building skills, his hands-on approach consistently delivers significant bottom-line results.

Prior to consulting, Mike played a key role in the Lean transformation at a number of Square D Company's facilities. A founder of San Diego State University's Lean Enterprise Certificate Program, he continues to teach in the program as well as SDSU's Lean Six Sigma Black Belt Program.

Fluent in Spanish, Mike earned his MBA in International Business from San Diego State University and holds a BS in Production and Operations Management. He is a Certified Trainer for the Implementation of Lean Manufacturing through the University of Kentucky, is a Six Sigma Black Belt and is CPIM certified through APICS. He can be contacted through www.mosterling.com.